SUCCESSION BETWEEN
INTERNATIONAL ORGANIZATIONS

A PUBLICATION OF THE GRADUATE INSTITUTE
OF INTERNATIONAL STUDIES,
GENEVA

Also published in this series:
The United States and the Politicization of the World Bank
Bartram S. Brown
World Financial Markets after 1992
Hans Genberg and Alexander K. Swoboda
Trade Negotiations in the OECD
David Blair

SUCCESSION BETWEEN INTERNATIONAL ORGANIZATIONS

Patrick R. Myers

Routledge
Taylor & Francis Group

LONDON AND NEW YORK

First published in 1993 by
Kegan Paul International

This edition first published in 2011 by
Routledge
2 Park Square, Milton Park, Abingdon, Oxfordshire OX14 4RN

Simultaneously published in the USA and Canada
by Routledge
711 Third Avenue, New York, NY 10017

First issued in paperback 2016

Routledge is an imprint of the Taylor & Francis Group, an informa business

British Library Cataloguing in Publication Data
A catalogue record for this book is available from the British Library

ISBN 13: 978-1-138-98336-6 (pbk)
ISBN 13: 978-0-7103-0457-5 (hbk)

Publisher's Note
The publisher has gone to great lengths to ensure the quality of this reprint
but points out that some imperfections in the original copies may be
apparent. The publisher has made every effort to contact original copyright
holders and would welcome correspondence from those they have been
unable to trace.

For Lucretia

CONTENTS

CONTENTS

INTRODUCTION

Succession between international organizations is a controversial topic. When the International Law Commission discussed adding the issue to its long-term program of work in 1971, it came to the conclusion that 'the scope for codification and progressive development of the law with regard to this matter would appear to be limited,' and that consequently there was no need to consider the subject any further.[1] It took an even more negative stance in 1982, declaring that 'strictly speaking, there can never be a "succession" of organizations.'[2]

This statement is curiously at odds with the International Court of Justice's 1971 advisory opinion on the *Legal Consequences of the Continued Presence of South Africa in Namibia*, where the Court flatly proclaimed the United Nations to be a 'successor' to the League of Nations in respect of certain supervisory functions over the mandate for the territory of South West Africa.[3] The Court did not use this word lightly. It had, in fact, carefully avoided using the term 'succession' in the five previous cases relating to the mandate, preferring instead more innocuous expressions such as 'taking over' functions and 'replacing' the League by the United Nations.[4]

Individual judges had no such scruples, and explicitly raised the issue of succession in their dissenting and separate opinions from the very first South West Africa case in 1950.[5] A number of legal writers also used the term in various studies that described the replacement of the League of Nations system of international organizations by the United Nations and its specialized agencies.[6]

Some authors, on the other hand, were uncomfortable with the word 'succession' and wrote about the 'supersession' of

1

organizations[7] and 'continuity' in the law of international organizations.

What is it about the topic that provokes such diverse reactions? Is there really such a thing as succession between international organizations? Does it ressemble any other form of succession or is it something completely different?

The present study is an attempt to shed some light on this little-known area of international law. Although it is true that many of the situations that prompted discussions about succession between organizations occurred during the period immediately following the Second World War, a host of more recent events tend to indicate that the subject has more than historical interest. Moreover, it would appear that the proliferation of regional organizations and mounting pressures to rationalize international cooperation has given rise to more issues relating to succession of organizations in recent years than to state succession.

The widely divergent views related above suggest that the word 'succession', like most general legal concepts, carries several meanings. The first step will therefore be to define the notion and show how it can be applied to international organizations. It will then be possible to examine the factual situations where succession may have occurred. This will naturally lead to an inquiry of the legal basis of succession, and, finally, to a discussion of the effects of succession between international organizations.

I

THE DEFINITION OF SUCCESSION BETWEEN INTERNATIONAL ORGANIZATIONS

A. INTRODUCTION

Succession is a concept that is found in all systems of law. An examination of private law succession and the doctrine of 'state succession' reveals certain common traits that characterize all forms of succession. This chapter briefly reviews how the notion has developed in municipal law and international law, and draws on this experience to define what is meant by the expression 'succession between international organizations.'

B. SUCCESSION IN MUNICIPAL LAW

Rights and obligations in municipal law are always the consequence of a person occupying a certain factual situation.[1] The owner of a tangible object, for example, enjoys certain rights and obligations which are recognized by the law as attaching to the fact of ownership. The owner may ordinarily give up the possession of the object to another person who assumes the same position over the object as the predecessor. The consequences attached by the law to the ownership of the object cease to be valid for the previous owner and become valid for the subsequent owner. This transfer of rights and obligations, or more precisely the substitution of one person for another in respect of certain rights and obligations, is commonly referred to as 'succession'.[2]

Legal doctrine sometimes distinguishes 'universal' succession, the transfer of all of a person's rights and obligations, from 'partial' succession, the transfer of specific rights and obligations. The concept of universal succession originated in primi-

3

tive societies where the family group formed the basic unit of society.[3] When the head of the household died, his entire personality survived and was continued by his heir.[4] This identity of the deceased and the heir was possible because the rights and obligations of the head of the household were considered to be not so much his own as those of the family.[5] A change at the head of the family, therefore, did not affect the continuity of the ownership of the family rights and obligations. This was not, strictly speaking, succession at all but rather the continuation of the subject of rights and obligations.[6]

In present day legal systems there are no perfect examples of universal succession.[7] Personal rights and obligations, such as those deriving from an individual's civil status or from agreements concluded *intuitu personae*, are normally not transferrable by any device.[8] In reality, therefore, municipal law admits only various forms of partial succession.[9]

Succession results either from an agreement between the predecessor and the successor or 'automatically' by operation of the law when certain conditions are fulfilled. Conventional succession typically arises in consequence of a sale, gift, assignment, exchange or other such contractual arrangements.[10] Automatic succession, on the other hand, takes place by virtue of pre-existing statutory law or rules developed by the courts and does not necessarily require the consent of the persons concerned.[11] Examples of this type of succession are the inheritance (succession *mortis causa*) and bankruptcy.

In whatever manner succession occurs, the effect is always the same: the successor steps into the shoes of the predecessor and assumes the very same rights and obligations which the predecessor enjoyed.[12] The change of subject does not modify the material content of the rights and obligations, nor does it give the successor greater rights and obligations than those which belonged to its predecessor. This rule is usually expressed by the Latin dictum *nemo plus iuris ad alium transfere potest quam ipse haberet*.[13]

Succession in municipal law, then, is a broad concept that is used in reference to any situation where there occurs at once a change of subjects and a continuation of a legal relationship. This continuity of rights and obligations is what sets succession apart from 'novation', a somewhat similar institution that requires both a change of subject and a replacement of old rights and obligations by new ones.[14]

C. STATE SUCCESSION

The expression 'state succession' is usually defined in terms of the replacement of one state by another in respect of sovereignty over a given territory.[15] Such replacement may occur when: (a) part or all of the territory of a state becomes part of the territory of another state, (b) part of the territory of a state separates from that state and forms a new state or (c) a dependent territory accedes to independence.[16]

This definition refers only to the factual situation of replacement. The legal consequences of a factual succession, that is the specific rights and obligations of the predecessor state which devolve to the successor state, are governed by a body of rules called the 'law of state succession'.[17]

Early writers on the subject of state succession drew their inspiration from Roman law. Grotius, Pufendorf, Vattel and other proponents of natural law regarded the successor state as a universal heir that continued the personality of the predecessor and received *ipso jure* all of its rights and obligations.[18]

This doctrine of universal succession reached its appogee in the late nineteenth century in the works of Max Huber. The state, according to Huber, was a social organism that differed from the individual in that its constituent elements did not necessarily disappear upon death. Its people and territory continued to exist and passed as a single unit to the successor state with all of the rights and obligations attached to those elements.[19]

By the early part of the twentieth century, however, it became apparent to many writers that the theory of universal succession was not at all consistent with the actual practice of states during the nineteenth century which resulted from the independence of the Spanish and Portuguese colonies in Latin America, the settlement of the Napoleonic wars and the dismemberment of the Ottoman empire. A new doctrine emerged that was based on the premise that a state exercised rights and assumed obligations by virtue of its own sovereign will and not as a result of a transfer of powers from another state. Political sovereignty was by its very nature not transmissible.[20]

For positivists like Cavaglieri, there was no such thing as 'state succession' and no general rule of law that required an annexing state to assume the legal consequences of the acts of the extinguished state.[21] If rights and obligations were maintained, such 'succession' was strictly voluntary, for reasons of equity, convenience or political interest.[22]

Most modern theorists have rejected these two extreme positions and recognized that some devolution does take place under customary international law in consequence of the very fact of one state replacing another.[23] The contemporary doctrine is less concerned with the philosophical underpinnings of state succession than with identifying through international practice which rights and duties do or do not devolve automatically to the successor state.[24] Many studies and international judicial decisions have confirmed that in some circumstances the public property, debts, and treaties establishing boundaries and regulating the use of the territory of the predecessor state devolve *ipso jure* to the successor state.[25]

The task of codifying the customary rules of international law relating to state succession was taken up by the International Law Commission in 1962.[26] For practical reasons, the Commission decided in 1967 to split the topic of 'succession in respect of treaties' from that of 'succession in respect of state property, archives and debts'.[27] The draft articles developed by the Commission served as the basis of the 1978 Vienna Convention on Succession of States in Respect of Treaties[28] and the 1983 Vienna Convention on Succession of States in Respect of State Property, Archives and Debts.[29]

It is not possible here to enter into a discussion of which provisions of the two conventions are codifications of existing customary international law and which represent a 'progressive development' of rules which have not yet been consolidated by past practice and *opinio juris*.[30] Suffice it to say that insofar as treaties, state property, archives and debts are concerned, the conventions confirm that when a succession of states occurs, territorial régimes established by treaties remain in effect for the successor state[31] and that state property, archives and debts pass to the successor state.[32]

In cases where no automatic succession takes place or where the predecessor and successor states wish to depart from an established rule of international law, the successor state must, depending on the circumstances, either consent to be bound by the obligations of the predecessor or agree with the predecessor to assume them. Except for treaties establishing boundaries and other territorial régimes and treaties in force when there is a merger or separation of states,[33] all other treaties relating to the territory of the successor state cease to be in effect on the date of succession, unless the successor state consents to be bound by their terms.[34] The public property, archives and debts of the predecessor state devolve automatically to the successor state unless the predecessor and successor otherwise agree.[35]

From this brief examination it may be concluded that the concept of state succession has the very same characteristics as succession in municipal law, namely: the substitution of one subject for another in respect of certain rights and obligations,[36] the transfer of rights and obligations either by agreement (conventional succession) or by operation of the law (automatic succession)[37] and, finally, the identity of the transferred rights and obligations.[38]

D. SUCCESSION BETWEEN INTERNATIONAL ORGANIZATIONS

The basic ingredients of succession identified above can be applied equally well to the transfer of rights and obligations between international organizations. Succession in this context, however, has a peculiar nature owing to the special character of such institutions.

1. The Characteristics of an International Organization

The origins of present day international organizations can be traced back to the Congress of Vienna in 1815. Although European powers had long been accustomed to holding peace conferences to settle territorial disputes and other issues arising from armed conflicts, the Congress of Vienna introduced two novel techniques that had a major influence on the development of international organizations.

The first was the practice of convening international conferences at regular intervals to deal with important political issues. Four such 'congresses' were held between 1815 and 1822,[39] after which differences between the great European powers put a stop to the practice. Nevertheless, throughout the remainder of the nineteenth century and into the early twentieth century, the major powers continued to meet whenever pressing political issues required concerted action.[40] This 'Concert of Europe', as it was called, evolved into a quasi-institutionalized 'exclusive club for great powers, whose members were self-appointed guardians of the European community and executive directors of its affairs.'[41]

The second innovation brought about by the Congress of Vienna was the multinational treaty. Until that time, peace settlements between more than two states had always taken the form of a series of bilateral treaties. The Peace of Westphalia of 1648, for example, consisted of two parallel treaties which the Holy Roman Empire signed with Sweden and France.[42] The Paris Peace Treaty of 1814 was a series of identical treaties signed simultaneously by France with each of the Allied Powers.[43]

The Final Act of the Congress of Vienna was the first treaty to be signed by all the states participating in a diplomatic conference. It was essentially a cover agreement that tied together all of the various bilateral treaties that had been negotiated in the course of the meeting. This practice of negotiating first a series of bilateral treaties and then a cover agreement continued until the middle of the nineteenth century when the initial phase was finally abandoned in favor of a single instrument.[44]

In the second half of the nineteenth century, the techniques of the international conference and the multilateral treaty were combined to create 'unions', which, were initially little more than multilateral treaties providing for regular conferences to promote coordination of national policies in specific fields such as commerce, communications and health.[45] Soon, however, these unions were endowed with permanent administrative organs.[46] Permanent secretariats called 'bureaux' were established for the International Telegraph Union in 1868,[47] the Universal Postal Union in 1878, the Union for the Protection of Intellectual Property in 1883, the Union for the Protection of Literary and Artistic Works in 1886, the International Union of Railway Freight Transportation in 1890, the International Radiotelegraph Union in 1906 and the International Office of Public Health in 1907.[48] By the eve of the outbreak of the First

World War, there were approximately fifty such permanent institutional organs operating on the international scene.[49]

The success of the administrative unions in dealing with limited, non-political activities made it possible in the aftermath of the First World War to envisage the creation of more complex and powerful institutions.[50] The establishment of the League of Nations constituted the first attempt of the international community to organize all international cooperation within the framework of a permanent, general-purpose institution.[51]

From the point of view of its structure, the League was a far more ambitious and complex international institution than any other previously created. Its Assembly resembled the annual conferences of the administrative unions, but its Council, an executive organ composed of the great powers and a limited number of other states, was a new idea.[52] The third organ, the Secretariat, had extensive responsibilities which required a large permanent staff, premises and financial resources.[53]

In addition to these three organs, the League was linked to two other major institutions, the International Labour Organisation and the Permanent Court of International Justice, as well as to three technical agencies[54] and several permanent advisory commissions.[55] A number of other autonomous international agencies were invited to enter under the umbrella of the League by vitue of Article 24, paragraph 1 of the Covenant, which provided that all international bureaux could be placed under the direction of the League.[56] Although a few agencies came under the ambit of the League,[57] the more important international institutions remained outside the sphere of the League, partly because the United States was hostile to any plans for placing institutions it was associated with under the direction of the League.[58]

During the inter-war period, under the influence of the League system, international agencies gradually acquired more autonomy from their member states. The idea emerged that these institutions could be regarded as distinct legal entities that could possess some of the attributes of international legal personality.[59] This element of separate personality was eventually affirmed by the International Court of Justice in its landmark advisory opinion of April 11th, 1949 on *Reparation for Injuries Suffered in the Service of the United Nations*, where it stated that the United Nations 'was intended to exercise and enjoy,

9

and is in fact exercising and enjoying, functions and rights which can only be explained on the basis of the possession of a large measure of international personality and the capacity to operate upon an international plane.'[60]

As a result of these developments, it is generally accepted today that an international organization possesses three essential characteristics. The first is that it is established by a treaty.[61] Variously called a convention, charter, covenant or constitution, this document defines its purposes, functions, powers and structure. The fact that the organization is based on a treaty necessarily entails that: (a) it is created under, and operates according to, international law,[62] and (b) its members are normally, though not always, states.[63]

The second characteristic is that an international organization has a permanent set of organs. A permanent institutional structure is what sets it apart from an international conference.[64]

Lastly, an organization possesses a certain degree of autonomy in the sense that it can act in its own name. Through its organs it expresses a separate and distinct will from that of its member states. This autonomy makes it possible for the organization to enjoy certain international rights and obligations and hence to be, to a limited extent, a subject of international law.[65]

An international organization can therefore be defined as an association of states established by a treaty for the purpose of performing certain functions, possessing permanent organs through which it expresses a will distinct from that of its members.[66]

2. The Concept of Succession as Applied to International Organizations

An international organization is created by states to perform specific functions which the states have found they are unable to do on an individual basis. It is not an end in itself but rather an instrument for the fulfilment of certain common ends.[67] Because each organization has its own particular purposes and functions, it is a unique entity, different from all other organizations.

The functional nature of an international organization was analyzed by the Permanent Court of International Justice in its advisory opinion of December 8, 1927 on the *Jurisdiction of the European Commission of the Danube*. The Court compared the territorial basis of the competence of sovereign states with the more limited capacities of the European Commission and concluded that although it exercised its functions in the territory of a sovereign state it was not state, 'but an international institution with a special purpose' and that 'it only has functions bestowed upon it by the Definitive Statute with a view to fulfilment of that purpose.'[68]

The same view was expressed by the International Court of Justice in its 1949 advisory opinion on the *Reparation for Injuries Suffered in the Service of the United Nations* where it stated that:

> Whereas a state possesses the totality of international rights and duties recognized by international law, the rights and duties of an entity such as the Organization must depend upon its purposes and functions as specified or implied in its constituent documents and developed in practice.[69]

Since the rights and obligations of an international organization are limited to its functions, the issue of succession necessarily arises when responsibility for certain functions is transferred from one organization to another. This functional succession has been compared by Mochi-Onory to state succession in the sense that 'instead of territory there is a function, and instead of a sovereignty, a competence.'[70]

Succession between international organizations differs from state succession in other respects. For example, only one state can exercise sovereignty over a piece of territory at any given time, while in the case of international organizations several institutions can exercise functions in the same field. It is quite common in fact for several organizations to coexist with similar purposes, competences and functions. Duplication of functions also occurs between substantially different organizations. In such circumstances, organizations usually resort to consultations and coordination agreements to avoid wasting efforts and resources.[71] Such coordination of activities does not raise issues of succession, however, unless it results in the transfer of functions.

Another factor complicating succession between organizations is the close relationship that always exists between an

11

organization and its members. Although it may possess capacities which are recognized as quite separate from those of states, it is never entirely independent of the will of its members. In the words of Reuter, 'the member states play a fundamental role in the pursuit of an organization's purposes and the execution of its resolutions.'[72] The transfer of functions, therefore, raises the issue of the consent of the states which are affected by such an event.

A further source of difficulty arises where the two organizations have identical memberships. When the purposes, structures, powers and functions of the organizations are radically different, it is usually quite obvious that the members intended them to be distinct legal entities. On the other hand, when an organization undergoes important constitutional changes, it may be questioned whether the identity of the organization has been maintained. In such situations, the continuity or discontinuity of the original organization may have to be sought in the circumstances surrounding the changes, the 'travaux préparatoires' and the texts of the constitutional amendments.

The transfer of functions from one organization to another is usually accompanied by other rights and obligations related to the functions which the successor organization may desire to take over in order to carry on the predecessor's activities. The fate of the predecessor organization's assets and liabilites is, however, dependent on and subordinate to the devolution of functions.

The expression 'succession between international organizations' will therefore be used in this study to mean the transfer of functions and their ancillary rights and obligations from one international organization to another.

II

THE FORMS OF SUCCESSION BETWEEN INTERNATIONAL ORGANIZATIONS

A. INTRODUCTION

The issue of succession between international organizations first arose in the closing days of the Second World War when the allied powers laid the foundation of an entirely new family of international organizations to replace the League of Nations system which had become thoroughly discredited.[1] The new United Nations Organization that emerged from the series of conferences held at Dunbarton Oaks, Yalta and San Francisco in 1944 and 1945 was, however, basically a revised version of the League.[2] Like the Covenant of the League, the Charter of the United Nations provided for a system of global institutions consisting of a general-function organization and a number of special-function institutions having broad international responsibilities in 'economic, social, cultural, education, health and related fields'.[3] These technical organizations were to be brought into relationship with the United Nations as its specialized agencies.[4] The system was designed to be decentralized in the sense that while the United Nations would assume the overall direction of international cooperation, each affiliated specialized agency would remain legally independent and autonomous.[5]

Because there was some uncertainty that all of the major powers would eventually ratify the Charter of the United Nations, the allied governments were eager to ensure the success of international cooperation in as wide a range of technical fields as possible.[6] Conventions were concluded to establish the Food and Agriculture Organization (FAO) and the United Nations Relief and Rehabilitation Administration (UNRRA) in

13

1943, the International Monetary Fund (IMF), the International Bank of Reconstruction and Development (IBRD) and the International Civil Aviation Organization (ICAO) in 1944, the United Nations Educational, Scientific and Cultural Organization (UNESCO) in 1945 and the World Health Organization (WHO) in 1946. Also during this period, the constituent instruments of three existing bodies, the International Telecommunications Union (ITU), the Universal Postal Union (UPU) and the International Labour Organization (ILO) were adapted to fit into the new international system.

The establishment of this new system of global institutions created a novel situation. Many of the post-war organizations, and in particular the FAO, the ICAO, UNESCO, the WHO, and of course the United Nations itself, were designed to operate in the same functional fields as a number of existing organizations. In order to eliminate the resulting duplication and confusion, it was necessary to dissolve the old organizations and transfer all or part of their functions and assets to the new institutions. The process by which this was accomplished provided the first examples of succession between international organizations.

Another situation that gave rise to problems of succession in the post-war period was the dismantling of UNRRA and the International Refugee Organization (IRO), two temporary organizations that had been set up to provide assistance to the victims of the war. Since some of their functions were considered to be useful and necessary to continue, other organs or specialized agencies of the United Nations were found to take them over.

The problem of succession between global institutions arose again in the 1960's when the International Bureau of Education (IBE) and the International Relief Union (IRU), two small global organizations whose fields of activity were too narrow to become specialized agencies of the United Nations but whose competences and activities overlapped with those of UNESCO in certain areas, found themselves in serious financial difficulty. The solution finally adopted resulted in the complete integration of the IBE into UNESCO and the transfer of part of the IRU's functions to UNESCO.

The proliferation of regional and partial[7] organizations in the 1950's and 1960's eventually led to situations where several organizations in the same part of the world performed the same or similar functions. In order to eliminate duplication and waste of scarce resources it became necessary to take measures to rationalize regional cooperation. In Europe, for example, the Council of Europe (CE) took over some of the functions of the Western European Union (WEU) in 1960, the European Space Research Organization (ESRO) and the European Launcher Development Organization (ELDO) were merged in 1975 to form the European Space Agency (ESA) and the International Patent Institute (IPI) was absorbed by the European Patent Organization (EPO) in 1978.

In Africa and the Caribbean, the many organizations that were established during the decolonization period to perpetuate colonial administrations, such as the West African Customs Union (UDEAO), the East African Common Services Organization (EACSO), the Malagasy Organization for Economic Cooperation (OAMCE), the African and Malagasy Union (UAM), the Commission for Technical Co-operation in Africa South of the Sahara (CCTA), the Caribbean Commission (CC) and the Caribbean Free Trade Association (CARIFTA), encountered serious difficulties owing to the rapidly changing political climate in their regions and differences between pace and model of the economic development of their member states. These problems eventually led to the dissolution of the institutions and the creation of new international organizations to carry on the same or similar functions.

From these historical developments it is possible to establish the following typology of situations where functional succession takes place:

(a) an organization is replaced by another organization which is created to fulfill the same general purposes and functions (replacement),

(b) a limited function organization is absorbed by a broader based organization and becomes one of its organs (absorption),

(c) two or more organizations are combined to form a single new entity (merger),

(d) a subsidiary organ is separated from its parent institution and becomes a new organization (separation), and

(e) specific functions of an organization are transferred to another organization without otherwise affecting its existence (transfer of specific functions).

In this chapter we will examine these five forms of succession.

B. REPLACEMENT

The replacement of organizations by new ones possessing essentially the same powers and functions has, in practice, been the most common form of succession. The following are examples of succession by replacement.

1. The Replacement of the League of Nations by the United Nations

The League of Nations never managed to become the central institutional framework for maintaining peace and directing international cooperation that its creators had intended it to be.[8] When war broke out in 1939, the League was placed in suspended animation under the care of a Supervisory Commission which was charged with maintaining the League's remaining nonpolitical activities, as well as its records and documentation with a view to transmitting them to 'whatever authority might be entrusted with these matters after the war.'[9]

The overwhelming majority of the states that gathered in San Francisco in 1945 to complete the work on the Charter of the United Nations were still at the time, or had formerly been, members of the League.[10] Since it was obvious to everyone that the new organization would replace the League,[11] and that a way needed to be found to ensure a smooth transition from the old to the new organization, the San Francisco Conference established a Preparatory Commission to formulate 'recommendations concerning the transfer of certain functions, activities and assets of the League of Nations which it may be considered desirable for the new Organization to take over on terms to be arranged.'[12]

The Preparatory Commission and the Supervisory Commission of the League entered into discussions and together developed a 'Common Plan' for the transfer of League assets to the United Nations.[13] This Plan was approved by the United Nations General Assembly on February 12, 1946[14] along with a resolution requesting the Economic and Social Council to 'survey the functions and activities of a non-political character which have hitherto been performed by the League of Nations in order to determine which of them should, with such modifications as are desirable, be assumed by organs of the United Nations or be entrusted to specialized agencies which have been brought into relationship with the United Nations.'[15]

The Economic and Social Council accordingly began to organize itself to take over the functions of certain League organs. Between February and December 1946 it created numerous commissions to deal with human rights, economics and employment, social issues, statistics, transportation and communications, narcotic drugs, the status of women, population and fiscal matters.[16] These were to follow in the footsteps of the League's committees, which had similar responsibilities.[17]

The Assembly of the League convened for its twenty first and final session in Geneva in April 1946 to discuss the dissolution of the organization and the transfer of certain of its functions and assets to the United Nations and its specialized agencies. On the final day of the meeting the Assembly adopted a resolution under the terms of which the Common Plan was approved,[18] the League was dissolved 'with effect from the day following the close of the present session . . . except for the sole purpose of the liquidation of its affairs'[19] and a Board of Liquidation was appointed and assigned the task of 'transferring to new or continuing organizations sections of active work as soon as the necessary arrangements could be made and, on the other hand, of liquidating matters which did not fall within the competence of new or continuing institutions or necessarily disappeared on the final closing down of the League.'[20]

The Assembly also passed several other specific resolutions concerning the transfer of functions to the United Nations. One dealt with the secretarial and custodial functions of the League with respect to the deposit of the original signed copies of treaties.[21] Another recommended that the members of the League 'facilitate the assumption without interruption by the United Nations, or by specialized agencies brought into relationship with that organization, of the functions and powers which have been entrusted to the League of Nations, under international agreements of a technical and nonpolitical character.'[22] Still another directed the Secretary-General of the League 'to afford every facility for the assumption by the United Nations of such non-political activities, hitherto performed by the League, as the United Nations may decide to assume.'[23]

The Board of Liquidation immediately set to work to implement these decisions. It transferred to the United Nations the League's custodial function with respect to treaties and related documents on August 1, 1946[24] and the League's library service, publications service and internal services by October 1, 1946.[25] The functions exercised by the various League committees relating to narcotic drug control, traffic in women and children and of obscene publications, economic statistics, transportation and communications, child welfare and health activities were assumed by the corresponding United Nations commissions under various arrangements worked out between the Board of Liquidation and the Secretary-General of the United Nations.[26]

At the time of its dissolution the League was responsible for the administration of eleven special funds, which included pension funds and various foundations established by private donations.[27] These were split among the United Nations, the World Health Organization and the International Labour Organisation.[28]

The buildings, furniture and office equipment which the League owned in Geneva, the Hague, London, Paris, Princeton, Washington D.C., New Delhi and Singapore were turned over to the United Nations on August 1, 1946, with the exception of the International Labour Office building which was transferred to the International Labour Organisation.[29]

The employment contracts of the League's staff were all terminated on July 31, 1946 but a number of ex-officials continued to work for the Board of Liquidation during the transition period. By the close of the liquidation over 250 former employees of the League had been hired by the United Nations and its specialized agencies.[30]

The Board of Liquidation spent a considerable amount of time and energy collecting overdue contributions from the members of the League. During its sixteen months of operations, it managed to recover over 28.2 million Swiss francs,[31] part of which was used to discharge the obligations of the League and the rest was distributed according to a scheme whereby members of the League which had not joined the United Nations received their share of the assets in cash and the others received a credit on the books of the United Nations.[32]

The last chapter of the League's history came to a close on

July 31, 1947 with the publication of the Board of Liquidation's final report.

2. The Replacement of the International Commission for Air Navigation by the International Civil Aviation Organization

The International Commission for Air Navigation (ICAN) came into being on July 11, 1922 under the Paris Convention Relating to the Regulation of Aerial Navigation of October 13, 1919.[33] Its main functions were to review and if necessary amend the technical annexes to the Convention which related to standards for aircraft markings, certificates of air worthiness, log books, rules on lights and signals, rules of the air, pilots licenses, aeronautical maps and ground markings, dissemination of meteorological information and customs procedures.[34]

The close connection of ICAN with the League of Nations prevented it from ever acquiring the universal character its founders had hoped for and throughout the inter-war period it remained primarily a European regional organization.[35]

In the course of the Second World War the allied powers developed a vast intercontinental air transportation network which they wanted to see maintained after the war. A regional approach for dealing with civil aviation problems no longer seemed adequate to deal with the revolutionary changes that had occurred in this form of transportation. The issue was discussed by the principal air powers in early 1944, and it was decided to convene an international conference to draft a new convention on air navigation.[36]

The delegations of the fifty states that met in Chicago in the fall of 1944 were fully aware that the new convention would replace the Paris and Havana Conventions. Various proposals were put forward by the United States, Canada and France on how to deal with the existing aeronautical conventions.[37] The solution finally adopted was to include a provision in the new Convention on International Civil Aviation which expressly stated that the Convention 'supersedes the Conventions of Paris and Havana' and that each contracting state 'undertakes, immediately, upon the coming into force of this Convention to give denunciation' of the two earlier conventions.[38]

Because it was realized that it would take considerable time to obtain the required number of ratifications for the new convention to come into force and that immediate action was necessary to avoid disrupting air service, the Chicago Conference set up a Provisional International Civil Aviation Organization (PICAO).[39] The PICAO quickly established links with ICAN, and in late August 1945 the Secretary General of ICAN, Dr. Albert Roper, was elected Secretary General of the PICAO with the understanding that he would continue as the head of ICAN 'until the two organizations were merged.'[40]

The ICAN Commission met in London in August 1945 to consider the situation that had arisen as a result of the Chicago Convention and made two important decisions. The first was to approve the arrangement under which Dr. Roper would serve as Secretary General of both the ICAN and the PICAO.[41] The second was to adopt a 'formula for denunciation' which the members of the organization could use to avoid being bound by both the Paris and Chicago Conventions.[42]

Fourteen months later, in late October 1946, the ICAN Commission convened in Dublin to make arrangements for the termination of its activities and the disposal of its functions, assets and liabilities. The Commission approved the transfer of documentation relating to eighteen topics to the PICAO[43] and established a liquidation committee to take charge of the liquidation of the organization.[44]

The liquidation committee elaborated a liquidation plan which was approved in January 1947[45] and implemented as from 4th April, the date on which the Chicago Convention came into force.[46] Under the liquidation plan, the ICAN library, office effects and certain residual funds were turned over to the ICAO.[47] Although the winding up procedures were supposed to have been completed on December 31, 1947,[48] the Liquidation Committee encountered certain difficulties which prevented it from closing the ICAN books until December 31, 1948.[49]

3. The Replacement of the International Institute of Agriculture by the Food and Agriculture Organization

The International Institute of Agriculture (IIA) was established by a convention signed in Rome on June 7, 1905.[50] Its functions included the study and publication of information relating to the production and sale of agricultural products, the salaries of farm workers, new plant diseases and problems of insurance

and agricultural credits.[51] The IIA also assumed certain administrative duties with regard to six international conventions.[52]

When the delegates of forty-three states assembled in Hot
Springs, Virginia in May 1943 to discuss post-war problems of
food and agriculture, there was early agreement that a new
permanent international organization should be created to promote 'concerted action among like-minded nations to expand
and improve production, to increase employment, to raise levels
of consumption, and to establish greater freedom of international commerce' in the field of food and agriculture.[53] To
this end, the conference set up an Interim Commission to draft
the constitution of the new organization[54] and to examine the
relationship between the new institution and existing bodies
exercising functions in the same field.[55]

The Interim Commission produced a draft constitution[56] and
a recommendation that since the functions of the proposed
Food and Agriculture Organization (FAO) would include all of
those previously exercised by the IIA and that such duplication
would be wasteful and confusing, the work of the IIA should
be 'merged with the Food and Agriculture Organization and its
library and archives transferred to it.'[57] It further urged those
governments which were members of both the Interim Commission and the IIA to exert their influence to make this project
possible.[58]

The issue of the future of the IIA was discussed at length
during the First Session of the FAO Conference in October 1945,
and on November 1st a resolution was adopted which requested
that the Institute draw up a protocol providing for the dissolution of the organization and the transfer to the FAO of its
assets and functions under certain international conventions.[59]

The Permanent Committee of the IIA accordingly prepared a
protocol along the lines suggested by Interim Commission
which the IIA Assembly approved on July 9, 1946.[60] According
to the terms of this document, the Permanent Committee would
announce the termination of the 1905 Rome Convention once
it had collected all the assets of the IIA and transferred them
to the FAO.[61]

The IIA Assembly also passed a motion authorizing the
appointment of a seven-member Liquidation Commission to
deal with all matters relating to the liquidation of the Institute.[62]
This commission encountered some difficulties recovering suf-

21

ficient arrears of contributions from the former member states to satisfy the obligations of the IIA towards its staff, and it was finally forced to turn over responsibility for completing the liquidation to the FAO as from February 28, 1949, three years after the new organization came into existence.[63]

4. The Replacement of the Office International d'Hygiène Publique by the World Health Organization

The Office international d'hygiène publique (OIHP)[64] was set up under a convention signed in Rome on December 9, 1907.[65] It was charged with the collection and publication of information concerning infectious diseases[66] and certain administrative functions under eleven multilateral agreements.[67]

The idea of creating a new international health organization was first raised at the San Francisco Conference in May 1945.[68] A recommendation was approved by one of the committees of the Conference which provided that 'in preparation of a plan for the international health organization, full consideration should be given to the relation of such organization to, and methods of associating it with other institutions, national as well as international, which already exist or which may hereafter be established in the field of health.'[69]

The issue was again discussed at the first meeting of the United Nations Economic and Social Council in February 1946, and a committee was appointed to draft the constitution of a new international health organization for consideration by a future international conference.[70] This committee prepared a convention establishing the World Health Organization (WHO) and recommended that the OIHP 'be absorbed in the proposed new organization.'[71] In order to accomplish this, the committee suggested that the delegates to the forthcoming International Health Conference be empowered to sign a protocol abrogating the Rome Agreement of 1907.[72]

The committee's suggestion was taken up at the International Health Conference when it convened in New York in June 1946. With the assistance of a representative of the OIHP, a protocol was drafted which provided for the transfer of the functions of the OIHP to the WHO,[73] the dissolution of the Office and the termination of the Rome Agreement of 1907.[74]

The International Health Conference adopted two other measures to facilitate the transfer of functions, assets and liabilities from the OIHP to the WHO. First of all, it included an article in the WHO Constitution which authorized the WHO to 'take over from any other international organization or agency whose purpose and activities lie within the field of competence of the Organization such functions, resources and obligations as may be conferred upon the Organization by international agreement or by mutually acceptable arrangements entered into between the competent authorities of the respective organizations.'[75] Secondly, it established an Interim Commission which was directed 'to take all necessary steps in accordance with the Protocol . . . for the transfer to the Interim Commission of the duties and functions of the Office, and to initiate any action necessary to facilitate the transfer of the assets and liabilities of the Office to the World Health Organization.'[76]

In the light of these developments, the Permanent Committee of the OIHP decided in October 1946 to entrust the task of winding up the organization to a Commission of Finance and Transfer.[77] This commission worked with Interim Commission of the WHO on the transfer of OIHP functions relating to the administration of certain health conventions,[78] the OIHP staff pension fund,[79] the publication of the monthly bulletin of communicable diseases[80] and certain epidemiological activities.[81]

When the OIHP Permanent Committee met in May 1950 to review the situation, it appeared that several states had still not acceded to the 1946 Protocol or denounced the Rome Agreement.[82] Rather than wait any longer, the Permanent Committee decided to proceed as from November 15, 1950 with the liquidation of the organization and the transfer of its remaining assets and property to the WHO.[83] The winding up procedures continued until April 1951, by which time the WHO had taken over the OIHP's library and archives, assets consisting of cash, securities, furniture and equipment[84] and the claims of OIHP against its members for contributions in arrears.[85]

5. The Replacement of the International Institute of Intellectual Co-operation by the United Nations Educational, Scientific and Cultural Organization

The International Institute of Intellectual Co-operation (IIIC) was established in December 1924 on the basis of an informal agreement between the French government and the League of Nations.[86] Its purpose was essentially to provide support for the League's Committee on Intellectual Co-operation.

In 1937 an international conference on intellectual cooperation recommended that the statute of the IIIC be transformed into a treaty in order that other countries could subscribe to the same obligations as France.[87] The League's Committee on Intellectual Co-operation accordingly drafted an International Act Concerning Intellectual Co-operation which was opened for signature on December 3, 1938.[88]

The IIIC officially became an international organization on January 31, 1940, but the invasion of France a few months later forced the Institute to suspend its activities until the end of the war.[89] By the fall of 1945, when the IIIC could resume its work, certain events occurred which put its future in doubt. First of all, the impending demise of the League of Nations threatened to deprive the Institute of its governing body, the Administrative Council, which was composed of the members of the League's Commission on Intellectual Co-operation.[90] Secondly, an international conference held in London in November 1945 had elaborated the constitution of the United Nations Educational, Scientific and Cultural Organization (UNESCO), a new international organization with basically the same purposes and functions.

Although it was evident that the IIIC would have to be dissolved, there was also a widespread feeling that measures should be taken to ensure the continuity of the work of intellectual cooperation in the framework of UNESCO. The League Assembly at its last session in April 1946 adopted a resolution to transfer to the United Nations its contingent rights over certain assets of the Institute.[91] The Economic and Social Council of United Nations adopted a resolution in October 1946 recommending that 'in view of the future transfer to UNESCO of the functions and activities of the International Institute of Intellectual Co-operation . . . the Preparatory Commission of UNESCO and the Institute be requested to undertake negotiations for this purpose forthwith.'[92] The United Nations General Assembly passed a similar resolution a few weeks later.[93]

An agreement between the IIIC and UNESCO was prepared by the UNESCO Preparatory Commission and approved by the first General Conference of UNESCO on December 9, 1946.[94]

The agreement provided that the IIIC would cease its activities as from December 31, 1946[95] and that UNESCO would take over certain functions of the Institute as well as its library, archives, copyrights, furniture and other office materials.[96]

The Institute ceased to exist at the end of 1946, but the final liquidation of its assets was not begun until 1952, when the United Nations transferred to UNESCO the assets of the IIIC which it had acquired from the League of Nations in 1946, and UNESCO accepted responsibility for the final liquidation of the Institute.[97] An official of the French administration was appointed by the Director-General of UNESCO to dispose of the remaining property of the IIIC.[98] The liquidator completed his work in November 1955, almost nine years after the dissolution of the organization.[99]

6. The Replacement of the East African Common Services Organization by the East African Community

The East African Common Services Organization (AECSO) was created under an agreement signed by Kenya, Tanzania and Uganda at Dar-Es-Salaam on December 9, 1961.[100] Its purpose was basically to continue the various services in the fields of telecommunications, aviation, railways, meteorology, customs, taxes, agriculture and fisheries research, medical research and statistics which had formerly been administered under the British colonial rule by an agency called the East African High Commission (EAHC). From the beginning, the EACSO experienced numerous difficulties owing to the differences in the rates of economic growth of Kenya and the other two members of the organization, Tanzania and Uganda.[101]

In order to rescue the organization, the leaders of the three member states met and appointed a commission in August 1965 to study the problem and propose solutions.[102] The commission's report served as the basis for the elaboration of a new Treaty for East African Cooperation which was signed in Kampala on June 6, 1967.[103]

The Kampala Treaty recalled the historical evolution of East African institutions from the EAHC to the EACSO[104] and provided that a new organization called the East African Community (EAC) would 'take over from the Common Services Organization such of those services as are in existence at the date of the coming into force of this Treaty.'[105] In order to facilitate the transition from the EACSO to the EAC a number of transitional provisions were annexed to the treaty.[106] For example, funds collected by the East African Income Tax Department which had not been transferred to the Distributable Pool Fund of the EACSO were to be paid to the corresponding organ of the EAC.[107] The rules of the Assembly of the EACSO were to apply to the Assembly of the EAC until it elaborated a new set of rules.[108] The Secretary-General and Legal Secretary of the EACSO were to assume the same functions in the EAC.[109]

In accordance with the terms of the Kampala Treaty, the EACSO ceased to exist on December 1, 1967, the date on which the new instrument came into force.[110] The EAC, however, was beset by the same problems that brought on the demise of its predecessor. Political disputes between the member states eventually caused its complete collapse in 1977. The funding necessary to finance its budget was cut off and the employees of the organization were sent home to their respective countries.[111]

C. ABSORPTION

Absorption resembles replacement in some respects. In both cases an institution is dissolved and some or all of its functions and assets are taken over by another organization which has the same or similar purposes and competences. The distinction between the two lies essentially in the scope of the functions of the predecessor and successor organizations. In the case of replacement, the functions of the two organizations are basically the same, and the successor body is regarded as an improved version of the old organization. In the case of absorption, on the other hand, there is a significant disproportion in the scope of the responsibilities and activities of the two organizations which usually results in the smaller institution being integrated into the larger body as one complete unit, becoming an organ or subsidiary agency of the successor institution.

The following are two examples of succession by absorption.

1. The Absorption of the International Bureau of Education by the United Nations Educational, Scientific and Cultural Organization

The International Bureau of Education (IBE) was established in June 1926 as a nongovernmental organization to serve as an information center for all matters relating to education.[112] In order to increase the financial resources of the IBE and broaden its legal basis, the statutes of the Bureau were incorporated in a treaty that was signed July 25, 1929.[113]

The IBE experienced serious financial difficulties in 1966 and appointed a commission to study how to remedy the situation.[114] The commission's recommendation was to integrate the IBE within the framework of UNESCO as an international center of comparative education.[115] Accordingly, the IBE entered into discussions with UNESCO,[116] and an arrangement was worked out between the two organizations whereby the Bureau would become a subsidiary organ of UNESCO.[117]

Under the terms of the agreement, the IBE was absorbed into UNESCO on January 1, 1969.[118] UNESCO took over all of the functions of the Bureau[119] as well as all of its the assets remaining after the liquidation and settlement of its liabilities.[120]

2. The Absorption of the International Patent Institute by the European Patent Organization

The International Patent Institute (IPI) was created by a convention signed at The Hague on June 6, 1947[121] to provide reasoned opinions regarding the novelty of inventions.[122] It was a relatively successful organization that eventually grouped eight European countries: Belgium, France, Italy, Luxembourg, Monaco, the Netherlands, Switzerland and the United Kingdom.[123]

The question of the future status of the IPI arose in 1973 when fifteen European States concluded the European Patent Convention which provided for the establishment of the European Patent Organization (EPO).[124] A protocol that accompanied the European Patent Convention called upon the signatories of the 1947 agreement to ensure that an agreement was concluded between the IPI and EPO to 'transfer to the

European Patent Óffice . . . all assets and liabilities and all staff members of the International Patent Institute.'[125]

An Agreement on the Integration of the International Patent Institute into the European Patent Organization was subsequently drafted by the Interim Committee of the EPO and approved by the IPI Board of Administration in September 1977.[126] In accordance with this agreement, the IPI became a branch of the EPO on January 1, 1978.[127] Its assets and liabilities existing on the date the agreement came into force passed to the EPO 'without exception or reserve'[128] and its staff members became permanent employees of the EPO.[129]

D. MERGER

The merger of organizations differs from replacement and absorption in two important respects. First of all, the organizations being combined have different functions and capacities but operate in fields that are closely related. Secondly, the two or more organizations being merged are dissolved and replaced by a single new body which incorporates elements from each of the predecessor institutions.

The following are illustrations of this form of succession.

1. The Merger of the European Launcher Development Organization and the European Space Research Organization to Form the European Space Agency

The European Launcher Development Organization (ELDO) was created by a convention signed in London on March 29, 1962 by Australia, Belgium, Denmark, France, the Federal Republic of Germany, Italy, the Netherlands and the United Kingdom.[130] As its name indicates, ELDO was charged with the development and construction of satellite launchers.

The European Space Research Organization (ESRO) was set up under another convention signed in Paris on June 14, 1962 by Belgium, Denmark, France, the Federal Republic of Germany, Italy, the Netherlands, Spain, Sweden, Switzerland and the United Kingdom.[131] Its purpose was to manage programs relating to the construction and application of satellites.

From the start, ELDO was handicapped by disputes over control of the various aspects of the program.[132] The problems of the organization came to a head in 1972 when the failure of the first test launcher led to a decision to abandon the development of the 'Europa' missile and the U.S. National Aeronautics and Space Administration (NASA) refused ELDO's offer to collaborate on the construction of a space laboratory.[133]

A European Space Conference was held in December 1972 to review the situation, at the end of which it was agreed to merge ELDO and ESRO into a single new organization to be called the European Space Agency (ESA).[134] The constitution of the new institution was drafted by a special working group in 1973 and signed at a ceremony in Paris on May 30, 1975.[135]

The signatories agreed that the ESA would begin functioning *de facto* on the basis of the ESRO and ELDO conventions until the new ESA convention came into force.[136] It was also decided that ESRO would continue its activities under the name 'European Space Agency' and would establish a detailed inventory of the rights and obligations of ELDO which might be taken over by the ESA.[137]

These measures presented no particular problems as the ESA was based almost entirely on the ESRO model.[138] The Councils of ESRO and ELDO began meeting together, acting in effect like the Council of the future ESA.[139] The Secretary-General of ESRO was made head of ELDO and took charge of the liquidation of that body.[140]

When the ESA convention came into effect on October 30, 1980, the new organization took over all of the rights and obligations of ESRO and certain of the rights and obligations of ELDO which were included in the inventory drawn up by ESRO.[141]

2. The Merger of the African and Malagasy Organization for Economic Cooperation and the Union of African and Malagasy States to Form the African and Malagasy Common Organization

Twelve newly independent French-speaking African States[142] held a conference at Tananarive in early September 1961 and signed instruments to create the African and Malagasy Organization for Economic Cooperation (OAMCE)[143] and the Union of African and Malagasy States (UAM).[144] The purpose of the OAMCE was to help raise the living standards of the member states through coordination of their economic development plans.[145] To this end, it was supposed to prepare international conventions, make recommendations to the member states, coordinate research programs and provide information and documentation services.[146]

The UAM was essentially a political institution established 'to organize the cooperation of its members in all domains of foreign policy in order to reinforce their solidarity, to assure their collective security, to foster their economic development, to maintain peace in Africa, in Malagasy, and in the world.'[147]

The establishment of the Organization of African Unity (OAU), a general-purpose regional organization, made it necessary to modify the objectives and functions of the OAMCE and the UAM to avoid duplication with the OAU.[148] The heads of state of the UAM met in Dakar in March 1964 and unanimously decided that the UAM and OAMCE and their specialized agencies[149] should be merged into a single body which would be called the African and Malagasy Union for Economic Cooperation (UAMCE).[150] The new organization would be charged with the coordination of the development plans of the members in the economic and social fields.[151]

Four members of the UAM, however, refused to sign the Charter of the UAMCE when it was opened for signature at Nouakchott on April 29, 1964. The ten other states merely initialed the document and applied it on a provisional basis while efforts were undertaken to reunite all of the members of the Afro-Malagasy group.[152] In order to accommodate the dissident states, the UAMCE project was abandoned in February 1965 in favor of a new institution, the African and Malagasy Common Organization (OCAM), which was supposed to promote the political, economic, social and technical development of the member states.[153]

The charter of the OCAM was drafted in January 1966 and signed in Tananarive on June 27, 1966.[154] The final text contained no references to political functions, and in the end the OCAM emerged as an almost identical reproduction of the ill-fated UAMCE.[155]

With the exception of the treaties concluded under the auspices of the two earlier organizations, which were the object of a resolution to ensure continuity under the new organization,[156] no specific measures were undertaken to transfer the functions, assets and liabilities of the UAM and the OAMCE to the OCAM.[157] The new body simply took possession of the head-quarters buildings and their contents in Yaundé and Cotonou and assumed the claims and debts of the previous organizations without any distinction or accounting.[158]

E. SEPARATION

The separation of a subsidiary organ to form a new international organization is a somewhat uncommon occurrence. The tendency has rather been in the direction of consolidating institutions to economize on ressources.

The following are some examples of the separation of organizations.

1. The Separation of the International Labour Organisation from the League of Nations

The International Labour Organisation (ILO) was established in 1919 under Articles 387 to 427 of the Treaty of Versailles. It was formally linked to the League through its membership[159] and budget,[160] and certain of its functions were entrusted to the League's Council and Secretary-General.[161]

From the very beginning, however, the ILO endeavoured to assert its independence from the League. Under the able leadership of its first director, Albert Thomas, the organization aggressively fought to become an effective instrument for achieving social justice rather than simply an office of the League responsible for distributing information about labour issues.[162]

The method the ILO adopted to become autonomous was to interpret the Treaty of Versailles in the broadest possible fashion. For example, according to Article 387, paragraph 2 of the Treaty, the memberships of the League and the ILO were in principle supposed to be identical. In reality, however, this was never the case. Austria, Egypt and Germany became members of the ILO before they joined the League. The United States was admitted to the ILO although it never belonged to the League. When Brazil, Haiti, Peru, China, Venezuela and Hungary withdrew from the League, they remained members of the ILO.[163]

Another area where the ILO circumvented the formal texts was with regard to its finances. Although the ILO's budget was supposed to be reviewed and approved by the Assembly of the League, in practice the Assembly, to avoid raising the ire of the ILO, simply accepted without discussion whatever the Administrative Council of the ILO proposed.[164]

There was no doubt by the eve of the Second World War that the ILO had in fact become one of the most successful international organizations. In twenty years it had elaborated more than fifty international labour conventions. Some of its supporters, however, felt that the ILO's constitutional ties with the League, tenuous though they were, could prove harmful to the organization in the event of the League's collapse, which by then had become a distinct possibility. A proposal was put forward to separate the two organizations formally, but war broke out before anything further could be done on the matter.[165]

Efforts to revise the ILO's charter had to wait until 1944, when a Constitutional Committee was appointed to review the question and make specific recommendations.[166] The work of this committee made it possible for the Twenty-seventh ILO Conference in November 1945 to adopt three amendments to the ILO Constitution dealing with membership, finance and the procedure for amending the Constitution.[167] Two more amendments were passed at the Twenty-nineth Conference in September 1946. One removed all the remaining references to the League of Nations from the Constitution and replaced certain League organs by ILO organs in respect of certain functions.[168] The second amendment modified the final articles of all the international labour conventions adopted by previous sessions of the ILO Conference so that they no longer referred to the Secretary General of the League.[169]

The League of Nations, for its part, facilitated the separation of the ILO by passing a resolution recognizing the right of the organization to make whatever constitutional changes were necessary as a result of the dissolution of the League and instructing the Liquidation Board to transfer certain funds and properties to the ILO.[170] Accordingly, an agreement was signed between the ILO and the liquidation board of the League under which the League turned over ownership of all the material assets which it had placed at the disposal of the ILO[171] and handed over responsibility for the administration of certain funds.[172]

The process of separating the ILO from the League was finally completed on April 20, 1948, with the coming into force of the revised Constitution of the ILO.[173]

2. The Separation of the Arab League Educational, Cultural and Scientific Organization from the League of Arab States

The League of Arab States (LAS) was created by a convention signed on March 22, 1945 for the purpose of strengthening relations between the member states, coordinating their political activities, defending their independence and protecting the interests of all Arab states.[174] Moreover, the LAS exercises activities in the fields of economics and finance, communications, social welfare, health and cultural affairs.[175]

Over the years, the cultural affairs activities of the LAS were dispersed among several subsidiary bodies which included the Cultural Department of the League Secretariat, the Institute of Arab Manuscripts and the Institute of Higher Arabic Studies.[176] In February 1964 the League drew up two instruments to consolidate the three organs into the Arab League Educational, Cultural and Scientific Organization (ALESCO), an independent international organization which would become a specialized agency of the LAS.[177]

The ALESCO Constitution came into effect on July 25, 1970, and on that day the functions and assets of the League's Cultural Department, the Institute of Arabic Manuscripts and the Institute of Higher Arabic Studies were taken over by the new organization.[178]

3. The Separation of the United Nations Industrial Development Organization from the United Nations

The General Assembly of the United Nations established the United Nations Industrial Development Organization (UNIDO) as an autonomous organ of the Assembly by a resolution adopted November 17, 1966.[179] Its purpose was to promote the industrialization of developing countries in accordance with Articles 1. b., 55 and 56 of the Charter of the United Nations.[180]

In order to better promote and implement the principles set

out in General Assembly resolutions relating to the establishment a new international economic order,[181] UNIDO's Second General Conference in March 1975 recommended the transformation of the organization into a specialized agency of the United Nations.[182] The General Assembly accepted the proposal at its seventh special session in September 1975 and created an Intergovernmental Committee of the Whole to draw up a constitution for the future specialized agency.[183]

The Committee prepared a draft constitution in 1976 and 1977 which was further elaborated at the United Nations Conference on the Establishment of the United Nations Industrial Development Organization as a Specialized Agency in February and March 1978.[184] The Conference, however, was unable to complete its work within the time limit set by the General Assembly. A second session was held in March and April 1979, at the end of which the constitution of UNIDO was adopted by consensus.[185]

According to Article 25, the constitution the new organization would enter into force when at least eighty states had deposited instruments of ratification, acceptance or approval.[186] The fulfillment of this requirement took until June 21, 1985, almost six years.

The separation of UNIDO from the United Nations actually took place in stages beginning in August 1985 under transitional arrangements adopted by the General Assembly in December 1979.[187] As soon as the members of the organs of the new specialized agency were elected, they took over the functions of the old United Nations organs which continued to exist, at least formally, until December 31, 1985.[188]

F. TRANSFER OF SPECIFIC FUNCTIONS

The transfer of specific functions occurs in two situations. The first is when organizations which have the same or similar memberships and overlapping functions and capacities decide that only one of the institutions should continue to perform certain functions. This is basically a rationalization of functions and does not otherwise affect the organizations. The second situation is when organizations are in the process of being dismantled. The transfer of a specific function in such case constitutes a stage in the dissolution or the liquidation of an organization.

The following are examples of each of these situations.

1. The Transfer of the Social and Cultural Functions of the Western European Union to the Council of Europe

The problem of overlapping responsibilities and duplication of efforts among the different European regional organizations became acute in December 1958 with the simultaneous meetings of the Committee of Ministers of the Council of Europe (CE), the Council of Ministers of the Western European Union (WEU) and the Council of Ministers of the North Atlantic Treaty Organization (NATO).[189] The Committee of Ministers of the CE decided that the situation had become so bad that measures needed to be taken 'to streamline the European institutions' and so they placed this issue on the agenda of its next meeting scheduled for the following April.[190]

In anticipation of that meeting, the Belgian government drew up a series of suggestions for rationalizing the activities of the various European organizations[191] which were examined by a special committee of representatives of the CE, the WEU, NATO and the Organization for European Economic Cooperation (OEEC). The report of the special committee recommended that the exercise of the powers of the WEU in the social and cultural field be transferred to the Council of Europe.[192] This recommendation was endorsed by the Committee of Ministers of the CE on April 20, 1959, and it issued a statement that the transfer of the WEU functions in the social and cultural field to the CE would be accomplished 'in accordance with procedures to be laid down by the Ministerial Committees of the two organizations.'[193]

Although the Assembly of the WEU objected to the fact that it had not been consulted on the matter before the decision was made, as required by the Treaty of Brussels of 1948,[194] the secretariats and councils of the WEU and CE nevertheless pressed forward with preparations to transfer the functions. The main social and cultural committees of the WEU were transferred to the CE between April 15 and May 27, 1960.[195] The custodial and administrative functions which the WEU had assumed under international agreements concluded in simplified form were taken over by CE as well, but those entrusted by formal instruments were not transferred because they required specific amendment procedures.[196]

2. The Transfer of Functions Relating to the Study of Natural Disasters from the International Relief Union to the United Nations Educational, Scientific and Cultural Organization

The International Relief Union (IRU) was established by a convention signed in Geneva on July 12, 1927 to provide assistance to victims of natural disasters and to encourage the study of preventive measures against disasters.[197] The IRU never possessed sufficient financial resources to achieve its objective of ensuring international assistance, and from an early date it was forced to limit its activities to scientific research and documentation.[198]

Chronic financial difficulties forced the IRU in 1950 to seek a merger with the United Nations, but its offer was turned down.[199] In December 1965 the Union once again asked the United Nations to take over its responsibilities and assets,[200] and this time the Secretary-General concluded that some of the IRU's functions and assets could be continued by UNESCO.[201] At the Secretary-General's suggestion the United Nations Economic and Social Council passed a resolution recommending that UNESCO make arrangements with the IRU to transfer the responsibilities of the IRU that were within its competence, as well as the remaining assets of the Union.[202]

UNESCO subsequently entered into consultations with the IRU and together the two organizations elaborated an agreement under which UNESCO took over the IRU's 'activities in connexion with the scientific study of natural disasters and the means for protecting against them',[203] its 'stock of publications, the materials in its documentation service and its archival documents relating to the scientific study of natural disasters, as well as the sums remaining at the time of liquidation'.[204]

Although the major portion of the IRU's functions and assets were transferred to UNESCO in accordance with the transfer agreement, the organization continued to exist and still had sixteen member states in 1984.[205]

G. CONCLUSIONS

Although all cases of succession between international organizations can be classified more or less easily as replacement, absorption, merger, separation or the transfer of specific functions,it is sometimes possible to find a mixture of several different types of succession. The winding up of the United Nations Relief and Rehabilitation Administration, for example, combined elements of both simple transfer of functions and replacement. When it was decided in 1946 that the UNRRA had achieved its purposes and should be dissolved, there began a process under which virtually all of its functions, assets and liabilities were split up among several other existing organizations. The WHO took over its health functions,[206] its food production program went to the FAO[207] and some of its social welfare functions were assumed by the United Nations.[208] The only organization that was actually created specifically to carry on certain UNRRA functions was the International Relief Organization.[209]

What characterizes replacement, absorption, merger, separation and transfer of specific functions is that in each case functions, assets and liabilities are transferred between different legal entities. This we saw earlier is the very essence of succession.

There have been many instances where international organizations have undergone major constitutional changes, but so long as such changes have not affected the identity of the subject of the rights and obligations there is no succession. The constitution of the Pan American Union, for example, has undergone several extensive revisions since 1889, but the member states always opted to modify the structure of the organization rather than to replace it with a new one.[210]

This was also the case for the Organization for European Economic Cooperation (OEEC) which was 'reconstituted' in 1960 and renamed the Organization for Economic Cooperation and Development (OECD). In the course of negotiating the revisions, several delegations had argued in favor of creating an entirely new organization, since the admission of Canada, Japan and the United States would change the European character of the organization and the proposed amendments would significantly expand its functions.[211] It was nevertheless decided to consider the revisions a 'reconstitution' of the OEEC in order to avoid having to contend with problems of succession.[212]

Another type of constitutional change that may resemble succession but cannot properly be classified as such is the merger of the organs of international organizations. This occurred in the European Communities in 1958 when the Assembly and Court of the European Coal and Steel Community were merged with the Court of Justice and the Parliamentary Assembly of the newly created European Economic Community and the European Atomic Energy Community ties.[213] In 1965 the councils and commissions of the three European Communities were merged to form a single Council and a single Commission.[214]

The merger of certain organs of the European Communities was presented at the time as a step in the direction of creating a single European Community that would be governed by one treaty that would replace the treaties of Paris and Rome. This goal, however, has not yet been achieved, and the three organizations continue to exist as separate legal entities.[215]

A somewhat similar situation occurred in the case of the Paris Union for the Protection of Industrial Property and the Bern Union for the Protection of Literary and Artistic Works. The administrative organization of the two unions were first united in 1898 and operated under various names, the last of which was called the United International Bureaux for the Protection of Intellectual Property (BIRPI).[216]

While other unions, like the Universal Postal Union and the International Telecommunications Union, were transformed into modern international organizations soon after the Second World War, the Paris and Bern Unions remained largely unchanged until 1967. Some early proposals for reform had envisaged the creation of a single new organization patterned on the specialized agencies of the United Nations,[217] but it was finally decided to maintain the Unions as independent entities and to create a new international organization, the World Intellectual Property Organization (WIPO) to coordinate the administration of the Unions and to promote the protection of intellectual property throughout the world.[218]

The convention establishing WIPO provided for a new International Bureau which functions at the same time as the Secretariat of the new organization and the BIRPI.[219] Aside from this common organ, WIPO and the Unions remain three distinct international organizations.

Because the merger of organs does not affect the identities of the organizations concerned, it cannot be considered true mergers of organizations. It cannot be considered a transfer of rights and obligations between organizations either, since the organs are common to each organization and cannot be identified with any single entity. These partial mergers should be considered a kind of federalism between international organizations.

III

THE LEGAL BASIS OF
SUCCESSION BETWEEN
INTERNATIONAL
ORGANIZATIONS

A. INTRODUCTION

Having established when problems of succession arise between international organizations, we turn now to the question of how devolution legally takes place, that is the principles and rules of international law that govern succession. One conclusion we reached earlier about the concept of succession is that it results either from an agreement between the predecessor and the successor, which is usually called 'conventional succession', or by operation of the law when certain conditions are fulfilled, which is commonly referred to as 'automatic succession'.[1] In this chapter we will examine these two basic types of succession in the practice of international organizations.

B. CONVENTIONAL SUCCESSION

There are many conventional ways to transfer rights and obligations between international organizations. The specific method chosen usually depends on the circumstances. Few problems arise when the memberships of the predecessor and successor organizations are the same. More complex arrangements are required when the memberships are different.

1. Methods Used When Memberships are the Same

(a) Constitutional Provisions A technique frequently used to transfer functions, assets and liabilities between organizations with identical memberships has been to include provisions to that effect in the constitutions of the successor bodies. The 1960

Agreement for the Establishment of the Caribbean Organization, for example, provided that the 1946 Agreement for the Establishment of the Caribbean Commission would terminate when the 1960 Agreement came into force,[2] and that:

> the assets of the Caribbean Commission shall be and are by virtue of this Agreement transferred to and vested in the Caribbean Organization. The Caribbean Organization is hereby authorized to assure at the same time the liabilities of the Caribbean Commission and shall be regarded as the successor body of the Caribbean Commission.[3]

The 1967 Treaty for East African Cooperation declared that the East African Common Services Organization Agreements of 1961 and 1966 were abrogated[4] and that the new East African Community was to take over those of the services of the EACSO as were in existence on the date the new convention came into force.[5] Annex XV of the Treaty also said that the funds collected by several subsidiary services of EACSO were to be paid to the corresponding organ of the EAC, the rules of procedure of the Assembly of the EACSO were to be applied by the EAC until such time as it elaborated new ones, and, lastly, the Secretary-General and Legal Secretary of the EACSO were to assume the same functions in the EAC.[6]

Another example is the 1975 Convention for the Establishment of a European Space Agency, which stipulated that the conventions of the European Space Research Organization and European Organization for the Development of Space Vehicle Launchers would terminate on the date of entry of the ESA convention,[7] and that on that same date all the rights of ESRO and ELDO would be taken over by the new organization.[8]

(b) Implied Succession   In some instances, the transfer of functions, assets and liabilities has taken place without any formalities whatsoever No special measures were employed, for example, when the International Committee for Coordination of Anti-Locust Activities in Central America and Mexico (CICLA) was replaced by the International Regional Organization of Animal and Plant Health (OIRSA) in 1955 and when the African and Malagasy Organization for Economic Cooperation (OAMCE) and the Union of African and Malagasy States (UAM)

merged to form the African and Malagasy Common Organization (OCAM) in 1966. The members of these organizations
seem to have considered succession to have been implicit and
that no special procedures were necessary.[9]

The 'implied abrogation' of a treaty is a well-established rule
of international law. Judge Anzilotti stated in the 1939 case of
the *Electricity Company of Sofia and Bulgaria* that 'it is generally
agreed that, besides express abrogation, there is also tacit abrogation resulting from the fact that the new provisions are incom-
patible with the previous provisions, or that the whole matter
which formed the subject of these latter is henceforward governed by the new provisions.'[10] This rule was eventually codified
in Article 59, paragraph of the 1969 Vienna Convention on the
Law of Treaties in the following terms:

> A treaty shall be considered as terminated if all the parties
> conclude a later treaty relating to the same subject matter
> and: (a) it appears from the later treaty or is otherwise
> established that the parties intended that the matter
> should be governed by that treaty; or (b) the provisions of
> the later treaty are so far incompatible with those of the
> earlier one that the two treaties are not capable of being
> applied at the same time.[11]

Although it might be clear from the circumstances that the
treaty establishing the predecessor organization has been tacitly
terminated, it does not necessary follow that all of the rights
and obligations of the predecessor organization are transferred
to the successor organization. In the two cases cited, however,
tacit succession can be presumed, since the successor organization did in fact take over the functions, assets and liabilities of
the predecessor organization and no objections were raised
from any quarter. Such informal succession may only work
for relatively small organizations with few functions, members,
assets and liabilities.

2. Methods Used When Memberships are Different

When the memberships of the predecessor and successor orgni-
zations are different, the principle of *pacta tertiis non nocent*
requires that the rights of the members of predecessor organization which have elected not to become members of the suc-

cessor organization be protected.[12] In such situations succession requires two operations: (a) the dissolution of the organization and liquidation of its assets and (b) the transfer of its functions to the successor organizations and disposal of its residual assets.

(a) The Dissolution of International Organizations The dissolution of international organizations can be accomplished in a number of ways. Sometimes detailed procedures are specified in their constitutions.[13] Often, however, there are no provisions at all, either through oversight or design. Even when constitutional provisions exist, experience has shown that they have usually proved to be too cumbersome and time consuming to follow.

(1) Dissolution Provisions in Constitutions

The most common type of termination clause that appears in constitutions provides for dissolution of the organization when its membership falls below a certain number. Article 10 of the constitution of the International Institute of Intellectual Co-operation, for example, stated that the 1938 Act would cease to be in force if the contracting parties fell below eight as a result of denunications.[14] A similar wording appeared in the 1947 Agreement Concerning the Establishment of an International Patents Bureau, which set the minimum membership at four.[15] According to the 1962 Convention for the Establishment of a European Space Research Organization, ESRO would be dissolved when the membership dropped to less than five.[16]

An unusual procedure that seems to have been unique to the 1907 Agreement for the Establishment of the Office international d'hygiène publique was to have a tacit renewal of the convention every seven years for those members who had not notified their intention to withdraw from the organization within one year before the expiration of each period.[17]

(2) Withdrawal of Members

The constitutions of many international organizations have no special dissolution procedures, but may allow individual member states to withdraw, subject to certain formalities. The notification period for withdrawal may be as short as six months, as in the case of the World Intellectual Property Organization,[18] and as long as two years, as in the case of the International Labour Organization.[19] Twelve months, however, seems to be the most frequently adopted period.[20]

Article 43 of the 1919 Convention Relating to the Regulation of Aerial Navigation stated that:

> The present Convention may not be denounced before January 1, 1922. In case of denunciation, notification thereof shall be made to the government of the French Republic, which shall communicate it to the other contracting Parties. Such denunciation shall not take effect until at least one year after the giving of notice, and shall take effect only with respect to the Power which has given notice.[21]

The International Commission for Air Navigation adopted this procedure, recommending in August 1945 that the member states denounce the 1919 Convention Relating to the Regulation of Aerial Navigation by using the following standard form of notification:

> In accordance with Article 43 of the Convention relating to the Regulation of Aerial Navigation signed in Paris on 13th October 1919, the Government of . . . . signatory gives notice of denunication of the said Convention; providing that such denunciation shall have effect on or at the expiration of one year from the date of notice or upon the entry into force, for the said Government of the Convention on International Civil Aviation signed at Chicago on 7th December 1944, whichever is the later.[22]

In practice, obtaining the denunciations of all the member states of a defunct organization has almost always turned out to be a very long and nearly impossible task. In almost every case, the liquidation of the organization went forward, and was in fact usually completed, long before the last notification of withdrawal was received.[23]

(3) Agreements Between Members

When the constitutions of international organizations contain no dissolution or withdrawal procedure, the member states have usually concluded special agreements providing for the termination of the treaty establishing the organization and the winding up of its affairs.

In the case of the International Institute of Agriculture, a special protocol was prepared by the Permanent Committee of the IIA according to which the Permanent Committee would announce the termination of the 1905 convention once it had collected all of the assets of the Institute and transferred them to the Food and Agriculture Organization.[24] The instrument came into force on January 28, 1948, when, as stipulated in Article VI, the thirty-fifth member state notified its acceptance.[25]

Less than one month later, the Permanent Committee declared the Institute to be dissolved.[26] In view of the fact that it took twenty-two months to obtain the thirty-five ratifications necessary for the protocol to come into effect, it is very unlikely that the seventeen remaining ratifications could have been received in so short a period of time.[27] Furthermore, the dissolution was announced a year before the liquidation was actually completed.[28]

The same technique was used to dissolve and wind up the Office international d'hygiène publique, although it would have been possible to terminate the 1907 Agreement on November 15, 1950 if all the member states had notified their intention to withdraw from the organization by November 15, 1949. Such a procedure, however, would have still left open the question of the transfer of functions and assets of the OIHP to the World Health Organization, which the members of both organizations wanted to take place. A special protocol promised to be a quicker and more efficient way to accomplish that objective.

The Protocol Concerning the Office international d'hygiène publique provided that the 1907 Agreement would be terminated when all the members had become parties to the Protocol or had denounced the Agreement in accordance with its terms.[29] As it turned out, a number of states did not accede to the Protocol or otherwise take steps to denounce the 1907 Agreement. In November 1948, more than a year after the Protocol came into effect, the Executive Board of the World Health Organization had to instruct the Director-General of the organization 'to inform the Member States parties to the Rome Agreement of the action that they should take in order to denounce the Agreement before November 1949.'[30] The following March the Executive Board again urged 'those parties to the Agreement of 1907 which have not already done so to denounce the said Agreement and, if possible to accept the Protocol of 1946.'[31] This invitation was reiterated in June by the Second World Health Assembly, and the Executive Board and Director-General of the WHO were called upon 'to keep in touch with the Office international d'hygiène publique and to give their assistance if required in settling the situation which might arise should certain governments, parties to the Rome Agreement of 1907, be unable to denounce the said Agreement.'[32]

Seven states had still not acceded to the 1946 Protocol or denounced the Rome Agreement by the last session of the OIHP Permanent Committee in May 1950.[33] The Committee observed, however, that none of the members had 'expressly and formally manifested their intention of opposing the definitive transfer of the duties and functions of the Office to the World Health Organization or to the transfer of its assets.'[34] It decided, therefore, that although the *de jure* dissolution could only be pronounced once the remaining parties to the 1907 Agreement had denounced it, the Office could be terminated *de facto*.[35] Concluding that the membership of the Office after November 15, 1950 would be reduced to a level such that it would no longer fulfill the purposes for which it was established, the Permanent Committee decided that on November 15, 1950 'without waiting for the legal dissolution of the Office international d'hygiène publique, the Chairman and Director shall terminate the activities of the Office.'[36]

Even after the final liquidation of the OIHP was completed, efforts continued to obtain the formal denunciations of Germany, Spain and Japan, the three remaining parties to the 1907 Agreement.[37] It was not until January 1952, at least a year after the Office had effectively ceased to exist, that the Executive Board of the WHO could announce that all the members of the OIHP had denounced the 1907 Agreement.[38]

(4) Resolutions of Organs of the Two Organizations

One of the most unusual procedures used to dissolve and liquidate an organization was the one adopted by the League of Nations. When the issue of the termination of the League was discussed at the twenty-first session of the Assembly in April

1945, the representative of the United Kingdom proposed that 'the best method would be for the Assembly to pass a resolution that as from the day after the last sitting the League should be deemed to have ceased to exist except for the purpose of winding up.'[39] The thirty-four states present endorsed the idea, and on April 18, 1945, the Assembly unanimously adopted the following resolution:

> The Assembly of the League of Nations, Considering that the charter of the United Nations was created, for purposes of the same nature as those for which the League of Nations was established, an international organization known as the United Nations to which all States may be admitted as Members on the conditions prescribed by the charter and to which the great majority of the Members of the League already belong;
>
> Desiring to promote, so far as lies in its power, the continuation, development and success of international co-operation in the new form adopted by the United Nations;
>
> Considering that, since the new organization has taken up its functions, the League of Nations may be dissolved; and
>
> Considering that under Article 3, paragraph 3, of the Covenant, the Assembly may deal at its meetings with any matter within the sphere of action of the League:
>
> Adopts the following resolution:
>
> **Dissolution of the League of Nations**
>
> (1) As from the day following the close of the present session of the Assembly, the League of Nations shall cease to exist except for the sole purpose of liquidation of its affairs as provided in the present resolution.
>
> (2) The liquidation shall be effected as rapidly as possible and the date of its completion shall be notified to all the Members by the Board of Liquidation provided for in paragraph 2 . . .[40]

Some legal experts have expressed reservations about this procedure, in particular the competence of the League's Assembly to take such measures on the basis of Article 3, paragraph 3 of the Convenant.[41] They argued that if the Convenant contained no express provision for the dissolution of the League, it was certainly because the founders intended it to be a permanent organization. Furthermore, it is very unlikely that the contracting states ever intended the Assembly to have the competence to dissolve the League.[42]

Although the Assembly probably acted *ultra vires* there is no question that all of the member states present at the final session approved the decision and that the other member states tacitly accepted the termination of the League by cooperating with the Board of Liquidation or acquiesced by not voicing any objections to the procedure. This is consistent with the long-established rule of treaty law that, unless a treaty stipulates otherwise, it may be terminated 'by consent of all the parties.'[43] The form of the consent is immaterial so long as the intention of the parties is evident.[44]

The same procedure was used to terminate the Permanent Court of International Justice, except that in this case the League Assembly passed a resolution to dissolve an institution that was based on a separate treaty from the Covenant and that had a different membership.[45] The resolution adopted by the Assembly on April 18, 1946 recalled an earlier resolution of the Permanent Commission of the United Nations recommending that the League take steps to dissolve the Permanent Court,[46] and then went on to declare that, since all of the judges of the Permanent Court had already resigned and no mechanism would exist to appoint new judges after the disappearance of the League, the Permanent Court was to be 'regarded as dissolved with effect from the day following the close of the present session.'[47]

Once again, it cannot be said that the resolution in and of itself abrogated the Protocol of Signature. It merely recorded the consent of the parties to the Protocol to the dissolution of the Permanent Court and stated the fact that the Protocol of Signature would legally cease to exist once its object became impossible to attain.

There must have been some lingering doubts about this method of dissolving the Permanent Court, because the Allied Powers continued their efforts to secure the formal agreement of the defeated countries to the measures that had been taken.[48] Such doubts were probably unfounded, because there were sufficient grounds under general international law to consider the Protocol of Signature to have been properly terminated.

Besides the impossibility of performance mentioned above and the acquiescence of the members not present at the last League Assembly, the consent of all the parties to the abrogation of the Protocol of Signature was implicit when they signed or acceded to the Charter of the United Nations. Article 92 of the Charter stipulates that the International Court of Justice 'shall function in accordance with the annexed statute, which is based upon the statute of the Permanent Court of International Justice.'[49]

(5) Conclusions Regarding Dissolution

We may conclude, then, that the dissolution of international organizations has been accomplished in many different ways. Even when specific constitutional procedures have existed, they have seldom been strictly followed. The main concern has always been expediency, that is to proceed with the liquidation of the organization without further delay.

Although attempts were often made to get all the members to agree to the dissolution, this was almost always a mere formality. By the time all of the consents had been obtained, the organization had already ceased to exist anyway, because it had no longer had the means to fulfill the purposes and functions for which it was created.[50]

(b) Transfer of Functions and Assets The transfer of functions and assets between organizations whose memberships are not identical takes place either by means of agreements between the predecessor and successor organizations or else as the result of agreements concluded between the member states of the organizations concerned.

(1) Agreements between the Predecessor and Successor Organizations

Once the decision has been made to dissolve an organization, the usual practice has been to appoint a liquidator to carry out the winding up procedures. This may be an individual, a special commission or one of the organs of the institution. In the course of performing its duties, the liquidator enters into contact with the successor organization or organizations and makes arrangements for the transfer of certain functions and assets. Such arrangements will consist of either formal or informal agreements.

(i) *Formal Agreements*   Formal transfer agreements are by far the most common method of transmitting rights and obligations between international organizations. The League of Nations and the United Nations, for example, signed eight such agreements between July 1946 and June 1947.[51] The United Nations Relief and Rehabilitation Agency concluded agreements with the WHO,[52] the FAO,[53] the PCIRO[54] and the United Nations[55] between December 1946 and September 1948. Similar arrangements were made between the League of Nations and the International Labour Organisation in May 1946,[56] the International Institute of Intellectual Cooperation and UNESCO in December 1946,[57] the Office international d'hygiène publique and the WHO in January 1948,[58] the International Bureau of Education and UNESCO in November 1968,[59] the International Relief Union and UNESCO in November 1968[60] and, finally, the International Patent Institute and the European Patent Organization in September 1977.[61]

The competence of the liquidator to conclude transfer agreements is usually based on resolutions of one of the organs of the organization or an agreement signed by the member states. In the case of the League of Nations, the authority was derived from the Resolution for the Dissolution of the League of Nations, which gave the Board of Liquidation full powers to 'make such agreements and take all such measures as in its discretion it considers appropriate for this purpose.'[62] This same resolution also directed the Board of Liquidation to transfer to the ILO certain funds[63] and certain properties of the League in Geneva.[64]

The UNRRA Council passed a series of resolutions, each relating to specific functions and activities of the organization in the fields of health,[65] social welfare,[66] agriculture,[67] displaced persons[68] and child welfare.[69] These served as the authority for the Director of UNRRA to negotiate transfer agreements with each of the successor organizations on behalf of the defunct organization.

The competence of the International Patent Institute to conclude an international agreement with the European Patent Organization was derived from a protocol signed by all of the member states which provided that they would:

> take all necessary steps to ensure the transfer to the European Patent Office . . . of all assets and liabilities and all staff members of the International Patent Institute. Such transfer shall be effected by an agreement between the International Patent Institute and the European Patent Organization . . .[70]

The competence of the successor organization to conclude a transfer agreement is sometimes specifically set out in its constitution. Article 72 of the Constitution of the WHO, for example, authorizes the organization to 'take over from any other international organization or agency whose purpose and activities lie within the field of competence of the Organization by international agreement or by mutually acceptable arrangements entered into between the competent authorities of the respective organization.'[71] Similar provisions can be found in Article XIII, paragraph 4 of the Constitution of the FAO,[72] Article XI, paragraph 2 of the UNESCO Constitution,[73] Article III,paragraph 5 of the UNRRA Constitution[74] and Article 14 of the IRO Constitution.[75]

In most instances, however, there is no express authority for the successor organization to conclude a transfer agreement. Such express authority would have been useful to dispel any doubts that might have existed at the end of the Second World War regarding the treaty-making capacity of international organizations, but it is generally agreed today that every organization has such capacity. Because each organization differs from every other organization in legal form, functions, powers and structures, its capacity to conclude agreements with other organizations depends on its constitutive treaty.[76] The relevant rules of the organization therefore determine whether the functions, assets and liabilities assumed by the successor institution are consistent with its purposes, functions and powers.

(ii) *Informal Agreements* The functions and assets of defunct organizations have sometimes been transferred to successor organizations by means of informal agreements. These usually consisted of arrangements negotiated by the representatives of the organizations which were subsequently approved by the competent organs of each institution.

This method was employed to transfer numerous functions of the League of Nations to the United Nations. On February 12, 1946 the General Assembly passed a resolution requesting the Economic and Social Council:

> . . . to survey the functions and activities of a non political character which have hitherto been performed by the League of Nations in order to determine which of them should, with such modifications as are desirable, be assumed by the organs of the United Nations or be entrusted to the specialized agencies which have been brought into relationship with the United Nations. Pending the adoption of the measures decided upon as a result of this examination, the Council should, on or before the dissolution of the League, assume and continue provisionally the work hitherto done by the following League departments: the Economic, Financial and Transit Department, particularly the research and statistical work; the Health Section, particularly the epidemiological service; the Opium Section and the secretariats of the Permanent Opium Board and Supervisory Body.[77]

The League Assembly responded on April 18, 1946 by directing the Secretary-General of the League 'to afford every facility for assumption by the United Nations of such non-political activities, hitherto performed by the League, as the United Nations may decide to assume.'[78]

At the request of the ECOSOC, the Secretary-General of the United Nations made a survey of the League's functions which the United Nations should take over and his recommendations were approved by the General Assembly on December 14, 1946 in a resolution entitled 'Transfer to the United Nations of Certain Non-Political Functions and Activities of the League of Nations, Other Than Those Pursuant to International Agreements.'[79]

As a result of these parallel resolutions, the original texts of treaties and other international instruments were transferred to the United Nations on August 1, 1946.[80] By October 1946 the United Nations had taken over the functions which had been conferred on the League by over fifty conventions on communications, transit, economics, finance, legal and social questions, as well as the League's library service and publications services.[81]

The same process was followed to transfer the duties of the League in respect of its staff pensions fund to the International Labour Organisation. Paragraph 16 of the Resolution for the Dissolution of the League provided that, subject to the agreement of the International Labour Organisation, the administration of the fund would be transferred to the ILO.[82] This offer was accepted by the International Labour Conference in a resolution approved on October 9, 1946 under which the ILO agreed to assume 'responsibility for financing and administering the staff pensions fund on the basis indicated in paragraph 16 of the Resolution adopted on April 18, 1946, by the twenty-first and last session of the Assembly of the League of Nations and on the understanding that arrangements would be made for the pensions fund to be examined again by the Consulting Actuary so that such financial provisions as circumstances indicated could be made from the League funds by the Liquidation Board before transfer was effected.'[83]

Other funds administered by the League transferred to the ILO in this manner were the Pensions Fund for the Members of the Permanent Court of International Justice, the Working Capital Fund and the Renovation Fund.[84]

Similar arrangements were used to transfer functions from the Office international d'hygiène publique to the World Health Organization. The President of the OIHP and the Commission of Finance and Transfer were supposed 'to take the steps necessary to effect the transfer to the World Health Organization or its Interim Commission of the duties and functions which were assigned to the Office.'[85] In accordance with its instructions, the OIHP's Notification Service and responsibility for publishing the *Bulletin Mensuel* were transferred to the Interim Commission of the WHO on January 1, 1947.[86] The Interim Commission of the WHO also agreed as from July 1, 1947 to take over the administration of the OIHP's staff pension fund.[87] An arrangement was concluded on January 23, 1948 under which the

Interim Commission of the WHO assumed the OIHP's functions relating to international epidemic control and the study of communicable diseases.[88] During the final phase of the liquidation, between November 1950 and April 1951, the OIHP turned over its library, archives, some furniture, certain funds and securities and responsibility for collecting overdue contributions from some of the OIHP's former members.[89]

Such informal transfer agreements are governed by the same rules as apply to formal agreements. The competence of the liquidators of the predecessor organization is usually derived from resolutions of the organ of the institution representing the consent of all the member states, while the authority of the successor organization is based on its mandate according to its constitutional law.[90]

(2) Agreements between States

Organizations may be entrusted with certain judicial, administrative or chancery functions under treaties or unilateral declarations. Such functions can be transferred to the successor organization either by inserting provisions to this effect in the constitution of the successor organization or else by amending each treaty and unilateral declaration. The following are some examples of these procedures.

(i) *Treaties and Declarations Conferring Jurisdiction on the Permanent Court of International Justice* The Permanent Court of International Justice was assigned jurisdictional functions under a large number of treaties and unilateral declarations. Since the Permanent Court had functioned well during the inter-war period, the allied powers thought it should be integrated in some manner in the new United Nations system of organizations. The San Francisco Conference considered making the Permanent Court an organ of the United Nations but concluded that this would entail certain complicated procedures. The Statute of Permanent Court would have to be modified, and with only 32 of the 41 states parties to the Statute present at the Conference, the negotiations between the parties concerned would probably be protracted and the outcome uncertain. Moreover, many of the states participating in the Conference were not parties to the Statute and would be excluded from the amendment process.[91]

In order to avoid such problems, the Conference decided to create a new court based on the Statute of the Permanent Court.[92] It sought to ensure the continuity of the judicial process begun by the Permanent Court, however, by including two provisions in the Statute of the International Court of Justice. Article 36, paragraph 5 related to unilateral acceptance of compulsory jurisdiction and states that:

> Declarations made under Article 36 of the Statute of the Permanent Court of International Justice and which are still in force shall be deemed, as between the parties to the present Statute, to be acceptances of the compulsory jurisdiction of the International Court of Justice for the period which they still have to run and in accordance with their terms.

Article 37 related to jurisdictional clauses in treaties and provides that:

> Whenever a treaty or convention in force provides for reference of a matter to a tribunal to have been instituted by the League of Nations, or to the Permanent Court of International Justice, the matter shall, as between the parties to the present Statute, be referred to the International Court of Justice.

These two clauses were intended to maintain in effect jurisdictional clauses and declarations which would otherwise have lapsed or become inoperative after the Permanent Court ceased to exist. To have left it up to the individual states to make the required modifications to all the various instruments would have been very cumbersome and disruptive.[93]

Although the two articles have similar language and cover similar objects, they have been interpreted very differently by the International Court of Justice. In the *Aerial Incident Case between Israel and Bulgaria*, the Court held that Article 36, paragraph 5 applied only to the original signatories of the Statute.[94] All the declarations of acceptance of the compulsory jurisdiction of the Permanent Court that had not been transformed into acceptances of the jurisdiction of the new Court by operation of Article 36, paragraph 5 before the dissolution of the Permanent Court were extinguished and could not be revived.[95]

The Court examined the temporal scope of Article 37 in the *Barcelona Traction Case (Preliminary Objections)* and concluded that jurisdictional clauses in treaties merely become dormant after the dissolution of the Permanent Court and were reactivated when the parties to the treaties became parties to the Statute of the International Court of Justice.[96] To interpret this provision in the same way as Article 36, paragraph 5 would have resulted in a situation where most of the jurisdictional clauses concerned would have lapsed, which was precisely what Article 37 was supposed to prevent.[97]

(ii) *The Narcotic Drug Conventions of 1912, 1925, 1931 and 1936*   The League of Nations was entrusted with administrative and chancery functions relating to six narcotic drug conventions. These included communicating to the parties the texts of regulations and statistical information regarding trade in drugs, determining whether the provision of the conventions applied to certain preparations containing narcotic substances and appointing the members and staff of technical bodies, the Permanent Central Opium Board and the Supervisory Body.[98] In September 1946, the United Nations Economic and Social Council recommended that the United Nations take over those functions and approved a draft protocol amending the narcotics conventions.[99] The General Assembly unanimously adopted the draft on November 19, 1946,[100] and the protocol was opened for signature on December 11, 1946.[101]

(iii) *The Conventions on the Suppression of Traffic in Women, Children and Obscene Publications of 1921, 1923 and 1933*   League of Nations exercised certain chancery functions in respect of three conventions on the suppression of traffic in women, children and obscene publications. These included the receipt of the instruments of ratification and denunciation of the conventions and publication of a special record showing which states had signed, ratified, acceded to or denounced the conventions.[102] As in the case of the narcotics conventions, the Economic and Social Council concluded that the United Nations should carry on these functions and proposed that the same procedure be followed as for the conventions on narcotic drugs.[103] Two protocols were drafted which the General Assembly approved on October 20, 1947.[104] The protocol amending the conventions on traffic in women and children was opened for signature on November 20, 1947,[105] while the protocol amending the convention on traffic in obscene publications was opened for signature on May 4, 1949.[106]

(iv) *The Convention Relating to Economic Statistics of 1928*   The Economic and Social Council expressed the desire in February 1947 'to assume formally the functions of the Committee of Experts set up under the International Convention Relating to Economic Statistics'[107]of December 14, 1928. These functions included calling for conferences to revise the Convention, receiving notices of changes in the territorial applicability of the Convention, receiving notices of ratification, accession and denunciation and inform the members of the League and certain other states of such notices.[108] In order to do this, a protocol amending the 1928 Convention was drafted by the Economic and Social Council and presented to the General Assembly for approval.[109] The protocol was adopted by the General Assembly on November 18, 1948[110] and opened for signature on December 9, 1948.[111]

(v) *The International Sanitary Conventions of 1926 and 1933*   The Office international d'hygiène publique was charged with certain epidemiological functions under the International Sanitary Convention of June 21, 1926[112] and the International Sanitary Convention for Aerial Navigation of April 12, 1933.[113] Since the OIHP was unable to carry out its functions during the Second World War, the United Nations Relief and Rehabilitation Agency prepared two protocols amending the sanitary conventions to permit UNRRA to exercise the functions hitherto performed by the OIHP.[114] The agreements signed on December 15, 1944 provided that the functions assumed by UNRRA would revert to the OIHP within eighteen months unless further amendments were adopted.[115] When the time came for the protocols to expire, UNRRA drafted two additional protocols to extend their duration.[116] The functions never did revert to the OIHP; instead they passed to the World Health Organization on November 1, 1946.[117]

(vi) *The Conventions Relating to Food and Agriculture*   The International Institute of Agriculture was entrusted with administrative functions under six conventions relating to food and agriculture.[118] Rather than prepare a special amendment to these conventions the members of the IIA chose to include a provision in the protocol dissolving the Institute which specified that the functions attributed to it by the six conventions would devolve upon the FAO 'and the parties to the said conventions shall execute such provisions, in so far as they remain in force, in all respects as though they refer to the Organization in place of the Institute.'[119]

(vii) *The International Labour Conventions* A multitude of international labour conventions were adopted during the inter-war period under the auspices of the International Labour Organisation which entrusted certain chancery functions to the Secretary-General of the League of Nations. The dissolution of the League made it necessary for the ILO to make arrangements to take over those functions. The procedure adopted once again was to prepare a protocol revising the international labour conventions which the ILO General Conference endorsed on October 9, 1946.[120]

Whether the instruments amending treaties conferring functions on international organizations are contained in the constitutions of the successor organization or in special agreements, they always have an *inter se* character which have effect only as between the parties.[121] The states that become parties to the amendment still remain bound by the terms of the original conventions with respect to the parties to the original convention that do not accept the amendment. However, when the organization that was entrusted with functions under the original agreement disappear, the parts of the agreement relating to the defunct organization become ineffective. According to the principle of the separability of treaty provisions, the obligations which did not depend on the existence of the predecessor organization remained binding for all the parties.[122]

3. Conclusions Regarding Conventional Succession

The foregoing examination of conventional succession has demonstrated how close the ties are between an organization and its member states. In the final analysis, it is the members who decide whether and how the transfer will be accomplished.

When the memberships of the predecessor and successor organizations are the same, there are relatively few problems.

The transfer of functions, assets and liabilities may even take place tacitly without any special procedures whatsoever.

On the other hand, when the memberships are not identical, the situation is somewhat more complex.[123] It is usually necessary in such circumstances to dissolve and liquidate the predecessor organization. Treaty law normally requires that all the member states consent to the modification or termination of the organization's constitution. The constitutive instrument of an organization, however, is not just an ordinary treaty; it is a very special kind of instrument that creates a living entity that depends on the continuous participation of its members to fulfill its aims and purposes. The implementation of the decisions of the majority of the member states to dissolve and liquidate an organization may eventually deprive the institution of the means to carry out its functions and activities. When such a point is reached, the constitutive treaty will be terminated because its object has become impossible to achieve.

The second observation that can be made regarding the practice of conventional succession is that there are many different procedures which can be used to transfer rights and obligations between international organizations. Which procedure is followed depends very much on the historical circumstances. In the end, though, the legal instruments that are used do not matter greatly so long as the states concerned manifest in some way or another their consent.

C. AUTOMATIC SUCCESSION

Automatic succession, as was explained earlier, does not result from an agreement but rather from a rule of law that recognizes the transfer of rights and obligations to have taken place when certain conditions are fulfilled.[124] In private law the legal basis of automatic succession can be found in the statutory laws and the decisions of courts. On the international level, the source is customary law as developed through international practice and the decisions of international tribunals.[125]

The issue of automatic succession between international organizations first arose shortly after the end of the Second World War when the Union of South Africa refused to place the territory of South West Africa under the United Nations Trusteeship System. For nearly three decades, the Union had exercised administrative and legislative powers over this former German territory under the terms of a Mandate confirmed by the Council of the League of Nations on December 17, 1920.[126] In order to ensure that the Mandate was properly executed, the Union was required to submit to the supervision of the Council of the League of Nations and to provide it with annual reports.

After the dissolution of the League in 1946, the Union of South Africa contended that since there was no longer any supervisory organ, the Mandate for South West Africa had lapsed. It therefore sought international recognition of the annexation of the territory into the Union in accordance with what it claimed were the wishes of the inhabitants.[127]

This the General Assembly refused to accept. Its competence to deal with the issue was, however, not clear since the supervisory functions of the League in respect of the mandated territories had not been formally transferred to the United Nations and was contested by the Union of South Africa. In order to settle the matter once and for all, the General Assembly turned to the International Court of Justice in December 1949 and requested an advisory opinion on the status of South West Africa.

1. The 1950 Advisory Opinion on the Status of South West Africa

The International Court of Justice was asked to give an opinion on several questions, the most important of which was whether the Union of South Africa continued to have international obligations under the Mandate for South West Africa, and if so what were those obligations?[128]

The Court first addressed the claim of the Union of South Africa that the mandate had lapsed because the League had ceased to exist. The Mandates System, it affirmed, was an 'international régime' that was governed by international rules, not by any principles of private law.[129] These international rules created an 'international status for the Territory recognized by all the Members of the League of Nations, including the Union of South Africa.'[130]

The mandate imposed two kinds of obligations. One related to the administration of the territory; the other related to the supervision and control of that administration by the League of

Nations.[131] The former obligations required the Union 'to promote to the utmost the material and moral well-being of the inhabitants,' which the Court considered 'the very essence of the sacred trust of civilization.'[132] Since the performance of this group of obligations did not depend on the existence of the League, there was no reason why they should come to an end when the League disappeared.

The Court found support for this conclusion in Article 80, paragraph 1 of the Charter of the United Nations which it said 'maintains the rights of States and peoples and the terms of existing international instruments until the territories in question are placed under the Trusteeship System.[133] As evidence that this was the intention of the framers of the Charter, the Court cited a resolution the League of Nations adopted on April 18, 1946 which noted that all of the mandatory powers had expressed their intention to continue to administer the territories under mandate 'in accordance with the obligations contained in the respective Mandates, until other arrangements have been agreed between the United Nations and the respective mandatory Powers.'[134] It also cited numerous statements made by the Union of South Africa before the League and the United Nations in which the Union declared that it would continue to discharge its obligations under the mandate.[135]

As regards the second group of obligations, the Court admitted that there might be some doubts whether the supervisory functions of the League could be exercised by the United Nations, since those functions 'were neither expressly transferred to the United Nations nor expressly assumed by that organization.[136] It affirmed, however, that there were 'decisive reasons' for concluding that the United Nations was qualified to exercise the supervisory functions.

The first reason was that the 'obligation incumbent upon a mandatory State to accept international supervision and to submit reports is an important part of the Mandates System.'[137] This obligation did not cease to exist 'merely because the supervisory organ ceased to exist, when the United Nations has another international organ performing similar, though not identical, supervisory functions.'[138]

The second reason was that Article 80, paragraph 1 of the Charter protected the rights of the inhabitants of mandated territories until Trusteeship Agreements were concluded. These could not be effectively protected without supervision by an international organ.[139]

The third reason was that the League of Nations resolution of April 18, 1946 had stated that the mandatories would agree on other arrangements for the mandated territories with the United Nations, and no other body. This the Court said 'presupposes that the supervisory functions exercised by the League would be taken over by the United Nations.'[140]

The last reason envoked by the Court was that the General Assembly of the United Nations had the competence under Article 10 of the Charter to discuss any matters within the scope of the Charter and to make recommendations to the members of the United Nations on such matters. It went on to cite several instances where the General Assembly had in fact exercised this supervisory function.[141]

All of these reasons led the Court to the conclusion that the 'General Assembly of the United Nations is legally qualified to exercise the supervisory functions previously exercised by the League of Nations with regard to the administration of the Territory, and that the Union of South Africa is under an obligation to submit to supervision and control of the General Assembly and to render annual reports to it.'[142]

2. Views Critical of the 1950 Advisory Opinion

The issue of the succession of the United Nations to the League of Nations in respect of the Mandate for South West Africa was addressed repeatedly in a long series of subsequent advisory opinions and judgments in which the Court upheld its initial conclusions. A number of judges, however, contested the Court's finding. The following are some of the major dissenting views that were published.

(a) *Judge Read* Judge Read agreed with Court in his separate Opinion in 1950 that the international status of South West Africa continued to have international obligations under the mandate, but contested the Court's assertion that the supervisory functions of the League had been transferred to the United Nations General Assembly.[143] The dissolution of the League, he affirmed, 'might weaken the Mandates System; but it would not bring it to an end.'[144] During the Second World War, he observed, the inhabitants had not suffered adversely from the lack of supervision.[145]

When the League disappeared, its obligations regarding supervision of the mandate become impossible to perform. The only way they could have been continued, Judge Read maintained, was if an arrangement had been agreed between the Union of South Africa and the United Nations, as authorized by the League resolution of April 18, 1946.[146] He could find nothing in the record to indicate that the Union and the United Nations had reached any such agreement.[147]

In support of this conclusion, the judge cited a statement that appeared in the report of the Fourth Committee of the General Assembly where the representative of the Union of South Africa declared that his government would submit reports to the United Nations on South West Africa on the condition that such reports 'would not be considered by the Trusteeship Council and would not be dealt with as if a trusteeship agreement had in fact been concluded.'[148]

The only other way the supervisory functions of the League could have been taken over by the United Nations would have been by succession. In Judge Read's view, however, succession required the 'consent, express or implied by the League, the United Nations and the Mandatory Power.'[149] There was no such consent, he felt, because the United Nations had established a specific procedure for assuming 'functions or powers entrusted to the League of Nations by treaties, international conventions, agreements and other instruments having a political character,'[150] and that this procedure had never been applied in the case of South West Africa.[151]

Since there was no agreement on this issue between the Union and the United Nations and no implied or express consent between the parties concerned to the transfer of the League's functions in respect of the mandates, the judge concluded that the Union of South Africa was under no obligation to render reports to the United Nations and to submit to the supervision of the Unted Nations.[152]

(b) *Judge McNair* Judge Sir Arnold McNair in his separate opinion in 1950 agreed that the mandate for South West Africa established a special international status that had 'more than a contractual basis.'[153] This status, he said, created certain 'real' rights and obligations that survived the dissolution of the League, because real rights and obligations 'acquire an objective existence which is more resistent than are personal rights to the dislocating effects of international events.'[154]

On the other hand, Judge McNair thought that the supervisory functions of the League had lapsed owing to the fact that the Council of the League and the Permanent Mandates Commission, the two organs charged with performing those functions, no longer existed. That part of the mandate had therefore become impossible to perform.[155]

As for the arguments the Court had invoked in support of its view that the Union was under an obligation to submit to the supervision of the United Nations, the judge had the following to say. First of all, there was no succession, because the framers of the Charter of the United Nations had failed to provide for the succession of the administrative functions of the League of Nations contrary to what they had done for the jurisdiction of the Permanent Court of International Justice.[156] There was, he said, ample evidence at the San Francisco Conference that the Union wished to terminate the mandate and annex the territory, and yet nothing had been done to address this issue.

Secondly, the argument that Article 80, paragraph 1 of the Charter protected the rights of the inhabitants of the mandate territories until they were placed under a trusteeship was without merit. The lapse of the supervisory functions of the League was caused by disappearance of that organization and had nothing to do with Article 80, paragraph 1 of the Charter.[157]

Thirdly, the various statements made by representatives of the Union of South Africa were on the whole 'contradictory and inconsistent' and did not prove that it had 'assented to an implied succession by the United Nations to the administrative supervision exercised by the League.'[158]

Lastly, it was not possible to construe the Resolution on Mandates adopted by the League Assembly on April 18, 1946 'as having created a legal obligation" for the Union 'to make annual reports to the United Nations and to transfer to that Organization the pre-war supervision of its mandate by the League.'[159] The only duty incumbent on the Union was to carry out the obligations of the mandate 'which did not involve the activity of the League.'[160]

Having found no legal grounds on which to base the replacement of the League of Nations by the United Nations, Judge McNair concluded that South Africa was under no obligation to accept administrative supervision by the United Nations.[161] This did not mean, however, that the mandatory was subject to no international accountability at all. There still remained a possibility of judicial supervision under Article 7 of the Mandate, which granted any member of the League the right to bring the mandatory before the Permanent Court of International Justice. This right had been maintained by Article 37 of the Statute of the International Court of Justice for the states that were still members of the League at the time of its dissolution. This article, Judge McNair affirmed, 'effected succession by the International Court to the compulsory jurisdiction conferred upon the Permanent Court by Article 7 of the Mandate.'[162]

(c) *Manley O. Hudson* Manley O. Hudson published an article in the Amercian Journal of International Law in 1951 in which he expressed the view that the declarations of the representatives of the Union of South Africa 'give scant support to the Court's conclusion that the Mandatory has an obligation to render reports to the General Assembly.'[163] The Court's statement that the League of Nations' Resolution on Mandates 'presupposed' that the supervisory functions exercised by the League would be taken over by the United Nations was, he wrote, 'hardly borne out by the text of the resolution.'[164]

Hudson went on to say that in his opinion the succession of the General Assembly to the League was not 'a necessary consequence of its competence under Article 10 of the charter to which the Court refers.'[165]

The Court's interpretation of Article 80, paragraph 1 of the Charter was wrong, Hudson declared, because the provision was intended to be 'entirely negative in character.'[166] This was evident from the fact that the League was still in existence at the time the Charter was drafted, and it was important to stipulate in Chapter XII that the terms of the Charter would not alter the existing situation relating to mandates. Any change to the mandates was a matter for the League to decide.[167]

(d) Judges Badawi, Basdevant, Hso Mo, Armande-Ugon and Moreno Quitana Judges Badawi, Basdevant, Hso Mo, Armando-Ugon and Moreno Quintana commented on the 1950 case in their dissenting opinion to the 1956 advisory opinion on the *Admissibility of Hearings of Petitioners by the Committee on South West Africa*. The Union of South Africa, they said, had never submitted to the General Assembly any request that it assume the functions of the Council of the League as provided in Resolution 24(I) of February 12, 1946.[168] In their view, the Court's opinion in 1950 'does not base itself on the idea of succession, on the idea of the transfer of powers,' but rather 'on the objective elements of the situation – the importance of international supervision under the Mandates System as well as the provisions of the Charter of the United Nations.'[169]

(e) Judges Spender and Fitzmaurice Judges Sir Percy Spender and Sir Gerald Fitzmaurice in their joint dissenting opinion to the judgement of the Court in the 1962 *South West Africa Cases* reviewed the historical background of the period between 1945 and 1946 and found that it 'seems to us impossible, on the facts as we have described them, and looking at the matter as a whole, to take any other view than that both the United Nations and the League assemblies were fully aware of and alerted to the whole implications of the mandates question, and of the dissolution of the League relative to that; or alternatively they must on the facts (and even simply as a presumption of law), be held to have been.'[170] For these two jurists the rejection by both assemblies of proposals to transfer the League's function relating to the mandates to the United Nations demonstrated their unwillingness 'to provide any specific way for the consequences of the termination of the League and its membership, for a possible eventual failure to bring a mandated territory into trusteeship.'[171] Whatever may have been the circumstances which prompted this omission, judges Spender and Fitzmaurice could find 'no legal principle which would enable a court of law to put the clock back and, by judicial action, make provision for a case which those concerned elected not to deal with, for

reasons which appeared to them good and sufficient at the time.'[172]

(f) Judge Van Wyk Ad Hoc Judge Van Wyk came to the same conclusion as judges Spender and Fitzmaurice in his dissenting opinion to the 1962 decision. He pointed out that no provision had been made in the Charter of the United Nations for the transfer of the supervisory functions of the Council of the League to the United Nations.[173]

In his view the various statements by South Africa's representatives and other members of the United Nations 'reveal that it was not assumed that the organs of the United Nations would automatically become heir to the powers and functions of the organs of the League in the Mandate instrument.'[174] As evidence of this, he cited the report of the United Nations Special Committee on Palestine submitted to the General Assembly in 1947 which stated that:

> . . . the League of Nations and the Mandates Commission have been dissolved, and there is now no means of discharging fully the international obligations with regard to a mandated territory other than by placing the territory under the International Trusteeship System of the United Nations. The International Trusteeship System, however, has not automatically taken over the functions of the mandates system with regard to mandated territories. . . . The most the mandatory could now do, therefore, in the event of the continuation of the Mandate, would be to carry out its administration, in the spirit of the Mandate, without being able to discharge its international obligations in accordance with the intent of the mandates system.[175]

Such statements, Van Wyk affirmed, 'effectively negative the suggestion that there was a tacit agreement between Members of the United Nations and the Mandatories that the organs of the United Nations would be substituted for the organs of the League relative to the supervision of the Mandates.'[176]

The judge repeated his argument in his separate opinion to the decision of the Court in the 1966 *South West Africa Cases (Second Phase)*, declaring that none of the members of the League and the United Nations during the period preceding and following the dissolution of the League 'thought that they were parties to any agreement which compelled' the mandatory powers 'to report and account to the General Assembly of the United Nations.'[177] If such an implied agreement had existed, he said, 'one would have expected that the states which are alleged to have been parties to such an agreement would have been aware thereof and would have made some reference thereto.'[178]

3. Views Supporting the 1950 Advisory Opinion

It is natural that the jurists who agreed with the reasoning of the 1950 advisory opinion did not repeat the arguments envoked by the Court. A few, however, published their own views on the question of the succession of the United Nations to the League in respect of the supervisory functions over mandates.

(a) Judge Alvarez Judge Alvarez in his dissenting opinion to the 1950 advisory opinion claimed that the United Nations had succeeded automatically to the League by virtue of a rule of what he called 'the new international law.'[179] This new international law required that when an 'international organization like the League of Nations disappears and another one is created, without any indication as to whether the latter replaced the former,' the latter must be 'considered as succeeding the former *ipso facto*,' on the condition that 'the first organization has created an institution, such as the Mandate, having for its purpose the same sacred trust of civilization as the Trusteeship created by the second institution.'[180]

In that judge's view, the basis for such automatic succession was the need to continue a 'social function which cannot terminate with the League of Nations, even if no other organ takes its place.'[181]

(b) Judge Lauterpacht Judge Lauterpacht wrote in his separate opinion to the 1956 advisory opinion on the *Admissibility of Hearings of Petitioners by the Committee on South West Africa* that the 1950 case must be read as an illustration of the principle of effectiveness. In his view, the mandate created an international status which had the character of an objective law, and 'which is

legally operative irrespective of the conduct of South Africa.'[182] Because the mandate 'transcends a mere contractual relation,'[183] it could not be allowed to become ineffective when one of the parties failed to fulfill its obligations. The substitution of the United Nations for the League of Nations as the supervisory organ was based, therefore, on the need to make the mandate work.[184]

This was, Lauterpacht concluded, 'the most important example of succession in international organization.'[185]

(c) Sir Gerald Fitzmaurice It is somewhat ironic that Sir Gerald Fitzmaurice, who become one of the staunchest critics of the Court's 1950 advisory opinion, published an article in the 1952 edition of the *British Year Book of International Law* in which he stated that:

> The Court found in effect that there had been an automatic or necessary devolution on to the United Nations of certain supervisory functions of the former League of Nations in regard to mandated territories.[186]

Although Fitzmaurice did not take a position on the correctness of the Court's reasoning, he nevertheless concluded that automatic succession could be presumed to take place when 'a given organization becomes extinct, but another organization intended generally to take its place comes or has come into being, having essentially the same purposes and principles, with a similar or analogous constitution and institutions, and carrying out broadly the same functions, in the same field.'[187] Of course, such devolution can only occur if the constituent instrument of the successor organization 'specifically authorizes or enables it to assume and carry out the functions in question.'[188]

Fitzmaurice went on to compare the automatic succession of the United Nations to state succession where all of the rights and obligations connected to a territory are transferred with it. In the case of an international organization, there is a 'functional field' which passes from one organization to another. The functional field 'carries with it the rights, obligations, and functions connected with that field, and appertaining to the capacity to act in it.'[189]

4. The 1971 Advisory Opinion on the Continued Presence of South Africa in Namibia

The General Assembly tried unsuccessfully for twenty years to get South Africa to submit to its supervisory authority over the Mandate for South West Africa. It finally concluded in 1970 that it would be useless to continue these efforts and that South Africa's defiant attitude was undermining respect for the United Nations. It therefore adopted Resolution 2145 (XXI) which declared that since South Africa had failed to fulfill its obligations under the Mandate, the Charter of the United Nations and the Universal Declaration of Human Rights 'the Mandate conferred upon his Britannic Majesty to be exercised by the Government of the Union of South Africa is therefore terminated.'[190]

The General Assembly had no powers under the Charter to ensure that South Africa withdrew from the territory of South West Africa (renamed Namibia), so it asked the Security Council to take appropriate action. The Security Council responded to this request and adopted Resolution 276 (1970), which declared that 'the continued presence of the South African authorities in Namibia is illegal', and that consequently all acts taken by the Government of South Africa 'on behalf or concerning Namibia after the termination of the Mandate are illegal and invalid.'[191]

The Security Council also acted on a recommendation of one of its sub-committees and requested an opinion from the International Court of Justice on 'the legal consequences for States of the continued presence of South Africa in Namibia, notwithstanding Security Council resolution 276 (1970).'[192]

This question gave the Court an opportunity to reexamine the issue of the survival of the mandate and the transfer of the supervisory functions of the League to the United Nations. First of all, it repeated its conclusions in the 1950 opinion that the mandate was an international institution, that South Africa was acting as a mandatory on behalf of the League and that the League 'had only assumed an international function of supervision and control.'[193]

The Court then went on to declare that when South Africa accepted the mandate it also accepted an obligation of 'legal accountability' for its performance, that is to render annual reports on the administration of the territory.[194] This obligation was an indispensable element of the mandate, which did not depend on the existence of the League.[195]

The trusteeship system was clearly intended to establish a more effective means of supervising the administration of territories not yet ready for independence.[196] The Court felt that:

> It would have been contrary to the overriding purpose of the mandates system to assume that difficulties in the way of the replacement of one régime by another designed to improve international supervision should have been permitted to bring about, on the dissolution of the League, a complete disappearance of international supervision. To accept the contention of the Government of South Africa on this point would have entailed the reversion of mandated territories to colonial status, and the virtual replacement of the mandates régime by annexation, so determinedly excluded in 1920.[197]

It was precisely for this reason, the Court affirmed, that the drafters of the charter introduced the safeguarding clause in Article 80, paragraph 1.[198] The participants at the San Francisco Conference realized that the adoption of the Charter would make it necessary to dissolve the League and had adopted Article 80, paragraph 1, for 'the purpose and effect of keeping in force all rights whatsoever, including those contained in the Covenant itself, against any claim as to their possible lapse with the dissolution of the League.'[199]

The Court rejected the argument of South Africa that Article 80, paragraph 1 must be interpreted as a saving clause, having only a negative effect of preventing the operation of Chapter XII from affecting existing rights. First of all, it pointed out that there is nothing in Chapter XII which would affect existing rights, and secondly that paragraph 2 of Article 80 presupposes that the rights referred to in paragraph 1 are preserved.[200] It could not accept an interpretation of Article 80 that would render it all meaningless.[201]

The Court therefore concluded, as it had in 1950, that South Africa had 'agreed to submit its administration of South West Africa to the scrutiny of the General Assembly.'[202] The agreement was manifested by many statements made by its representatives before the Assembly of the League and the General Assembly of the United Nations, which the Court had cited in

71

this and previous cases, as well as by accepting Article 80, paragraph 1 on the preservation of rights and Article 10 on the competence of the General Assembly to deal with all questions falling within the perview of the Charter. The 'transfer of the obligation to report, from the League Council to the General Assembly, was merely a corollary of the powers granted to the General Assembly.'[203]

5. Dissenting Opinion of Judge Fitzmaurice to the 1971 Advisory Opinion

Judge Sir Gerald Fitzmaurice in his lengthy, dissenting opinion to the 1971 Namibia case stated that there was no general rule of international law which would operate to allow the United Nations to succeed automatically to the functions of the League, the only way the United Nations could have taken over the League's functions in respect of the mandates would have been by express or implied agreement. In his view, there had never been any such agreement.[204]

Judge Fitzmaurice argued that consent could not be implied from Articles 10 and 80, paragraph 1 of the Charter for the following reasons. In the first place, Article 10 may have empowered the General Assembly to exercise supervisory functions in respect of the mandates, but it did not oblige 'mandatories to accept the Assembly in that role and regard themselves as accountable to it.'[205] A right conferred on one party, he affirmed, does not 'automatically and *ipso facto* create an obligation' for another party.[206]

The only way South Africa could have become obligated to accept the supervision the General Assembly and submit reports to it concerning the mandated territory would have been if Article 10 contained express language to that effect.[207] In the absence of any such wording, Fitzmaurice concluded that Article 10 could not 'bear the weight thus put upon it.'[208]

As far as Article 80 is concerned, the judge echoed the views of McNair and Hudson that the changes contemplated by that provision 'are clearly those, and only those that might result from Chapter XII' and not from changes 'resulting from the operation of causes wholly outside that chapter.'[209] The real intention of Article 80, he said, was:

to guard against the possibility that the setting up of the trusteeship system might be regarded as an excuse for not continuing to observe mandates obligations, whatever these were, and continued to be. But it did not define what these were, or say whether they continued to be.[210]

Consequently, if the obligations of mandates lapsed from causes other than those of Chapter XII, 'Article 80 did not and was never intended to prevent it' from happening.[211]

On the question whether the actions of the League of Nations, the United Nations and South Africa indicated an implied agreement, Judge Fitzmaurice declared that the historical record showed that the League had a 'bad name politically', which prompted the founders of the United Nations to avoid any formal link with the League.[212] This attitude was reflected in the General Assembly's Resolution XIV of February 12, 1946 concerning the functions or powers entrusted to the League by treaties, international conventions, agreements and other instruments having a political character.

Fitzmaurice saw this same attitude prevailing also at the final meeting of the League Assembly where proposals by several delegations to avoid a hiatus between the mandates and trusteeships systems were rejected. He cited in particular the 'Chinese' or 'Liang' draft resolution which noted that not all mandated territories under the League had been transformed into trusteeship territories and that 'the League's function of supervising mandated territories should be transferred to the United Nations, in order to avoid a period of inter-regnum in the supervision of the mandatory régime in these territories.'[213] The rejection of such a resolution, he said, made it impossible to presume that the resolutions eventually adopted could be 'interpreted as having the same effect as those that were not.'[214]

Since Fitzmaurice could not find any evidence that the United Nations had assumed the supervisory functions of the League during the critical period between 1945 and 1946, the only way he thought it could have become invested with those functions later on would have been if South Africa had consented to this.[215] In his view, however, the various statements that had been made over the years by the representatives of South Africa could not be considered as acceptance of an obligation to account to the United Nations, but only as a commitment to continue to administer the territory of South West Africa in accordance with the mandate. This, he said, was 'a separate thing from reporting *about* the process.'[216]

Judge Fitzmaurice therefore arrived at the conclusion that because South Africa had never explicitly or implicitly consented to the transfer of obligations relating to the mandate from the League to the United Nations, the United Nations had never lawfully assumed the functions of the League.[217]

6. Conclusions

The Court in 1971 found that South Africa had consented to the transfer of supervisory functions to the General Assembly of the United Nations in two ways. First of all it had agreed to Articles 10 and 80, paragraph 1 of the Charter when it became a member of the United Nations. Article 80, paragraph 1 had maintained the obligations of the mandatories, while Article 10 had empowered the General Assembly *inter alia* to supervise the administration of the mandates.[218] Secondly, it had recognized the competence of the General Assembly to deal with the mandate for South West Africa when it declared that it would submit 'the question of the future international status of the Territory to the "judgment" of the General Assembly.'[219]

Since there was sufficient evidence to show that the transfer of supervisory functions in this case was based on conventional succession, the Court had no need to justify succession on the ground of automatic succession. The question can still be posed, however, whether an argument for automatic succession could have been sustained.

In its 1950 opinion the Court stated that the mandates established an 'international régime' and an 'international status'.[220]. In 1962 it affirmed that the mandate for South-West Africa 'in fact and in law, is an international agreement having the character of a treaty or convention'[221] which instituted a 'novel international régime.'[222]

There is strong support in international law for the proposition that some treaties having a 'territorial,' 'dispositive' or 'real' character are not affected by a succession of states. Such treaties are said to establish 'objective régimes.'[223]

The issue of treaties creating objective régimes was addressed by the International Law Commission in the course of its work on succession of states in respect of treaties. The Commission took the view that a treaty establishing an objective régime would not be binding on a successor state, and the beneficiary of such an objective régime would not be entitled to claim rights under the treaty, 'unless such a treaty were considered to fall under a special rule to that effect.'[224] As evidence that a special rule regarding objective régimes existed, the Commission cited the *Aland Island* and *Free Zones* cases, where the judges had found that the treaties in question had established territorial régimes which were part of an international settlement included in the general interest of the international community.[225] The successor states had succeeded to the legal situation resulting from the implementation of treaties and not to the contractual obligations of the treaties themselves.

The Commission therefore adopted the position that the rule regarding objective régimes 'should relate to the legal situation – the régime – resulting from the dispositive effects of the treaty rather than to succession in respect of the treaty.'[226] This legal situation, it said, attaches to the territory instead of to the beneficiary or burdened state.[227] The rule was therefore drafted in the negative form to provide that a succession of states does not affect the rights or obligations relating to the use of a territory established by a treaty for the benefit of a state or a group of states.[228]

The wording of the draft article on 'territorial régimes' proposed by the Commission in 1974 was adopted as Article 12 of the 1978 Vienna Convention on Succession of States in Respect of Treaties.[229] Only one minor change was made to introduce an exception for treaties establishing foreign military bases, which many countries wished to exclude from the application of the rule.[230]

In view of the large measure of support for the provision on territorial régimes within the International Law Commission and the 1978 Vienna Conference on Succession of States in Respect of Treaties, it may reasonably be concluded that there is general acceptance of a rule of customary international law that certain treaties of a territorial character constitute a special category which are not subject to the clean slate principle. Since the mandate for South West Africa can clearly be considered a treaty establishing a territorial régime, the issue that must be resolved is which rights and obligations under the mandate remained in force after the demise of the League of Nations.

Judge McNair contended that the 'provisions' of the Mandate are in part contractual and in part 'dispositive'.[231] The rights and obligations relating to the administration of the territory were, he said, 'valid *in rem – ergo omnes*',[232] while those relating to the administrative supervision by the League Assembly were of a contractual nature and became extinct upon the dissolution of the League.[233] The same argument was invoked by South Africa in the 1962 *South-West Africa Cases*.[234]

The Court, on the other hand, arrived at the conviction in the 1950 case that the administrative supervision was 'an important part of the Mandates System.'[235] In 1962 it said that:

> The findings of the Court on the obligation of the Union Government to submit to international supervision are thus crystal clear. Indeed, to exclude the obligations connected with the Mandate would be to exclude the very essence of the Mandate.[236]

When South Africa claimed in 1971 that the mandate had 'lapsed as a whole by reason of the falling away of supervision by the League,'[237] the Court replied that:

> . . . by South Africa's own admission, 'supervision and accountability' were of the essence of the Mandate, as the Court had consistently maintained. The theory of the lapse of the Mandate on the demise of the League of Nations is in fact inseparable from the claim that there is no obligation to submit to the supervision of the United Nations, and vice versa. Consequently, both or either of the claims advanced, namely that the Mandate has lapsed and/or that there is no obligation to submit to international supervision by the United Nations, are destructive of the very institution upon which the presence of South Africa in Namibia rests. . . .[238]

If, then, the obligation to submit to international supervision remained in effect, another international organ had to take over the functions previously exercised by the League. Noting that the 'authors of the Charter had in mind the same necessity (for international supervision) when they organized the International Trusteeship System,'[239] that 'Chapters XI, XII and XIII

76

of the Charter of the United Nations embody principles corresponding to those declared in Article 22 of the Covenant,'[240] that the mandatory states had declared their intentions 'to continue to administer the territories in accordance with the obligations contained in the Mandates until other arrangements should be agreed upon between the United Nations and the mandatory Powers,'[241] and, finally, that under Article 10 of the Charter the General Assembly of the United Nations had the competence to exercise such supervision,[242] the Court concluded that the General Assembly was the proper international organ to 'safeguard the sacred trust of civilization through the maintenance of effective international supervision of the administration of the Mandated Territory.'[243] No other institution existing at the time could have performed this function.

It is clear from the foregoing that the consent of South Africa in this case was not a *condictio sine qua non* for the transfer of supervisory functions to take place. The obligation of the mandatory to submit to international supervision remained in effect, because it was an essential element of an international régime. The United Nations succeeded to the responsibilities of the League, because it had 'another international organ performing similar, though not identical, supervisory functions.'[244] This, we have seen, is automatic succession.

The general conclusion that can be drawn from this case is that automatic succession may be deemed to occur when the following conditions are present:

1. the functions exercised by an international organization have the character of or are derived from an objective régime which survives the dissolution of the organization;
2. another international organization exists which has essentially the same structure, powers and purposes as the defunct organization and wishes to take over the functions relating to the said objective régime; and
3. the functions that attach to the régime are an essential element of the régime.

IV

THE EFFECTS OF SUCCESSION BETWEEN INTERNATIONAL ORGANIZATIONS

A. INTRODUCTION

Succession, we have already seen, has profound effects on organizations. In most cases, the predecessor organization disappears altogether. The successor takes over some, but usually not all, of the functions and other related rights and obligations of the predecessor. In this final chapter we will examine the consequences of succession on functions, treaties, assets, liabilities, subsidiary institutions and employees.

B. FUNCTIONS

1. Types of Functions Transferred

The functions of an international organization, that is its responsibilities for performing certain tasks, are derived basically from its constitution, sometimes complemented by other international agreements. Although a distinction is sometimes made between political and technical functions, there is no theoretical obstacle to the transfer of political functions between international organizations.[1] It is often difficult in practice to separate political from technical considerations.[2] What may be true, however, is that the members of the predecessor and successor organizations are more apt to agree to the transfer of technical functions than of political functions.

In some cases, the successor organization may assume all of the functions of the predecessor, while in others it may only take over certain specific functions. The choice depends essentially on the convergence of the purposes and powers of the organizations in question, as well as on political considerations.

The founders of the United Nations, for example, did not

want the new organization to be tainted by the bad image of the League. It was primarily for this reason that each function of the League was examined individually in order to decide which organ or specialized agency of the United Nations should take it over. As it turned out, virtually all the functions of the League were continued within the United Nations system.

On the other hand, the tendency for technical organizations has been to assume all the functions of their predecessors. This is what happened in the case of the succession of the FAO to the International Institute of Agriculture,[3] the WHO to the Office international d'hygiène publique,[4] UNESCO to the International Bureau of Education,[5] the East African Community to the East African Common Services Organization[6] and the European Space Agency to the European Space Research Organization and the European Space Vehicle Launcher Organization.[7]

Many of the functions performed by international organizations are conferred by multilateral treaties to which they may or may not be parties. We have already said much about the supervisory functions entrusted to the League of Nations by the mandate for South West Africa. The League, in fact, exercised functions under more than fifty conventions relating to economics, finance, narcotic drug control, health, social questions, communications and transit.[8]

The most common responsibilities attributed to international organizations by treaties are chancery or depository functions. These usually involve keeping custody of the original signed texts of treaties, the instruments of ratification, denunciation, objections and reservations as well as transmitting copies of such documents to governments. These types of functions, we saw earlier, are relatively easy to transfer to another organization.[9]

2. Limitations on the Exercise of Transferred Functions

The characteristic feature of succession in whatever context it occurs is that there is a continuity of rights and obligations when a change of subjects takes place. This necessarily implies that the successor assumes no more rights and obligations than the predecessor enjoyed. This principle is usually expressed by the ancient legal adage *nemo plus iuris ad alium transfere potest quam ipse haberet.*

The International Court of Justice recognized this rule as applying to succession between international organizations when it stated in its 1950 advisory opinion on the International Status of South West Africa that although the General Assembly of the United Nations was 'legally qualified to exercise the supervisory functions previously exercised by the League of Nations,'[10] the 'degree of supervision to be exercised by the General Assembly should not . . . exceed that which applied under the mandates system, and should conform as far as possible to the procedure followed in this respect by the Council of the League of Nations.'[11]

The General Assembly was forced in 1954 to ask the Court for an interpretation of its 1950 opinion when the Union of South Africa objected to the use of the two-thirds majority rule to decide questions relating to the territory of South West Africa on the grounds that the rule of unanimity had governed the proceedings of the Council of the League of Nations.[12] A two-thirds majority rule, South Africa contended, would 'lead to a degree of supervision exceeding that which applied under the Mandates System.'[13]

The Court admitted that the voting system of the General Assembly had not been considered when it held in its 1950 opinion that 'supervision should conform as far as possible to the procedure followed in this respect by the Council of the League of Nations.' It found, however, that:

> The constitution of an organ usually prescribes the method of voting by which the organ arrives at its decisions. The voting system is related to the composition and functions of the organ. It forms one of the characteristics of the constitution of the organ. Taking decisions by a two-thirds majority vote or by a simple majority vote is one of the distinguishing features of the General Assembly, while the unanimity rule was one of the distinguishing features of the Council of the League of Nations. These two systems are characteristic of different organs, and one system cannot be substituted for the other without constitutional amendment. To transplant upon the General Assembly the unanimity rule of the Council of the League would

not be simply the introduction of a procedure, but would amount to a disregard of one of the characteristics of the General Assembly. Consequently the question of conformity of the voting system to the General Assembly with that of the Council of the League of Nations presents insurmountable difficulties of a juridical nature. For these reasons, the voting system of the General Assembly must be considered as not being included in the procedure which, according to the previous Opinion of the Court, the General Assembly should follow in exercising its supervisory functions.[14]

In its 1950 opinion the Court had affirmed that 'The competence of the General Assembly of the United Nations to exercise such supervision and receive and examine reports is derived from the provisions of Article 10 of the Charter, which authorizes the General Assembly to discuss any questions or any matters within the scope of the Charter and to make recommendations on these questions or matters to the Members of the United Nations.'[15] After repeating this point, the Court stated that:

> . . . the authority of the General Assembly to exercise supervision over the administration of South-West Africa as a Mandated Territory is based on the provisions of the Charter. While, in exercising that supervision the General Assembly should not deviate from the Mandate, its authority to take decisions in order to effect such supervision is derived from its own constitution.[16]

The Court was again requested to give another opinion in December 1955 on the question whether it was consistent with the 1950 opinion for the General Assembly's Committee on South-West Africa to grant oral hearings to petitioners on matters relating to the territory.[17] Since it was clearly established that oral hearings had in fact never been granted to petitioners by the League's Permanent Mandates Commission,[18] the problem here was one of determining if the United Nations had assumed not just those supervisory functions which the League had actually exercised, but also those it could have applied if the opportunity had arisen. The Court held in this case that:

> There is nothing in the Charter of the United Nations, the

81

Covenant of the League, or the Resolution of the Assembly of the League of April 18, 1946 relied upon by the Court in its Opinion of 1950, that can be construed as in any way restricting the authority of the General Assembly to less than that which was conferred upon the Council by the Covenant and the Mandate; nor does the Court find any justification for assuming that the taking over by the General Assembly of the supervisory authority formerly exercised by the Council of the League had the effect of crystallizing the mandates system at the point which it had reached in 1946.[19]

The Court further stated that when the General Assembly 'replaced the Council of the League as the supervisory organ,'[20] it assumed 'the same authority as the Council.'[21] The scope of that authority, the Court declared, 'could not be narrowed by the fact that the Assembly had replaced the Council.'[22]

In this case the Court did not think it was possible to contend that the grant of oral hearings to petitioners would exceed the degree of supervision which had applied under the League, because of South Africa's refusal to cooperate with the General Assembly's Committee on South West Africa. Oral hearings, it said, were the only way that the Committee could test whether the contents of the petitions were well-founded or not.[23] In a sense, Judge Lauterpacht stated in his separate opinion, 'such hearings are to the advantage of the mandatory' and do not increase his obligation under the mandate because they 'may disclose the spurious or fraudulent nature of some petition.'[24]

To remove any doubts as to the scope of the transferred functions it is always possible to make special arrangements to that effect. This was done in the case of the transfer of the social and cultural functions of the Western European Union to the Council of Europe. According to the arrangement worked out by the two organizations, the transferred functions would be exercised on the basis of partial agreements which would limit the effect of the transfer to the seven Council of Europe states which were also members of the WEU.[25] It was decided that any 'activity covered by a partial agreement could, as required, be extended to other member states of the Council of Europe.'[26] The arrangement further provided that the 'working methods hitherto employed by the WEU would be maintained,'[27] which required the Council of Europe to introduce procedures that would make it possible for committees to continue direct consultations with member governments as had been done in the past.[28] Finally, the two organizations agreed that committees 'set up under a Partial Agreement would report on their activities to the Committee of Ministers of the Council of Europe, which, at meetings limited to representatives of member states party to the Partial Agreement, would decide what action to take on such reports.'[29] In short, the Council of Europe elected to apply a different procedure when it dealt with the inherited functions.

It may be concluded, then, that in the absence of any special arrangements, the successor organization may exercise the transferred functions in accordance with its own constitutional rules. The only limitation is that the successor organization may not exercise more rights than the predecessor actually possessed.

C. TREATIES

The effects of succession between international organizations on treaties depends very much on the type of treaty and the nature of the functions attributed by the treaty to the predecessor organization. In the case of multilateral treaties entrusting administrative functions to an organization, the disappearance of the organization causes some parts of the treaty to become inoperative. If the part that becomes inoperative is an essential element, the entire treaty could be considered abrogated because its object could no longer be fulfilled.[30]

This is generally not a problem when the treaty only confers custodial functions on an organization. On the other hand, when the defunct organization is, for example, responsible for appointing the members of supervisory or technical bodies, the object of the treaty may be placed in jeopardy. In both cases it is a relatively simple matter to amend such treaties by means of protocols, substituting the organs of the successor organization for those of the predecessor.[31]

Where this procedure proves impractical, as was the case with the multitude of bilateral treaties conferring judicial functions on the Permanent Court of International Justice, an alternative solution is to insert a transfer provision in the constitution of the successor organization.[32]

Treaties to which a defunct international organization was a party present a different problem. The 1986 Vienna Convention on the Law of Treaties Between States and International Organizations or Between International Organizations excludes consideration of 'any question that may arise in regard to a treaty . . . from the termination of the existence of the organization.'[33] A similar reservation also appears in the Vienna Convention on the Law of Treaties regarding 'any question that may arise in regard to a treaty from a succession of states.'[34]

In the absence of any codified rules on this subject, it is useful to examine the extent to which the terms of the Vienna Convention on Succession of States in Respect of Treaties may be applicable by analogy.

As far as multilateral treaties are concerned, the accepted rule is that the disappearance of one of the parties does not ordinarily cause the treaty to terminate, unless the object and purpose of the treaty thereby become impossible to attain. The agreement thus continues in force for the other parties.[35] There is no reason why this would not likewise apply to international organizations. The successor organization would not automatically accede to the treaty but would have to accede to it like any other state or organization.[36]

We have already examined in some detail the special case of multilateral treaties that create objective régimes.[37] The rule, we said, was that such régimes do not terminate even if an international organization party to the convention,[38] and exercising essential functions under it, should happen to disappear.[39]

The question of bilateral treaties is quite different. Ordinarily treaties having a contractual character necessarily become extinct upon the dissolution of the organization party to it, because the contractual relationship cannot continue with only one party.[40] The successor organization can very well enter into a headquarters agreement with the state on whose territory the organization is located, which agreement may have virtually identical terms as the predecessor's headquarters agreement. It is, however, a new treaty having different parties.

84

D. ASSETS

The purpose of transferring functions from one international organization to another is to ensure the continuity of activities which a community of states considers useful and desirable to maintain. In order to achieve such continuity, it is usually necessary for the successor body to assume a variety of assets which are ancillary to the functions. These provide the successor the material means to exercise the inherited functions.

As we pointed out earlier, all of the assets of the predecessor are usually taken over by the successor organization without distinction or accounting when the predecessor is replaced by a new organization that has the same membership. On the other hand, when the memberships are different, the predecessor organization is usually liquidated and special arrangements are made by the liquidators to transfer certain specific assets and liabilities to the successor organization. The following are examples of the way in which specific categories of assets and liabilities are disposed of.

1. Immovable Property

International organizations often own their headquarters buildings and other real property. The League of Nations, for instance, owned all of the buildings situated on the Ariana site in Geneva but possessed only a leasehold on the land.[41] It also had a freehold over of the land and buildings assigned to the International Labour Organisation in Geneva[42] and 'various plots of land with villas and their buildings' in Geneva and Pregny,[43] leasehold property in the Sécheron district[44] and servitudes over certain other properties in the Petit-Saconnex district of Geneva.[45]

In accordance with the 'Common Plan' for the transfer of League assets to the United Nations, all the real property rights of the League in the Canton of Geneva were turned over to the United Nations in July 1946,[46] except the land and buildings occupied by the ILO, which were transferred to that body by virtue of an agreement signed May 17, 1946.[47]

The African and Malagasy Union owned the premises of its headquarters at Cotonou but leased the land on which it stood from the government of Dahomey.[48] The building devolved to the African and Malagasy Common Organization (OCAM) by a tacit agreement and was subsequently leased to the Afro-American Labor Center.[49] In this same manner OCAM also took over the headquarters of the African and Malagasy Organization for Economic Cooperation (OAMCE) in Yaundé.[50]

The headquarters of the International Patent Institute were transferred to the European Patent Organization on January 1, 1978 in accordance with the integration agreement signed the previous October.[51]

Sometimes when the predecessor organization rented its offices, an offer was made to transfer the lease to the successor organization. This happened in the case of the International Commission for Air Navigation, the Office international d'hygiène publique and the Commission for Technical Cooperation South of the Sahara. The ICAO and the Organization of African Unity accepted the offers to take over the leases of their predecessors,[52] but the WHO declined to assume the lease for the OIHP's premises in Paris.[53]

2. Movable Property

When the successor organization takes over the premises of the predecessor organization, it usually accepts the contents of the buildings as well, which may include such things as documentation, archives, libraries, furniture, office equipment and supplies, and technical installations. Sometimes the transfer agreements specify in detail the items of movable property that will be handed over to the successor body, and sometimes they provide for a general transfer of all the assets of the predecessor to the successor.

The agreement between the League of Nations and the United Nations, for example, provided that the transfer of movable property would include the 'fittings, furniture, office equipment and books and the stock of supplies' which were in the Secretariat building, the Assembly Hall, the Library building, the International Labour Office building, the Peace Palace in The Hague and the League's branch offices in London, Paris, Princeton, Washington, D.C., New Delhi and Singapore, as well as 'the archives of the League and of the Permanent Court of International Justice.'[54]

Similarly, the liquidation plan of the International Commission for Air Navigation envisaged that the furniture, fixtures, books and publications would be transferred to the ICAO, if that body wished to purchase them.[55] The library had been acquired at no charge to the ICAN and it was therefore decided to hand it over to the ICAO without compensation.[56]

The Protocol for the Dissolution of the International Institute of Agriculture charged the liquidator with collecting the assets of the Institute and transferring to the FAO possession of and full title to the 'libraries, archives, records and movable property' of the IIA.[57] These assets were accepted by the FAO on August 1, 1946.[58]

The Agreement on the integration of the International Patent Institute into the European Patent Organization listed the contents of IPI's building in The Hague as technical installations, fixtures, equipment, fittings, office furniture, research documentation, office supplies, spare parts and cleaning materials.[59] All of these objects became the property of the EPO on January 1, 1978.[60]

When the successor organization sets up its headquarters in a different city from that of the predecessor organization, it usually has no use for the premises, furniture, office equipment and supplies of the predecessor. This was the case for the Office international d'hygiène publique. The WHO turned down the OIHP's offer to take over the lease of its premises in Paris[61] and the liquidator was forced to sell off most of OIHP's furniture and equipment,[62] leaving only a part of the furniture and equipment, the library and archives. A portion of the library was transferred to Geneva in December 1948 to be held on loan.[63] The remainder of the library and the archives as well as the remaining furniture and equipment were taken over by the WHO on November 15, 1950.[64]

3. Funds

The liquid assets of an international organization may originate from the contributions of its member states, the proceeds of the sale of its movable and immovable property and special funds placed under its administration.

(a) Contributions of the Member States   One of the main preoccu-

pations of the liquidators of an international organization is the collection of arrears of contributions of the member states. In the case of the League of Nations, the Board of Liquidation spent sixteen months negotiating the settlement of the outstanding debts of the member states, at the end of which time it reported that it had managed to collect slightly over twenty-eight million Swiss francs, representing about ninety-three percent of the arrears of the members.[65]

The liquidators of the International Institute of Agriculture and the Office international d'hygiène publique had many more difficulties collecting contributions in arrears. At the start of the winding up operation the IIA had claims of over seven million Swiss francs against its members.[66] The United States, Great Britain and other powers vowed at the last meeting of the General Assembly to settle their outstanding debts towards the IIA and to exert pressure on the other members to do likewise.[67] A few countries, however, subsequently declined to discharge their obligations for the period of the Second World War.[68] Others were experiencing serious financial problems and asked to be allowed to settle only a portion of their debts.[69] When the Liquidation Commission realized it could not complete this part of the winding up operations, it made arrangements so that the FAO could take over the responsibility for collecting the remaining arrears as from February 28, 1978.[70]

The same predicament befell liquidators of the OIHP, who were likewise forced to turn over the claims of the OIHP against its members to the WHO. The efforts of the WHO to collect the unpaid contributions of the former members of the OIHP lasted until May 1971, twenty years after the Office had disappeared.[71]

(b) Proceeds of the Sale of Movable and Immovable Property The sale of an organization's movable and immovable property is usually necessary when the successor organization decides not to take over the premises of the predecessor.[72] In the case of Office international d'hygiène publique, the arrangement worked out with the Interim Commission of the WHO provided that the WHO would select the furniture and equipment it wished to use.[73] An expert engaged by the liquidators of the Office had previously estimated the value of the organization's movable property at 2,250,545 French francs.[74] The furniture

and equipment that the WHO did not want and were no longer needed by the OIHP were gradually sold off and the proceeds of 1,138,926 French francs were credited to the Reserve Fund.[75]

(c) *Special Funds Administered by Organizations* International organizations often exercise administrative functions relating to special funds that they technically do not own. In the event that the administrator is dissolved, another international organization is usually found to take over responsibility for the funds.

The League of Nations, for example, administered a large number of special funds which included the Darling Foundation, the Léon Bernard Fund, the Account of the Eastern Health Bureau in Singapore, the Forstall Fund, the Working Capital Fund, the Pension Fund for the members of the Permanent Court of International Justice, the Staff Pension Funds, the Reserve Fund, the Exchange Fund and the Staff Provident Fund.

The Darling Foundation and the Léon Bernard Fund had been established to commemorate men who had died in the service of the League Health Organization. Income from these funds was used for awards for work in the field of public health. The funds were transferred to the Secretary-General of the United Nations who acted as custodian until arrangements could be made to turn them over to the World Health Organization.[76]

The liquidators of the League offered the Eastern Health Bureau Account to the United Nations, but responsibility for that fund also eventually went to the World Health Organization.[77]

The Forstall Fund had been created by a private donation to facilitate the printing and publication of information on the activities of the League.[78] Although the liquidators of the League realized that the donor had no legal right to a refund of his gift, they decided that, in view of the exceptional circumstance brought on by the dissolution of the League, the assets of the fund should be divided into two parts in proportion to the contributions made by Mr. Forstall and the League. Mr. Forstall received 13,123.30 Swiss francs and the League 14,102.25 Swiss francs, which it turned over to the United Nations.[79]

Responsibility for the Working Capital Fund went to the International Labour Organisation. This was a fund that had been set up with contributions of the members of the League to meet the expenses of League agencies when the League was short of funds.[80] The liquidators deducted the sums each state owed to the League and then transferred the remaining 3.8 million Swiss francs to the ILO to be used for working capital.[81]

The International Labour Organisation also assumed responsibility for the administration of the Pension Fund for the Members of the Permanent Court of International Justice which amounted to approximately 2.4 million Swiss francs. The transfer was made subject to the condition that, in the event of a deficit, the members of the ILO which were also members of the League would contribute to make up any deficiency through the ILO's budget.[82] On the other hand, any surplus remaining after the pensions of the judges ceased would accrue to the ILO.[83]

The Reserve Fund, the Staff Provident Fund and the Exchange Fund were liquidated, and the proceeds were added to the Staff Pensions Fund.[84] The total assets transferred amounted to 25,507,672 Swiss francs, of which 23,295,798.97 Swiss francs came from the fund itself and 2,216,873.03 Swiss francs were added by the League.[85] As in the case of the judges pension fund, the ILO assumed responsibility for covering any shortfall through additional contributions from its budget.[86]

Another case of the transfer of a staff pension fund was that of the Office international d'hygiène publique. Under an arrangement between the liquidators of the OIHP and the Interim Commission of the World Health Organization, the capital required to service the pensions of the former OIHP staff members was furnished to the WHO, and no financial obligations were assumed by the Interim Commission.[87] Later on, however, when these funds proved to be insufficient, the WHO decided that it had 'a moral responsibility to ameliorate the situation of the OIHP pensioners with regard to the increase of cost of living' and provided supplemental payments to these pensioners similar to the ones granted to pensioners of the United Nations Joint Staff Pension Fund.[88]

Sometimes an international organization transfers part of its liquid assets to the successor organization under the condition that the funds be used exclusively to continue specific activities. This was the case especially for the United Nations Relief and

Rehabilitation Administration which transferred three million dollars in 1947 and 1948 to permit the Interim Commission of the WHO to carry on UNRRA's functions relating to furnishing technical advice in the field of health.[89] The FAO received 1,135,000 U.S. dollars from UNRRA's agricultural advisory services.[90] By far the largest share of UNRRA's residual assets went to the International Children's Emergency Fund which was created by the United Nations at the instigation of UNRRA. UNICEF eventually received approximately 34.5 million dollars in cash.[91]

The Office international d'hygiène publique followed the example of UNRRA and financed the continuation by the WHO of its functions relating to international epidemic control and the study of communicable diseases. Under an arrangement signed with the Interim Commission of the WHO on January 27, 1948, the OIHP transferred approximately 47.6 million French francs to defray the expenses of these activities.[92]

4. Distribution of Assets

When the memberships of the predecessor and successor organizations are identical, the transfer of the assets of the predecessor organization to the successor organization poses few problems. On the other hand, when the memberships are different, the usual procedure is to determine the value of all the assets of the predecessor organization, divide that mass into shares and allocate the shares to each member state in proportion to its total contributions since the organization's creation. The shares of states which do not become members of the successor organization are paid in cash, while those of the states which have joined the successor organization are credited towards the contributions of those states in the books of the successor organization. The following are some examples of this practice.

(a) *The League of Nations* According to the 'Common Plan' for the transfer of the League of Nations assets to the United Nations, the proceeds of the liquidation of the League would be 'credited or distributed to Members of the League under a scheme to be determined by it.'[93] The 'Scheme of Distribution'

91

elaborated at the last League Assembly meeting in April 1946 provided in substance that:

1) the shares of the members of the League in the material and liquid assets would be based on the proportion of each member's total contributions;
2) the debts of the members towards the League would be deducted from their claims in respect of the material and liquid assets;
3) the shares in the material assets would be calculated and credited in the books of the United Nations;
4) the members of the League which were not members of the United Nations could receive cash in lieu of material assets; and finally
5) any liquid assets remaining after the final liquidation would be distributed to all the members in cash.[94]

The total value of the assets apportioned under this scheme amounted to 61,433,363.60 Swiss francs of which 46,194,569.29 Swiss francs consisted of material assets and 15,238,794.32 Swiss francs consisted of cash.[95] Finland, Portugal and Switzerland were the only members of the League which did not join the United Nations and which received repayment in cash.[96]

(b) The International Commission of Air Navigation   The liquidation plan approved by the Liquidation Committee in January 1947 provided that the funds collected from the disposal of ICAN assets and contributions in arrear would be divided among the members of ICAN in shares computed 'according to the proportion of contributions paid by each Contracting State to the total contributions received by ICAN since its creation.'[97] The shares of members which had not settled their contributions in arrear would be reduced by the amounts they owed.[98]

The members of ICAN which had not become members of the ICAO prior to the conclusion of the liquidation procedures would receive reimbursement in cash, in so far as their debts towards ICAN did not exceed their shares.[99] The twenty-five other members of ICAN which were also members of the ICAO received credits towards their contributions to the ICAO when the ICAO Council accepted from the ICAN Liquidation Committee in October 1948 assets consisting of 12,500 U.S. dollars worth of furniture and equipment and cash balances of approximately 6,000 pounds sterling and 5,000,000 French francs.[100]

(c) The International Institute of Agriculture   No provisions were made in the Protocol dissolving the IIA or in the resolution of the last General Assembly for the allocation of whatever sums remained at the end of the winding up process. As it turned out, virtually all of the assets of the IIA had been 'absorbed in liquidating the liabilities of the Institute.'[101] Several members of the IIA, however, made reservations when they settled their arrears of contributions that any cash remaining after all the liabilities of the IIA had been settled should be either returned to them or credited to their accounts with the FAO.[102]

E. LIABILITIES

There have been cases where the constituent instruments of the successor organizations or a special arrangement between the predecessor and successor organizations have provided expressly for the transfer of liabilities. The agreement for the Integration of the International Patent Institute into the European Patent Office, for example, provided that the 'Institute transfers to the Organization without exception its assets, and the Organization accepts without exception or reserve responsibility for the sum of the liabilities being those existing on the date on which this agreement comes into force.'[103] Likewise, the Convention for the Establishment of a European Space Agency specified that 'On the date when this Convention enters into force, the Agency shall take over all rights and obligations of the European Space Research Organization and the European Organization for the Development and Construction of the Space Vehicle Launchers.'[104]

Where the memberships of the predecessor and successor organizations have been identical, liabilities and assets have usually been assumed by the successor organization by tacit agreements. This occurred, as pointed out earlier, when the African and Malagasy Common Organization and the International Regional Organization of Animal and Plant Health replaced their predecessor organizations.[105]

In most instances, however, the successor organization agrees to accept only the assets remaining after the liquidation and settlement of the liabilities of the predecessor. The United Nations, for example, did not regard itself responsible for the collection of the debts owed to the League of Nations nor for the liabilities of the League with respect to its staff. According to the 'Common Plan' the League was supposed to discharge all its obligations, settle the question of contributions in arrears and make arrangements with regard to the administration of its staff pension fund and the pension fund for the judges of the Permanent Court of International Justice.[106]

The United Nations adopted the same position when UNRRA proposed to turn over its remaining assets for the benefit of the International Children's Emergency Fund. According to the transfer agreement signed on September 27, 1948, the Administrator for the liquidation of UNRRA was 'to strive to reduce to cash all assets, including any then outstanding accounts receivables and to discharge all known liquidated liabilities.'[107] At the end of the liquidation period, the liquidator was to provide the United Nations with sufficient cash to cover any outstanding claims.[108]

In the few instances where the successor organization agreed to complete the liquidation of the predecessor organization, it performed these tasks as a trustee and did not assume any liabilities for the debts of the defunct organization.[109] This was confirmed by the Superior Court of New York in the case of *Wencak v. United Nations* of January 18, 1956 when it found that the United Nations had undertaken to administer the liquidation of UNRRA but that such 'administration was not an assumption of liabilities upon succession to the assets as is frequently found with business corporations.[110]

F. SUBSIDIARY INSTITUTIONS

The subsidiary organs and agencies of an international organization generally share the fate of the parent institution. The League of Nations' High Commissioner for Refugees, Far-Eastern Epidemiological Intelligence Service, Permanent Opium Board and Drug Supervisory Body were terminated[111] as were the International Commission for Air Navigation's International Radio Committee[112] and the International Institute of Agriculture's International Forestry Center.[113]

The dissolution of the League, however, had no effect on the International Bureau for Information and Enquiries Regarding Relief to Foreigners, the International Hydrographic Bureau, the Central International Office for Control of Liquor Traffic in Africa, the International Commission for Air Navigation and the International Exhibitions Bureau, which were independent organizations that had entered into relationship with the League under Article 24 of the Covenant.[114] This was also the case for the International Labour Organisation, which, as was seen earlier, had become an autonomous organization by the end of the Second World War.[115]

The question of what to do with subsidiary bodies when the parent organization disappears has arisen more recently in the context of African regional organizations. The organizations that emerged during the early part of the decolonization period were characterized by a number of specialized administrations grouped around a central institution. When a specialized agency was based on a separate treaty, its existence was not affected by the dissolution of the central organization.[116] When the subsidiary institution was based on the same constituent instrument as the central organization some measures had to be taken to ensure the continuity of their functions and activities. In the case of the twenty-seven odd services administered by the East African Common Services Organization, for example, it was necessary to provide in the treaty establishing the East Africa Community, the successor to the EACSO, for the creation of departments to take over the various services of the predecessor.[117]

G. EMPLOYEES

The relationship between an organization and its personnel is defined by a contract of employment which is always entered into *intuitu personae*, that is it presupposes certain strictly personal considerations. As a general rule, therefore, the rights and obligations deriving from an employment contract are not transmissible to a new employer and are ordinarily terminated when the organization ceases to exist.

In practice, however, the successor organization has usually elected to engage some of the staff members of the predecessor organization to secure the benefit of their experience. Over

95

250 former employees of the League were hired by the United Nations and its specialized agencies.[118] A few of the key staff members of the International Commission for Air Navigation joined the Provisional International Civil Aviation Organization, including its General Secretary.[119] It must be remembered that during the period of the Second World War the staffs of most international organizations were reduced to a minimum. At the end of the war, the Office international d'hygiène publique had only nineteen employees. Three of them were hired by the Interim Commission of the WHO and the rest were dismissed gradually.[120]

Sometimes the entire staff of the predecessor organization has been offered contracts of employment with the successor organization. This was notably the case for the personnel of the International Institute of Agriculture[121] and the International Patent Institute.[122] Under such arrangements the contracts of the employees of the defunct organization are terminated and new contracts are signed with the successor organization under its own terms and conditions of employment.

A slight departure from this practice, however, was the decision of UNESCO to take on all the staff members of the International Bureau of Education under the same 'regulations and contractual provisions' as their former employer for a period of two years.[123] This arrangement can be considered a novation: the legal relationship with the predecessor organization was terminated and a new relationship under identical terms was established with the new employer.

V

GENERAL CONCLUSIONS

The purpose of this study was to investigate an aspect of succession that has received little attention in the past but that has become in practice one of the the most prevalent forms of succession on the international level. In order to understand the concept of 'succession between international organizations' it was necessary first of all to examine the meaning of 'succession' as it has evolved in municipal law and international law. The conclusion reached was that whatever form it takes succession is characterized by the transfer of certain rights and obligations from one natural or artificial person to another. There occurs at once a continuity of rights and obligations and a discontinuity of the subject of those rights and obligations.

Succession, we found, takes place by virtue of an agreement between the parties or else a rule that recognizes the change of subject when certain conditions are fulfilled. The former is called 'conventional succession', while the latter is known as 'automatic succession'.

Which rights and obligations are transferred to the new subject depends very much on their nature. Those that are intimately connected with the person of the predecessor are ordinarily not transmissible, while those that have a patrimonial character are in general easily transferred.

The last characteristic of succession we saw was that the rights and obligations assumed by the successor have exactly the same material content as those previously held by the predecessor. The principle accepted in all systems of law is that a person can transmit only the rights that he possesses.

The peculiarity about succession between international organizations is that it relates essentially to the transfer of functions,

which are the jurisdiction, duties and activities of a public institution, rather than of private rights and obligations, which
characterizes succession in municipal law. Functions are conferred on an organization when states decide that they cannot
deal with an issue on an individual or bilateral basis. Whatever
may happen to the particular organization to which the functions are entrusted, an attempt is almost always made to pre-
serve the functions and leave them in the hands of some
international body. When functions are transferred from one
organization to another, it has usually been found useful or
necessary to transfer as well certain resources that are connected
with those functions. In practice, therefore, succession to functions entails succession to some or all of the assets and liabilities
of the predecessor organization.

A review of the history of international organizations made
it possible to establish a typology of situations which give rise
to problems of succession. We saw that devolution takes place
when (a) an organization is replaced by another which is created
to carry out the same or similar functions, or (b) an organization
is absorbed by or merged with another, or (c) a subsidiary organ
or agency of an organization is separated from its parent and
forms an independent legal entity, or, finally, (d) an organization transfers a specific function to another institution but
continues to carry out its other functions.

The procedures used to transfer functions and their associated
rights and obligations have varied greatly and usually depended
on whether the memberships of the predecessor and successor
were identical or not. When the memberships were different,
as was frequently the case for replacement, merger or absorption, it was usually necessary to dissolve and liquidate the old
organization. In such circumstances, the transfer of functions,
assets and liabilities was accomplished by formal or informal
agreements between the members of the organization or
between the organizations themselves.

When the memberships of the predecessor and successor
organizations were identical, the procedures were much sim-
pler. In most instances the practice was to include special transfer provisions in the constitutions of the successor organizations, but sometimes the successor entities assumed all of the
functions, assets and liabilities of the defunct organizations
without any formalities at all. In such cases the similarities

between the old and new organizations were apparently so great that succession was considered to have taken place by tacit agreements between all of the parties concerned. Having established how conventional succession between organizations is accomplished, we then turned to the question of automatic succession. The only case where the issue has arisen was the succession of the United Nations to the supervisory functions of the League of Nations in respect of the mandate for South West Africa. A review of the many advisory opinions and judgments of the International Court of Justice led us to the conclusion that the Court, although it had alluded to automatic succession earlier, relied exclusively on the conventional basis of the transfer of functions in its final pronouncement on the subject in 1971. Since it could demonstrate that all the parties concerned had expressly or tacitly consented to the succession, the Court did not feel compelled to reiterate or expand on the argument it had put forward in 1950 that the obligation of the mandatory to submit to international supervision continued to exist, because the United Nations possessed an organ exercising similar supervisory functions.

Although the Court did not base its opinion in 1971 on the concept of automatic succession, it did make a number of statements in this and earlier cases which support the view that the supervisory functions over the mandate for South West Africa devolved automatically to the United Nations. First of all, it confirmed that the mandate established a territorial régime which had an objective character. Secondly, it found that the obligation to submit to administrative supervision was an essential part of mandate which survived the extinction of the League. Finally, it confirmed that there existed on the international scene an organ which had the competence to exercise the supervisory functions and which was entitled to do so in spite of the objections of the mandatory and in spite of the absence of any specific transfer agreement. This by definition is automatic succession.

The last part of the study was devoted to the consequences of succession between organizations. We examined the types of functions that can be transferred and the extent to which the successor organization can exercise the inherited functions and arrived at the conclusion that there are, in principle, no restrictions regarding the types of functions transferred between organizations but that certain limitations apply as to the exercise of the inherited functions.

Experience has shown that in virtually every case where an organization was dismantled, nearly all of its functions and resources were taken over by another institution that was better equipped to do the job. The reason for this is obvious: once states have determined that a certain task must be performed by an international organization, they are almost never willing to go back to dealing with the matter on an individual or bilateral basis.

Rudolph von Jhering once described succession as the condition for all human progress. The successor, he said, uses the experience of its predecessor to build a better life. We have no doubt that this holds true as well for succession between international organizations.

NOTES

ABBREVIATIONS

AFDI	*Annuaire français du droit international*
AJIL	*American Journal of International Law*
BDARO	*Basic Documents of African Regional Organizations*
BYBIL	*British Yearbook of International Law*
EY	*European Yearbook*
GBTS	*Great Britain Treaty Series*
ICJ	International Court of Justice
ICLQ	*International Comparative Law Quarterly*
IGO	*International Governmental Organizations*
IL	*International Legislation*
ILM	*International Legal Materials*
ILR	*International Law Review*
LNTS	*League of Nations Treaty Series*
NRG	*Martens' Nouveau recueil général des traités*
NILR	*Netherlands International Law Review*
OZFOR	*Oesterreichische Zeitschrift fürs Offentliches Recht*
PCIJ	Permanent Court of International Justice
RCADI	*Recueil des Cours professés l'Académie de droit international de La Haye*
RGDIP	*Revue général de droit international public*
RHDI	*Revue hellénique de droit international*
UNTS	*United Nations Treaty Series*
UST	*United States Treaties*
YBUN	*Yearbook of the United Nations*
YILC	*Yearbook of the International Law Commission*

INTRODUCTION

1 'Review of the Commission's Long-Term Programme of Work.' *YILC*, vol. II, Part Two, 1971, pp.79–80. For some earlier discussions of the topic within the International Law Commission see: 'Report by Mr. Manfred Lachs, Chairman of the Sub-Committee on Succession of States and Governments (Approved by the Sub-Committee).' Summary Records of the Fourth Meeting, *YILC*, vol. II, 1963, p. 264. See also Elias T.O. 'Delimitation of the Scope of "Succession of States and Governments".' *Ibid.*, p. 282. Castren, Erik. 'The Succession of States and Governments: The Limits and Methods of Research.' *Ibid.*, p. 291. Lachs, Manfred. 'Working Paper.' *Ibid.*, p. 298. 'Relations between States and Inter-Governmental Organizations.' First Report by Mr. Abdullah El-Erian, Special Rapporteur, *Ibid.*, p. 184. 'Report of the International Law Commission Covering the Work of its Fifteenth Session.' *Ibid.*, p. 224. 'Report of the International Law Commission on the Work of Its Sixteenth Session.' *YILC*, vol. II, 1964, p. 240.

2 'Question of Treaties Concluded between States and International Organizations or between Two or More International Organizations.' *YILC*, vol. II, 1982, p. 69.

3 *Legal Consequences for States of the Continued Presence of South Africa in Namibia (South West Africa) Notwithstanding Security Council Resolution 276 (1970)*, ICJ Reports 1971, p. 49.

4 *International Status of South West Africa*, ICJ Reports 1950, p. 137. *Admissibility of Hearings of Petitioners by the Committee on South West Africa*, ICJ Reports 1956, p. 29.

5 *International Status of South-West Africa*, Dissenting Opinion of Mr. Alvarez, *ICJ Reports*, 1950, p. 181. Separate Opinion by Judge Read, *Ibid.*, pp. 172–173. Separate Opinion by Sir Arnold McNair, *Ibid.*, pp. 159–161.

6 Fitzmaurice, Sir Gerald 'The Law and Procedure of the International Court of Justice: International Organizations and Tribunals.' *BYBIL*, vol. 29, 1952, pp. 8–10. Oppenheim. *International Law*, vol. 1, 8th edition, edited by H. Lauterpacht, 1955, p. 168. Hudson, Manley O. 'The Succession of the International Court of Justice to the Permanent Court of International Justice.' *AJIL*, vol. 51, 1957, pp. 569–573. Kiss, Alexandre-Charles. 'Quelques aspects de la substitution d'une organisation une autre.' *AFDI*, vol. VII, 1961, pp. 463–491. Chiu, Hungdah. 'Succession in International Organizations.' *ICLQ*, vol. 14, 1965, pp. 83–120. Mochi-Onory, Andrea G. 'The Nature of Succession between International Organizations: Functions and Treaties.' *RHDI*, vol. 21, 1968, pp. 33–48. Ranjeva, Raymond. *La succession d'organisations en Afrique*, Paris, Pedone, 1978, xiii – 418 p. See also Wodie, Francis. *Les institutions internationales régionales en Afrique occidentale et centrale*, Paris, Librairie générale de droit et de jurisprudence, 1970, pp. 61–65. Wodie, Francis. *Les institutions internationales régionales en Afrique*

occidentale et centrale. Paris, Librairie générale de droit et de jurisprudence, 1970, pp. 61–65.

7 Jenks, Wilfred C. 'Some Constitutional Problems of International Organizations.' *BYBIL*, 1945, pp. 68–71. Hahn, Hugo J. 'Continuity in the Law of International Organizations.' *OZOR*, 1964, pp. 167–239. Schwarzenberger, Georg. *International Law as Applied by International Courts and Tribunals*, vol. III, London, Stevens and Sons Ltd., 1976; pp. 99–144 ('Continuity and Discontinuity in the Law of International Institutions').

CHAPTER I THE DEFINITION OF SUCCESSION BETWEEN INTERNATIONAL ORGANIZATIONS

1 Du Pasquier, Claude. *Introduction la théorie générale et la philosophie du droit*. 4e édition, Neuchâtel et Paris, Delachaux et Niestlé, 1967, p. 106. Holmes, Oliver Wendell, Jr. *The Common Law*. Boston, Little Brown and Co., 1881, p. 340.

2 Capitant, Henri. *Introduction l'étude du droit civil*. 5e édition, Paris, Pedone, 1929, p. 269. Holmes, Oliver Wendell, Jr. *loc. cit.* Jolowicz, H.F. *Historical Introduction to the Study of Roman Law*. Cambridge, University Press, 1952, p. 72. Kelsen, Hans. 'Théorie générale du droit international public, Problèmes choisis.' *RCADI*, vol. 42, 1932 IV, p. 312. Ripert, Georges et Boulanger, Jean. *Traité général de droit civil de Planiol*. Tome IV, Paris, Librairie générale de droit et de jurisprudence, 1959, p. 471. Roguin, Ernest. *Traité de droit civil comparé. Les successions*. Tome I, Paris, Librairie générale de droit et de jurisprudence/Lausanne, Librairie F. Rouge et Cie., 1909, p. 3. Rossel, Virgile et Mentha, F. H. *Manuel de droit suisse*. 2e édition, Tome II, Lausanne, Payot, 1931, p. 5. Savigny, Frédéric Charles de. *Traité de droit romain*. Traduit de l'allemand par Charles Guenoux, 2e édition, tome 3, Paris, Librairie de Firmin Didot Frères, 1956, pp. 17–18. Udina, Maulio. 'La succession des Etats quant aux obligations internationales autres que les dettes publiques.' *RCADI*, vol. 44, 1933 II, p. 671.

3 Coissaro, Narana. *The Customary Laws of Succession in Central Africa*. Lisbon, 1966, p. 5. Kaser, Max. *Römisches Privatrecht*. 3. *Auflage*, München, C. H. Beck'schen Verlagsbuchhandlung, 1976, pp. 2, 60.

4 Holmes, Oliver Wendell, Jr. *op. cit.*, p. 343. Maine, Sir Henry Sumner, *Ancient Law. Its Connection with the Early History of Society and its Relation to Modern Ideas*. London, John Murray, 1916, p. 195.

5 Kaser, Max. *op. cit.*, p. 245. Maine, Sir Henry Sumner. *op. cit.*, p. 197.

6 Capitaine, Georges. *La liquidation officielle d'une succession en droit suisse*. Genève, Imprimerie Atar, 1935, p. 15. Cuq, Edouard. *Manuel des institutions juridiques des romains*. 2e édition, Paris, Librairie Plon/ Librairie générale de droit et de jurisprudence, 1928, p. 678. Maine, Sir Henry Sumner. *Ancient Law*. London, John Murray, 1916, p. 198. Paton, George Whitecross. *A Text-Book of Jurisprudence*. Oxford, Clarendon Press, 1946, p. 414.

7 Capitant, Henri. *loc. cit.* Kelsen, Hans. *op. cit.*, p. 314. Paton, George Whitecross. *op. cit.*, p. 415. Roguin, Ernest. *op. cit.*, p. 47. Weill, Alex. *Droit civil. Les biens.* Paris, Dalloz, 1970, p. 316.

8 Holmes, Oliver Wendell, Jr. *op. cit.*, p. 341. Mazeaud, Henri Léon et Jean. *Leçons de droit civil.* Tome IV, vol. II, 2e édition, Paris, Editions Montschestrin, 1971, pp. 606 and 610. Parry, David Hughes. *The Law of Succession.* 6th edition, London, Sweet & Maxwell, Ltd., 1972, p. 225. Redmond, P.W.D. *General Principles of English Law.* 2nd edition, London, MacDonald & Evans, Ltd., 1966, p. 251. Roguin, Ernest. *op. cit.*, pp. 32–33.

9 Paton, George Whitecross. *loc. cit.*

10 Austin, John. *Lectures on Jurisprudence.* 5th edition, revised and edited by Robert Campbell, vol. I, London, John Murray, 1929, p. 56. Capitant, Henri. *loc. cit. Corpus Iuris Civilis,* edited by Paul Krueger and Theodor Mommsen, Berlin, Weidmannsche Verlagsbuchhandlung, 1954: Ulpian. D. 43.19.3.2. 'Ab eo . . . in cuius hereditate vel emptione aliove quo iure successi.' Ulpian. D. 50.17. 156.2–3. 'Cum quis in alii locum successorit non est aequum ei nocere hoc, quod adversus eum non nocuit, eujus locuum successit. Perumque emptoris eadem causa esse debet circa petendum ac defendendum, que fuit autoris.' Ulpian. D. 50.17.143. 'Quod ipsis qui contraxerunt obstat, et successoribus eorum obstabit.' Paulus. D. 50.17.177. 'Qui in ius dominiumue alterius succedit, iure ejus uti debet.' Scaevola. D. 44.3.14.1–2. '(Accessiones possessionem) plane tribuuntur his qui in locum alisorum succedunt sive ex contractu sive voluntae: heredibus enim et his, qui successorum sive habentur, datur accessio testatoris. Itaque si nihil vendideris serum utar accessione tua.' Cuq, Edouard. *op. cit.*, pp. 678–679. Holmes, Oliver Wendell, Jr. *op. cit.*, pp. 363, 366. Jolowicz, H. F. *Roman Foundations of Modern Law.* Oxford, The Clarendon Press, 1957, p. 72. Kaser, Max. *op. cit.*, p. 21. Kelsen, Hans. *loc. cit.* Redmond, P.W.D. *op. cit.*, p. 251. Ripert, Georges et Boulanger, Jean. *loc. cit.* Roguin, Ernest. *loc. cit.* Rossel, Virgile et Mentha, F. H. *loc. cit.* Savigny, Frédéric Charles de, *op. cit.*, pp. 10–11.

11 Hahn, Hugo. *op. cit.*, p. 198. Waldock, Sir Humphrey 'Second Report on Succession in Respect of Treaties.' *YILC*, vol. II, 1969, p. 50.

12 Capitant, Henri. *op. cit.*, p. 270. Cuq, Edouard. *op. cit.*, p. 680. Holmes, Oliver Wendell, Jr. *op. cit.*, pp. 368, 430.

13 Corpus Iuris Civilis. *op. cit.* Ulpian. D. 50.17.177.

14 *Black's Law Dictionary* by Henry Compbell Black, revised 4th edition, St. Paul, Minn., West Publishing Co., 1968, pp. 1212–1213. Kaser, Max. *op. cit.*, pp. 214–215. Thomas, J.A.C. *Textbook of Roman Law.* Amsterdam/New York/Oxford, NorthHolland Publishing Co., 1976, p. 345. *Words and Phrases Legally Defined.* 2nd edition, edited by John B. Saunders, vol. 3, London, Butterworths, pp. 352–353.

15 Kelsen, Hans. *loc. cit.*: 'Il n'est question de succession des Etats que dans le cas d'une modification territoriale, lorsque notamment le territoire d'un Etat devient territoire d'un autre Etat'. O'Connell,

D.P. *State Succession in Municipal Law and International Law.* Cambridge, University Press, Volume I., 1967, p. 3: 'The significance of the term is to be limited . . . to the factual situation which arises when one State is substituted for another in sovereignty over a given territory . . .'. Udina, Maulio, *op. cit.*, p. 679: 'La modification territoriale est un fait, dont la succession constitue l'un des effets juridiques.' Waldock, Sir Humphrey. 'Second Report on Succession in Respect of Treaties'. *YILC*, vol. II., 1969, p. 51: ' . . . the Special Rapporteur considers it advisable to use the term 'succession' exclusively as referring to the fact of replacement of one State by another in sovereignty of territory or in the competence to conclude treaties with respect to territory.' Also see Article 2, para. 1(b) of the 1978 Vienna Convention on the Succession of States in Respect of Treaties. (U.N. Doc. A/CONF. 80/31) and Article 2, para. 2(a) of the 1983 Vienna Convention on Succession of States in Respect of State Property, Archives and Debts (U.N. Doc. A/CONF. 117/ 14), which define succession of States as 'the replacement of one State by another in the responsibility for the international relations of territory.' The expression 'in the responsibility for the international relations of territory' was preferred to 'sovereignty in respect of territory' because it was considered more general and could apply equally well to States and dependent territories. See *YILC* vol. II, 1981, pp. 21–22.

16 Kelsen, Hans. *op. cit.*, pp. 315–316. Oppenheim, L. *International Law. A Treatise.* ỽol. I, 8th edition, edited by Hersch Lauterpacht, London, Longmans, Green & Co., Ltd., 1963, pp. 157–158. See also Articles 15, 16, 31 and 34 of the 1978 Vienna Convention on the Succession of States in Respect of Treaties. *loc. cit.* and Articles 13, 14, 15 and 16 of the 1983 Vienna Convention on Succession of States in Respect of State Property, Archives and Debts. *loc. cit.*

17 O'Connell, D.P. *loc. cit.*

18 Grotius, Hugo. *De jure belli et pacis.* lib. II, cap. ix, tit. xii, in *The Classics of International Law.* Washington, D.C., the Carnegie Endowment for International Peace/Oxford, the Clarendon Press, 1916: 'Heredes personam quod dominii tuum publici quam privatii continuationem pro eadem censerii cum defuncti persona, ceri est juris.' Pufendorf, Samuel, *De jure naturae et gentium.* lib. VIII, cap. xiii, tit. i-v and vii-ix, *Ibid.*, 1934. Vattel, Emer de, *Le droit des gens ou principes de droit naturel.* vol. II, cap. xii, tit. 191, *Ibid.*, 1916. See also Caflisch, Lucius 'The Law of State Succession. Theoretical Observations.' *NILR*, vol. 4, 1963, pp. 338 and 352. Kelsen, Hans. *op. cit.*; p. 312. Marcoff, Marco. *Accession l'indépendance et succession d'Etat aux traités internationaux.* Fribourg, Editions Universitaires, 1969, p. 17.

19 Huber, Max. *Die Staatensuccession.* Leipzig, Verlag von Dunker & Humblot, 1898, p. 24. Marcoff, Marco G. *op. cit.*, p. 17. O'Connell, D.P. *op. cit.*, pp. 12–13.

20 Mériboute, Zidane. *La codification de la succession d'Etats aux traités. Décolonisation, cession, unification.* Paris, Presses universitaires de France, 1984, p. 25. O'Connell, D.P. *op. cit.*

21 Cavaglieri, Arrigo. 'Règles générales du droit de la paix.' *RCADI*, 1929, vol. I, p. 378: ' . . . il n'y a dans la plupart des cas aucune règle de droit général qui oblige l'Etat annexant de prendre sur lui les conséquences des actes de l'Etat disparu.' See also Strupp, Karl. 'Règles générales du droit de la paix.' *RCADI*, 1934, vol. I, p. 473.

22 Cavaglieri, Arrigo. 'Effets juridiques des changements de souveraineté territoriale.' *Revue de droit international et de législation comparée.* vol. XV, 1934, p. 225. O'Connell, D.P. *op. cit.,* pp. 16–17, and the authors cited therein.

23 Even Cavaglieri admits that the principle of consent does not apply to the debts of the predecessor state. *op. cit.,* p. 379: 'La liberté de l'Etat annexant rencontre toutefois une exception très importante et universellement reconnue. Il est tenu reconnaître et prendre sur lui les obligations patrimoniales, les dettes de l'Etat disparu, quelles qu'en soient la nature et la forme.'

24 Marcoff, Marco. *op. cit.,* pp. 36–37. O'Connell, D.P. *op. cit.,* pp. 28–29. Oppenheim, L. *op. cit.,* p. 158.

25 O'Connell, D.P. *op. cit.,* vol. I, pp. 199–236 and vol.I, pp. 1–381. Oppenheimer, L. *op. cit.,* p. 159. Marcoff, Marco. *op. cit.,* pp. 113–357.

26 Report of the International Law Commission on the Work of its Thirty-Third Session (4th May - 24th July 1980). *YILC*, vol. II, 1981, p. 9.

27 *Ibid.,* p. 10.

28 UN Doc. A/CONF. 80/31.

29 UN Doc. A/CONF. 117/14.

30 On the question of 'progressive development'of international law see Jennings, R. Y., 'The Progressive Development of International Law.' *BYBIL*, vol. 24, 1958, pp. 344–345. Lauterpacht, Sir. Hersch. 'Codification and Development of International Law.' *AJIL*, vol. 49, 1955, pp. 16–43. Summary Records of the Third Session of the International Law Commission, *YTLC*, vol. I, 1951, pp. 132–135.

31 Article 11 and 12 of the Vienna Convention on Succession of States in Respect of Treaties read as follows:

Article 11, Boundary régimes. A succession of States does not as such affect: (a) a boundary established by a treaty, or (b) obligations and rights established by a treaty and relating to the régime of a boundary.
Article 12, Other territorial régimes.
1. A succession of States does not as such affect: (a) obligations relating to the use of any territory, or to restrictions upon its use, established by a treaty for the benefit of any territory of a foreign State and considered as attaching to the territories in question; (b) rights restablished by a treaty for the benefit of any territory and relating to the use, or to restrictions upon the use, of any territory of a foreign State and considered as attaching to the territories in question.
2. A succession of States does not as such affect: (a) obligations

relating to the use of any territory, or to restrictions upon its use, established by a treaty for the benefit of a group of States or of all States and considered as attaching to that territory; (b) rights established by a treaty for the benefit of a group of States or of all States and relating to the use of any territory, or to restrictions upon its use, and considered as attaching to that territory.

3. The provisions of the present article do not apply to treaty obligations of the predecessor State providing for the establishment of foreign military bases on the territory to which the succession of States relates.

32 Articles 9, 14, 15, 16, 17, 18, 21, 27, 28, 29, 30, 31, 34, 37, 39, 40 and 41 of the Vienna Convention on Succession of States in Respect of State Property, Archives and Debts, *loc. cit.* The only exception to his rule provided for is in the case of debts when the successor state is a newly independent state. According to Article 38, 'no State debt of the predecessor State shall pass to the newly independent State, unless an agreement between them provides otherwise.' *Ibid.* For a detailed discussion of the reason for this exception see *YILC*, vol. II, 1981, pp. 91–105.

33 Articles 31, 34 and 35 of the Vienna Convention on Succession of States in Respect of Treaties, *loc. cit.*

34 See for example Articles 17, 18, 24, 27 and 28, *Ibid.*

35 Articles 14, 17, 18, 27, 30, 31 and 37, *Ibid.* As previously noted, a newly independent State does not become responsible for the debts of the predecessor unless it so agrees. See Article 38, *Ibid.*

36 Lauterpacht, Hersch. *Private Law Sources and Analogies of International Law.* London, Longmans Green and Co., Ltd., 1927, p. 125. Marek, Krystyna. *Identity and Continuity of States in Public International Law.* 2nd edition, Geneva, Librairie Droz, 1968, pp. 9–10: 'It should be clearly understood that whereas the problem of State identity and continuity bears on the *identity of the subject* . . . , the problem of succession relates to the identity of *certain* rights and obligations between *different subjects.*' Udina, Manlio. *op. cit.*, p. 671: 'La succession juridique, c'est-à-dire la substitution d'un sujet un autre dans un rapport juridique donné qui demeure identique.'

37 Bedjaoui, Mohammed. 'First Report on Succession of States in Respect of Rights and Duties Resulting from Sources other than Treaties.' *YILC*, vol. II, 1968, p. 97. 'Report of the International Law Commission on the work of Its Twentieth Session, *Ibid.*, p. 216.

38 Ago, Roberto. 'Summary Records of the TwentyFifth Session of the International Law Commission.' *YILC*, vol. I, 1973, p. 127: 'Once the successor State had replaced the predecessor State in its rights, it was, of course, free to act as it wished, but at the actual moment of the transfer the successor State received only what the predecessor State had possessed. In that respect there was complete equivalence.' Caflisch, Lucius. *op. cit.*, p. 358: ' . . . the territorial

successor is bound to assume rights and duties which are – at least materially – identical with the rights and duties formerly belonging to the territorial predecessor . . . .' Marek, Krystina, *loc. cit.* Yassen, Mustafa. 'Summary Records of the Twenty-Fifth Session of the International Law Commission.' *YILC*, vol. I, 1973, p. 109: 'The transfer of a right presupposed the existence of that right and its continuation.'

39 Aix-la-Chappelle (1818), Troppau (1870), Laibach (1821) and Verona (1822).

40 Approximately thirty such diplomatic conferences took place. The most significant were the Congress of Paris (1856), London Conferences (1871, 1912–13), Berlin Congresses (1878, 1884–85) and Algeciras Conference (1906).

41 Claude, Inis L. Jr. *Swords to Plowshares*. Third edition, New York, Random House, 1965, p. 21. See also Abi-Saab, Georges. 'The Concept of International Organization: A Synthesis.' *The Concept of International Organization*. Paris, UNESCO, 1981, p. 10. Bowett, D.W. *The Law of International Institutions*. Fourth edition, London, Stevens & Sons, 1982, p. 2. El-Erian, Abdulah, 'First Report on Relations Between States and Inter-Governmental Organizations.' *YILC*, vol. II, 1963; p. 162.

42 Treaty of Peace betwen Sweden and the Empire, signed at Osnabruck, 14 October 1648, *CTS*, vol. 1, pp. 121–269. Treaty of Peace between France and the Empire, signed at Münster, 14 October 1648, *CTS*, vol. 1, pp. 271–355.

43 Definitive Treaty of Peace and Amity between Austria, Great Britain, Portugal, Prussia, Russia and Sweden, and France, signed at Paris, 30 May 1814, *CTS*, vol. 63, pp. 171–202.

44 'Les Puissances . . . avec les Princes et Etats, Leurs Alliés . . . désirant maintenant de comprendre dans une transaction commune les différents résultats de Leurs négociations . . . ont autorisé Leurs Plénipotentiaires à réunir dans un Instrument général, les dispositions d'un intérêt majeur et permanent, et joindre cet Acte, comme Parties intégrantes des arrangements du Congrès, les Traités, Conventions, Déclarations, Règlements, et autres Actes particuliers, tels qu'ils se trouvent cités dans le présent Traité.' See also 'Traité général de paix entre l'Autriche, la France, la Grande-Bretagne, la Prusse, la Russie, la Sardaigne et la Porte Ottomane', Paris, 30 mars 1856, in Martens, G.Fr., *NRG*, XV, pp. 770–781 and Guggenheim, Paul. 'Contribution à l'histoire des sources du droit des Gens.' *RCADI*, 1958 II, pp. 70–71. Lachs, Manfred. 'Le développement et les fonctions des traités multilatéraux.' *RCADI* 1957 II, pp. 238–239.

45 See for example the Treaty between Austria, Bavaria, Prussia and Saxony for the Establishment of a German Telegraphic Union, Dresden, 25th July 1850, *CTS*, vol. 104, 1850, pp. 163–213 and the Treaty Establishing a Union between Belgium, France, Sardinia, Spain and Switzerland, Paris, 29th December 1855, *CTS*, vol. 114, 1855–1956, pp. 139–149.

46 The first permanent international organ was the European Danube Commission. See Article XVII of the Paris Peace Treaty of 30th March 1856, *op. cit.*, p. 777: 'Une Commission sera établie et se composera des Délégués de l'Autriche, de la Bavière, de la Sublime Porte et du Wurtemberg (un pour chacune de ces Puissances) . . . Cette Commission, qui sera permanente, 1. élaborera les règlements de navigation et de police fluviale; 2. fera disparaître les entraves . . . 3. ordonnera et fera exécuter les travaux nécessaires sur tout le parcours du fleuve; et 4. veillera, après la dissolution de la Commission Européenne au maintien de la navigabilité des embouchures du Danube et des parties de la mer y avoisinantes.'

47 A proposal was made to set up a permanent commission at the time of the creation of the International Telegraph Union in May 1865. The first conference of the Union, in July 1868, approved a motion to set up a Bureau international des administrations télégraphiques. See International Telegraph Convention, Paris, 17th May 1965, *CTS*, vol. 130, 1864–1865, pp. 198–231 and Article LXI of the International Telegraph Convention, Vienna, 21st July 1868, *CTS*, vol. 136, 1867–1868, p. 305: 'Une Administration télégraphique désignée par la Conférence prendra les mesures propres à faciliter, dans l'intérêt commun, l'exécution et l'application de la Convention. A cet effet, elle organisera, sous le titre de 'Bureau International des Administrations Télégraphiques' un service spécial qui fonctionnera sous sa direction, dont les frais seront supportés par toutes les administrations des Etats Contractants et dont les attributions sont déterminées ainsi . . . .'

48 Bowett, D. W. *op. cit.*, pp. 6–9. Nussbaum, Arthur. *A Concise History of the Law of Nations.* New York, the MacMillan Company, 1947, pp. 193–194.

49 Gerbet, Pierre. 'Rise and Development of International Organizations.' *The Concept of International Organizations.* Paris, Unesco, 1981, p. 38.

50 Reuter, Paul. *Institutions Internationales.* Paris, Presses Universitaires de France, 1963, pp. 186–187.

51 Claude, Inis, Jr. *op. cit.*, p. 60.

52 Oppenheim, L. *op. cit.*, p. 388. Reuter, Paul. *op. cit.*, p. 187.

53 Reuter, Paul. *op. cit.*, p. 188.

54 The Economic and Financial Organisation, the Organisation for Communication and Transit and the Health Organisation.

55 Mandates Commission, Opium Commission, Advisory Committee of Experts for Slavery, Intellectual Co-operation Commission.

56 Covenant of League of Nations. Part I of the Treaty of Peace, Versailles, 28th June 1919, *CTS*, vol. 225, p. 204: 'There shall be placed under the direction of the League all international bureaux already established by general treaties if the parties to such treaties consent.'

57 The following bureaux were placed under the direction of the League pursuant to Article 24, paragraph 1: the International Hydrographic Bureau, the Central International Office for the Con-

trol of the Liquor Traffic in Africa, the International Commission for Air Navigation, the International Bureau for Information and Inquiries regarding Relief to Foreigners, the Nansen International Office for Refugees, the International Exhibitions Bureau, the International Institute of Intellectual Co-operation, the International Institute for the Unification of Private Law, the International Educational Cinematographic Institute and the International Centre for the Study of Leprosy. Oppenheim, L., *op. cit.*, pp. 391–392.

58 Morley, Felix. *The Society of Nations*. Washington, The Brookings Institution, 1932, p. 172.

59 Jenks, Wilfred P. 'The Legal Personality of International Organizations.' *BYBIL*, vol. XXII, 1945, p. 1. Oppenheim, L. *op. cit.*, p. 379, note 3. See also the Advisory Opinion on Jurisdiction of the European Commission of the Danube, 8th December 1927, where the Permanent Court of International Justice observed that 'Although the European Commission exercises its functions 'in complete independence of the terrtorial authorities' and although it has independent means of action and prerogatives and privileges which are generally withheld from international organizations, it is not an organization possessing exclusive territorial sovereignty.' *PCIJ*, Series B, No. 14, p. 63.

60 ICJ Reports, 1949, p. 179.

61 Abi-Saab, Georges. *op. cit.*, p. 12. Bastid, Suzanne. *Le droit des organisations internationales*. Paris, Cours de droit, 1968/69, p. 26. Reuter, Paul. *op. cit.*, p. 204. Virally, Michel. 'Definition and Classification of International Organizations: A Legal Approach.' *The Concept of International Organization*. Paris, Unesco, 1981, p. 53.

62 Schwarzenberger, Georg. *International Law as Applied by International Courts and Tribunals*. vol. III, London, Stevens & Sons, Ltd., 1976, p. 5.

63 'Report of the International Law Commission on the Work of its Thirty-Fourth Session.' *YILC*, vol. III, 1982, p. 21. Reuter, Paul. *op. cit.*, pp. 192–193. Virally, Michel. *loc. cit.*, pp. 52–53.

64 Detter, Ingrid. *Law-Making by International Organizations*. Stockholm, P.A. Norstedt & Söners Förlag, 1965, p. 19.

65 Bastid, Suzanne, *op. cit.*, pp. 23 and 30. Cahier, Philippe. *Etude des accords de siège conclus entre les organisations internationales et les Etats ou elles résident*. Genève, Milano, Dott. A. Giuffrè, 1959, p. 6. Virally, Michel. *L'Organisation Mondiale*. Paris, Librairie Armand Colin, 1972, p. 24.

66 For a comparison of the different definitions proposed by legal scholars, see Abi-Saab, Georges, *op. cit.*, pp. 11–20. Cahier, Philippe. *loc. cit.* El-Erian, Abdullah. *op.cit.*, pp. 164–167. Virally, Michel. 'Definition and Classification of International Organizations: A Legal Approach.' *op. cit.*, pp. 51–56.

67 Chaumont, Charles M. 'La signification du principe de spécialité des organisations internationales.' *Mélanges Rolin*, Paris, 1964, p. 57. Virally, Michel, *loc. cit.*

68 *PCIJ*, Series B. No. 14, p. 64.

69 *ICJ Reports*, 1949, p. 180.
70 Mochi-Onory, Andrea G. 'The Nature of Succession Between International Organizations: Functions and Treaties.' *RHDI*, vol. 21, 1968, p. 37. See also Fitzmaurice, Sir Gerald. 'The Law and Procedure of the International Court of Justice: International Organizations and Tribunals.' *BYBIL*, vol. 29, 1952: 'If, for the concept of territorial area, there is substituted that of functional field, then the position might be stated as follows: that just as a territorial area passing from one state to another carries with it all rights and obligations specifically appertaining to that area in a territorial manner, so a functional field 'passing' from one international organization to another . . . carries with it the rights, obligations and functions connected with that field, and appertaining to the capacity to act in it,' and O'Connell, D.P. *International Law*. vol. I, London, Stevens & Sons, 1970, p. 396: 'Whereas state succession gives rise to a body of doctrine designed to minimize the impact of a change of sovereignty on the human beings associated with a distinct territory, the most that can be derived from the notion of a succession of organizations is a functional substitution.'
71 Bastid, Suzanne. 'Sur quelques problèmes juridiques de coordination dans la famille des Nations Unies.' *Mélanges offerts Paul Reuter*, Paris, Pedone, 1981, pp. 78–79. Bowett, D. W. *op. cit.*, p. 69. Jenks, C. Wilfred. 'Coordination: A New Problem of International Organizations.' *RCADI*, vol. II 1950, pp. 244–248.
72 Reuter, Paul. 'First Report on the Question of Treaties concluded Between States and International Organizations.' *YILC*, vol. II, 1972, p. 193.

CHAPTER II THE FORMS OF SUCCESSION BETWEEN INTERNATIONAL ORGANIZATIONS

1 Claude, Inis L. Jr. *op. cit.*, p. 73.
2 *Ibid.*, p. 66.
3 Article 57, paragraph 1 of the Charter of the United Nations.
4 Article 63, *Ibid.*
5 Jenks, C. Wilfred. *op. cit.*, pp. 172–173.
6 It was still fresh in the minds of most people that the failure of the United States to become a member of the League was one of the major causes of the League's failure to become the center piece of international cooperation. *Ibid.*, p.172.
7 Virally has suggested that the term 'partial' be used in reference to organizations which have exclusive memberships but are not restricted to a specific geographic region. Examples of such partial organizations are the Organization for Economic Cooperation and Development (OECD). See Virally, Michel. *L'organisation Mondiale*, Paris, Librairie Armand Rolin, 1972, p. 26.
8 Long before the outbreak of hostilities in 1939, the League had ceased to represent an effective instrument for maintaining peace. It was unable to stop the Japanese invasion of China in 1932, the

Italian attack on Ethiopia in 1936 and the German intervention in the Spanish Civil War between 1935 and 1939. It remained power-less when Germany seized the Sudetenland in 1938, absorbed Austria in 1939 and annexed Danzig, a territory which had been placed directly under its protection by the Versailles Treaty. See Colliard, Claude-Albert, *Institutions des relations internationales*. 7e édition, Paris, Dalloz, 1978, p. 373 and Articles 100–108 of the Treaty of Peace, *CTS*, vol. 225, pp. 246–249.

9 LN Doc. No. A. 5 (1946)X, Supervisory Commission. General Summarized Report on its Work during the Period of Emergency 1940–1946, p. 1.

10 Myers, Denys P. 'Liquidation of League of Nations Functions.' *AJIL*, vol. 42, 1948; p. 321: 'Of the 50 states represented at the San Francisco conference, 32 were members of the League of Nations, and 12 had previously been members. Of the 6 others only the United States might have been a League member. The current members of the League of Nations not represented at the confer-ence were 13 in number, the political status of some not being entirely certain.'

11 *Ibid.*

12 Article 4(c) of the Interim Arrangements Concluded by the Govern-ments Represented at the United Nations Conference on Inter-national Organization, San Francisco, June 26, 1945, in Goodrich, Leland M. and Hambro, Eduard. *Charter of the United Nations, Commentary and Documents*. Boston, World Peace Foundation, 1946, p. 379.

13 LN Doc. No. A. 8 (1946) Annex. Common Plan for the Transfer of League of Nations Assets Established by the United Nations Committee and the Supervisory Commission of the League of Nations. See also UN Doc. No. A/18, February 12, 1946. Report of the Committee set up by the Preparatory Commission to Discuss and Establish with the Supervisory Commission of the League of Nations a Common Plan for the Transfer of the Assets of the League of Nations.

14 UNGA Res. No. A/24. Transfer of Certain Functions, Activities and Assets of the League of Nations: 'The General Assembly, having considered the report of the Committee set up by the Preparatory Commission to discuss and establish with the Super-visory Commission of the League of Nations a common plan for the transfer of the assets of the League of Nations, approves of both the report of the Committee set up by the Preparatory Commission and the common plan submitted by it.'

15 *Ibid.*

16 Economic and Social Council, Official Records, 1st session, pp. 163–169.

17 The League of Nations Committees consisted of the following: Economic Committee, Coordination Committee on Economic and Financial Questions, Fiscal Committee, Financial Committee, Committee of Statistical Experts, Committee of Experts for the

Study of Demographic Problems, Committee for Communication and Transit, Health Committee, Advisory Committee for the Eastern Bureau of the Health Organization, Advisory Committee on Traffic in Opium and Other Dangerous Drugs, Advisory Committee on Social Questions, Advisory Committee of Exports on Slavery, International Committee on Intellectual Cooperation.

18 LN Doc. No. A. 32 (1946). Resolution for the Termination of the League of Nations: Paragraph 5: 'The Assembly approves and directs that effect shall be given in the manner set out in the Report of the Finance Committee to the "Common Plan for the Transfer of League of Nations Assets" which was drawn up jointly by the United Nations Committee and the Supervisory Commission, acting respectively on behalf of the United Nations and the League of Nations and was approved by the General Assembly of the United Nations on February 12, 1946.'

19 *Ibid.*, Paragraph 1(1).

20 *Ibid.*, Paragraph 2. L. N. Doc. No. C.5.M.5, July 31, 1947, Final Report of the Board of Liquidation, p. 6.

21 Resolution on Custody of the Original Texts of International Agreements, 18 April 1946, in *LN Official Journal*, Special Supplement No. 194, p. 278.

22 Resolution on Functions and Powers Arising Out of International Agreements of a Technical and Nonpolitical Character, *Ibid.*

23 Resolution on the Assumption by the United Nations of Activities Hitherto Performed by the League, *Ibid.*

24 LN Doc. No. C.5.M.5. *op. cit.*, p. 16. The Final Report of the Board of Liquidation notes that the originals of international labour conventions had previously been handed over to the ILO. *Ibid.*

25 *Ibid.*

26 *YBUN*, 1947–48, p. 11.

27 The Darling Foundation, the Léon Bernard Fund, the International Press House Fund, the Account of the Eastern Health Bureau (Singapore), the Working Capital Fund, the Pensions Fund for Members of the Permanent Court of International Justice, the Staff Pensions Fund, the Reserve Fund, the Staff Provident Fund, the Exchange Fund and the Forstall Fund.

28 LN Doc. No. C.5.M.5. *op. cit.*, pp. 13–19.

29 *Ibid.*, p. 11. Agreement concerning the Execution of the Transfer to the United Nations of Certain Assets of the League of Nations, Geneva, July 19, 1946, *UNTS*, vol. 1, pp. 111–117. Protocol (No. I) concerning the Execution of Various Operations in the Transfer to the United Nations of Certain Assets of the League of Nations, Geneva, August 1, 1946, *UNTS*, vol. 1, pp. 131–133. Protocol (No. II) on the Transfer of Certain Services from the League of Nations to the United Nations, Geneva, August 1, 1946, *UNTS*, vol. 1, pp. 135–137.

30 LN Doc. No. C.5.M.5. *op. cit.*, p. 21.

31 *Ibid.*, p. 28.

32 *Ibid.*, pp. 8–9. For the Scheme of Distribution see LN Doc. No. A. 32(I), 1946, Report of the Finance Committee, 18 April 1946.
33 Convention Relating to the Regulation of Aerial Navigation, Paris, October 13, 1919, *LNTS*, vol. 11, pp. 195–196.
34 Annexes A, B, C, D, E, F, G and H, *Ibid.*, pp. 243–272.
35 *Ibid.*, p. 195: 'There shall be instituted, under the name of the International Commission for Air Navigation, a permanent Commission placed under the direction of the League of Nations . . .'. The United States decided to remain outside of ICAN largely because of the formal link between the organization and the League. Other important countries that refused to join ICAN were the Soviet Union, Germany, China, Brazil, Hungary and Turkey. See Jennings, R. Y. 'Some Aspects of the International Law of the Air.' *RCADI*, vol. II, 1949, p. 517 and Schenkman, Jacob. *International Civil Aviation Organization*. Geneva, Libraire E. Droz, 1955, p. 47. Other regional arrangements were the stillborn Ibero-American Commission for Air Navigation sponsored by Spain and several Latin American countries in 1926 and the 1928 Havana Convention on Commercial Aviation concluded under the auspices of the Pan American Union. Unlike the Paris Convention, however, the Havana Convention did not establish an international organization. The Ibero-American Convention for Air Navigation, Madrid, November 1926, *IL*, vol. III, pp. 2027–2029. The Pan-American Convention on Commercial Aviation, Havana, 1928, *IL*, vol. IV, pp. 2256–2369.
36 'History of the PICAO.' *PICAO Journal*, vol. I, No. 1, 1945, p. 9. Peaslee, Amos J. *International Governmental Organizations. Constitutional Documents*. Revised third edition, Part V, The Hague, Martinus Nijhoff, 1974, p. 390.
37 See Doc. No. 16. United States Proposal of a Convention on Air Navigation. *Proceedings of the International Civil Aviation Conference*, Chicago, November 1–December 7, 1944, Washington, United States Government Printing Office, 1948, vol. I, p. 566: Article 32.' The present Convention supersedes, as between the Contracting States, the Convention Relating to the Regulation of Aerial Navigation signed at Paris on October 13, 1919, and the Convention on Commercial Aviation signed at Havana on February 20, 1928. Each of these two last-named Conventions will remain in force as between any High Contracting Party and any State which is a party thereto and is not a party to the present Convention.' Doc. No. 50. Canadian Revised Preliminary Draft of an International Air Convention. *Ibid.*, p. 588: Article XLVII. Other Agreements and Arrangements. Section 1. 'As between member states this convention shall replace the International Aerial Navigation Convention signed at Paris in 1919, the Ibero-American Convention on Air Navigation signed at Madrid in 1926, and the Pan-American Convention on Commercial Aviation signed at Havana in 1928.' Doc. No. 398. Minutes of the Meeting of the

Joint Subcommittee on Committee I, II and IV, November 25, 1944, *Ibid.*, p. 472.

38 Article 80 of the Convention on International Civil Aviation. Proceedings of the International Civil Aviation Conference, *op. cit.*, p. 169. For a summary of the evolution of this article see Appendix 2, Commentary on the Development of the Individual Articles of the Convention on International Civil Aviation, *Ibid.*, vol. II, p. 1398 and Doc. No. 398, Minutes of the Meeting of the Joint Subcommittee of Committee I, II and IV, November 25, *Ibid.*, vol. I, p. 472.

39 Interim Agreement on International Civil Aviation. *Ibid.*, vol. I, p. 132.

40 *PICAO Journal*, vol. 1, No. 1, 1945, p. 20.

41 ICAN Res. No. 1167. *Official Bulletin of the ICAN*. No. 28, 1945, p. 22: 'The Commission decides to authorize its General Secretary, Mr. Albert Roper, to assume the duties of Secretary General of the 'Provisional International Civil Aviation Organization'. For the duration of these duties he will receive only 25% of the amount of his indemnities as Secretary General of the Commission.'

42 *Ibid.*

43 ICAN Res. No. 1218. *ICAN Official Bulletin*, No. 29, p. 43. 'The Commission, having regard to the eventual liquidation of the ICAN, decides to transmit to PICAO, for further consideration and action, the documentation for the following items.' These included maps for air navigations, air traffic statistics, recognition of aircraft at sea, a signal book, seaplanes, symbols and terms used in aeronautical technology, model journey log of aircraft, use of oxygen inhalers on civilian aircraft, graduation of altimeters, firearms in aircraft, symbols and terms used in air navigation.

44 ICAN Res. No. 1222. *Ibid.*, pp. 44–45.

45 Liquidation Plan of the International Commission for Air Navigation Adopted by the Liquidation Committee During its Meeting of January 7 and 8, 1947, ICAO Doc. No. 4813, C/603, October 26, 1947, p. 11.

46 According to the ICAN Res. No. 1222, 'In the absence of opposition, the plan will become applicable on April 1, 1947, or on the date of the coming into force of the Convention on International Civil Aviation signed at Chicago on December 7, 1944, whichever is later.'

47 ICAO Doc. No. 4813, paragraphs 6 and 7, ICAO Doc. No. 6280, C/717 and ICAO Doc. No. 6437, A3–P/3.

48 ICAN Res. No. 1222, *loc. cit.*

49 ICAO Doc. Nos. C-WP/233 and 6772.

50 Convention for the Establishment of an International Institute of Agriculture, Rome, June 7, 1905, *NRG*, 3rd Series, vol. 2, pp. 238–243.

51 Article 9, *Ibid.*, p. 241.

52 For a list of these conventions see the Annex to the Protocol for

115

the Dissolution of the International Institute of Agriculture, *GBTS*, No. 29, Cmd. 7413, p. 8.

53 United Nations Conference on Food and Agriculture. Text of the Final Act in *AJIL*, Supplement, Official Documents, vol. 37, 1943, p. 159.

54 *Ibid.*, pp. 164–165.

55 *Ibid.*, p. 165.

56 First Report to the Governments of the United Nations by the Interim Commission on Food and Agriculture, Washington, July 1945, p. 3.

57 Second Report to the Governments of the United Nations by the Interim Commission on Food and Agriculture, Washington, July 1945, pp. 2–3.

58 *Ibid.*, p. 3.

59 FAO Doc. No. 206. in *Proceedings of the First Session of the Conference*, Washington, 1946.

60 'Rapport sur le projet de résolution présenté au nom du Comité permanent pour l'extinction de la Convention internationale de 1905.' *Actes de la Seizième Assemblée générale*, 8 et 9 juillet 1946, p. 41.

61 Article III of the Protocol. *loc. cit.*, p. 3: 'When the duties assigned to it by Article II of this Protocol have been completed, the Permanent Committee of the Institute shall forthwith, by circular letter notify the Members of the Institute of the dissolution of the Institute . . . and of the transfer of the functions and assets thereof to the Organization. The date of such notification shall be deemed to be the date of termination of the Convention of 7th June 1905, and also the date of the dissolution of the Institute . . . '.

62 IIA Res. No. 8. Tasks in Connection with the Liquidation of the IIA, *Actes de la Seizième Assemblée générale*, p. 71.

63 FAO Doc. No. 61, paragraph 15, Report of Committee I of Commission B. Second Session. FAO Doc. No. 1249, Report of the Activities of the FAO European Regional Office, 1948/1949, Fifth Session, p. 33. The Permanent Committee announced the dissolution of the IIA on February 27, 1948, although it had not yet completed all of its tasks under Article II of the Protocol.

64 International Office of Public Health.

65 Agreement for the Establishment of the International Office of Public Health, Rome, December 9, 1907, *AJIL Supplement*, vol. 3, 1909, pp. 152–158.

66 Article IV of the Organic By-Laws. *Ibid.*, p. 155.

67 Agreement Concerning Facilities to be Given to Merchant Seamen for the Treatment of Venereal Disease, December 1, 1924. Convention on Traffic in Opium and Drugs, February 19, 1925. International Sanitary Convention, June 21, 1926. Sanitary Convention for Aerial Navigation, April 12, 1933. Convention Concerning Anti-Diphtheritic Serum, August 1, 1930. Convention for Limiting the Manufacture and Regulating the Distribution of Narcotic Drugs, July 13, 1931. Convention for the Mutual Protection Against

Dengue Fever, July 25, 1934. Agreement concerning the Transport of Corpses, February 10, 1937. Agreement for Dispensing with Consular Visas on Bills of Health, December 22, 1931. Convention Amending the International Sanitary Convention of June 21, 1926, October 31, 1938.

68 Doc. No. 614. *United Nations Conference on International Organization*, vol. VIII, United Nations Information Organization, London and New York, 1945, p. 95.

69 Doc. No. 658, *Ibid.*, vol. X, pp. 120–121.

70 ECOSOC Res. No. 1/1, Calling for an International Health Conference.

71 UN Doc. No. E/772, Resolutions Adopted by the Technical Preparatory Committee of Experts on April 5, 1946. *Report of the International Health Conference*, Annex 2, p. 47.

72 *Ibid.*

73 Article 1, Protocol Concerning the *Office international d'hygiène publique*, New York, July 22, 1946, *UNTS*, vol. 9, p. 66.

74 Article 3, *Ibid.*

75 Article 72, Final Instruments of the Conference, *Report of the International Health Conference*, Annex 2, p. 61.

76 Article 2(e), Arrangement Concluded by the Governments Represented at the International Health Conference Establishing an Interim Commission of the World Health Organization. *Ibid.*, p. 64.

77 OIHP Permanent Committee, Resolution of October 31, 1946, *Procès-verbaux des séances du Comité permanent*, Session Ordinaire, October 1946, p. 140.

78 WHAI Res. No. 84. Denunciation of Rome Agreement and Transfer of IOHP Assets to WHO. *Handbook of Resolutions and Decisions of the World Health Assembly and Executive Board*, vol. I, 1948 1972, p. 360. *Yearbook of the United Nations, 1947–1948*, p. 911.

79 WHA Res. No. I/84, *loc. cit.*

80 *Official Records of the World Health Organization*, No. 5, pp. 110–111. Rapport du Président de la Commission des finances et du transfert sur le fonctionnement de l'Office international d'hygiène publique, novembre 1946–avril 1950. *Procès-verbaux des séances du Comité permanent*, Session mai 1950, p. 26.

81 For text of this Arrangement see *Official Records of the World Health Organization*, No. 7, Annex 28, pp. 203–204.

82 Compte rendu de la révision de la Commission des finances et du transfert de l'Office international d'hygiène publique, 4 mai 1950, *Procès-verbaux des séances du Comité permanent*, Session de Mai 1950, p. 4.

83 *Ibid.* WHO Doc. No. A3/46, Add. 1, Rev. 1, p. 3.

84 *Ibid.* WHO Doc. No. A4/27, Transfer of the Assets of the Office international d'hygiène publique, April 30, 1951, pp. 1 and 2.

85 *Handbook of Resolutions and Decisions of the World Health Assembly and Executive Board*, p. 363.

86 Article 1, Statut organique de l'Institut international de coopération

intellectuelle, Paris, 8 décembre 1924, *LNOJ*, 6th year, No. 2, 1924, pp. 285–289: 'Un Institut international de coopération intellectuelle, mis à la disposition de la Société des Nations, est fondé, à Paris, par le gouvernement de la République française, conformément aux termes de sa lettre au président du Conseil de la Société des Nations, en date du 8 décembre 1924.'
87 Institut international de coopération intellectuelle 1925–1946. 1956, p. 87.
88 *Ibid.*, p. 102.
89 LN Doc. No. A/6, 1946. Report on the Work of the League During the War submitted to the Assembly by the Acting Secretary-General, pp. 126 and 128.
90 LN Doc. No. A/33, 1946. Report of the First Committee to the Assembly, pp. 3–4.
91 *Ibid.*, Annex E: '2. The Assembly, Being desirous of facilitating by all means in its power the continuity of the work of intellectual cooperation; Considering that paragraph 7 of the letter of December 8th, 1924, from the French Government to the President of the Council of the League of Nations provides that, in the event of the abolition of the Institute, any articles and in particular, the archives and collections of documents deposited in the premises by the Governing Body, as well as any property which has been acquired by the Institute during its period of operation, shall remain the property of the League of Nations, Instructs the Secretary-General of the League of Nations to take in due time, in conjunction with the Directorate of the Institute, the necessary measures for the execution of the present resolution.'
92 ECOSOC Res. No. 24 (III). Utilization of the Property Rights of the League of Nations in the International Institute of Intellectual Cooperation. 3 October 1946.
93 UN Res. No. A/7 (I). Utilization by UNESCO of the Property Rights of the League of Nations in the International Institute of Intellectual Co-operation: 'as soon as possible after UNESCO has been definitively established, it shall take over in accordance with Article XI, paragraph 2, of its Charter, such of the functions and activities of the International Institute of Intellectual Co-operation as may be performed within the scope of the programme adopted at the UNESCO General Conference . . . and that an agreement be concluded between UNESCO and the Institute before 31st December 1946, in order to facilitate the assumption by UNESCO of the functions and activities referred to in paragraph 1 of the present Resolution . . . '.
94 UNESCO Doc. No. 1C/30. General Conference. First Session, 20 November to 10 December 1946, pp. 68–69.
95 Preamble, Agreement Between UNESCO and the IIIC, *Ibid.*, p. 241.
96 Article 2 and 3 of the Agreement, *Ibid.*
97 UNGA Res. No. A/591 (VI), Questions Concerning the Liquidation of the International Institute of Intellectual Co-operation.

98 UNESCO Doc. No. 29 EX/Decisions, Item 10.1. UNESCO Doc. No. 30 EX/Decisions, Item 14.1.
99 UNESCO Doc. No. 42 EX/41 and UNESCO Doc. No. 42 EX/ Decisions, Item 13.1. 'The Executive Board . . . Takes note of the final report of the Director-General on the liquidation of the International Institute of Intellectual Co-operation and authorizes him to discharge the liquidator and to accept transfer of the balance of the Institute's account . . . '.
100 Agreement for the Establishment of the East African Common Services Organization, Dar-Es-Salam, December 9, 1961, *UNTS*, vol. 437, p. 48. For the history of the EAHC see *BDARO*, vol. III, 1972, pp. 1095–1096 and Ranjeva, Raymond. *loc. cit.*, pp. 32–33.
101 *BDARO*, vol. III, 1972, p. 1097. Ranjeva, Raymond. *loc. cit.*, p. 33.
102 *Ibid.*
103 Treaty for East-African Co-operation, Kampala, June 6, 1967, in *BDARO*, vol. III, pp. 1145–1269.
104 Preamble, *Ibid.*, p. 1145: 'And whereas provision was made by the East African (High Commission) Orders in Council 1947 to 1961 for the control and administration of certain matters and services of common interest to the said countries and for that purpose the East African High Commission and the East African Central Legislative Assembly were thereby established: And whereas provision was made by the East African Common Services Organization Agreements 1961 to 1966 (upon the revocation of the East African (High Commission) Orders in Council 1947 to 1961) for the establishment of the East African Common Services Organization with the East African Common Services Authority as its principal executive authority and the Central Legislative Assembly as its legislative body . . . '.
105 Article 43, para. 2(a), *Ibid.*, p. 1171.
106 Annex XV, *Ibid.*, p. 1268.
107 Annex XV, para. 1, *Ibid.*
108 Annex XV, para. 2, *Ibid.*
109 Annex XV, para. 4, *Ibid.*
110 Articles 91, para. 1 and 94, *Ibid.*, p. 1198.
111 The Annual Register, edited by H.V. Hudson, London, Longman, 1977, p. 353 and 1978, p. 353. Other examples of this form of succession are the International Committee for Coordination of Antilocust Activities of Central American and Mexico by the International Regional Organization of Animal and Plant Health, the Caribbean Commission by the Caribbean Organization, the West African Customs Union by the West African Economic Community and the Commonwealth Telecommunications Board by the Commonwealth Telecommunications Organization.
112 Le Bureau international d' éducation au service du mouvement éducatif. Paris, Unesco, 1979, pp. 53–55.
113 *Bulletin of the International Bureau of Education*, No. 13, September 1929, pp. 3–5. Statutes of the International Bureau of Education,

Geneva, July 25, 1929. *United States Treaties and Other International Agreements*, vol. 14, Part 1, TIAS, 5312, 1963, p. 315.

114 *Le Bureau international d'éducation au service du mouvement éducatif*, *op. cit.*, p. 108.

115 *Ibid.*, p. 109.

116 *Ibid.*, pp. 110 and 113.

117 Article 3, Agreement between the United Nations Educational, Scientific and Cultural Organization and the International Bureau of Education. UNESCO Doc. No. 15. C/83, November 14, 1968, Annex II, p. 2: 'The Bureau shall be established at Geneva, within the framework of UNESCO, of which it shall be an integral part, an international center of comparative education, hereafter referred to as "the center" which will bear the name "International Bureau of Education" and which will enjoy a large intellectual and functional autonomy.'

118 Article VIII, Statutes of the International Bureau of Education, in UNESCO. *Records of the General Conference*, Fifteenth Session, 1968, Resolutions, pp. 109–110.

119 Article 2, Agreement between the United Nations Educational, Scientific and Cultural Organization, UNESCO Doc. No. 15/83, Annex II, p. 2.

120 Article 8, *Ibid.*, p. 3.

121 Agreement Concerning the Establishment of the International Patents Bureau, The Hague, June 6, 1947, *UNTS*, vol. 46, pp. 258–261.

122 Article 1, *Ibid.*, p. 259.

123 *ILM*, vol. 13, 1974, p. 268.

124 European Patent Convention, Munich, October 5, 1973, *IGO*, Parts III–IV, p. 90.

125 Protocol on Centralization of the European Patent System and on its Introduction. *Ibid.*, p. 151.

126 Draft Agreement on the Integration of the International Patent Institute into the European Patent Office, Interim Committee of the European Patent Organization, Doc. No. CI/Final 23/77.

127 Article 29, *Ibid.* Benthem, J.B. Van. 'The Current State of the European Patent System.' *Revue et Bulletin de la Fédération internationale des Conseils en propriété industrielle*, No. 31, March 1979, pp. 69–91.

128 Article 1, para. 1, *loc. cit.*

129 Article 4, *Ibid.* Another case of absorption was the integration of the Commission de Coopération Technique en Afrique au Sud du Sahara (CCTA) into the Organization of African Unity (OAU) as the main element of the OAU Scientific and Technical Research Committee (STRC).

130 *EY*, 1962, p. 1179.

131 *EY*, 1962, pp. 1115–1141.

132 Chappez, Jean. 'La cessation des activités de l'ELDO et la relance de l'Europe spatiale.' *AFDI*, vol. XIX, 1973, p. 948. *IGO*, Part II–IV, p. 163.

133 Annual Report of the European Space Vehicle Launcher Development Organization. *EY*, 1972, pp. 833–835.

134 *Ibid.*, p. 833.

135 Chappez, Jean. 'La création de l'Agence spatiale européenne,' *AFDF*, vol. XXI, 1975, p. 801. *EY*, 1975, p. 821.

136 Res. No. 1, Final Act of the Conference of Plenipotentiaries for the Establishment of a European Space Agency, *ILM*, vol. XIV, No. 4, 1975, pp. 857–858: 'The Conference . . . Recommends, in order to enable the Agency to function de facto as from the aforementioned day (the day following the date of signature of the Final Act), that in the application of the Convention for the Establishment of ESRO and ELDO the provisions of the Convention for the Establishment of a European Space Agency should be taken into account to the greatest possible extent . . . '. See also *European Yearbook*, 1975, p. 823.

137 Res. No. 2, Assumption of the Rights and Obligations of ELDO. *ILM*, vol. XIV, No. 4, 1975, p. 858.

138 Chappez, Jean. *loc. cit.*, p. 805.

139 *Ibid.*

140 *Ibid.*, p. 806.

141 Article XIX, *ILM*, vol. XIV, 1975, p. 882.

142 Cameroon, Congo-Brazzaville, Ivory Coast, Dahomey, Gabon, Upper Volta, Mauritania, Niger, Central African Republic, Senegal, Chad and Madagascar.

143 Treaty Establishing the African and Malagasy Organization for Economic Cooperation. Tananarive, September 12, 1961, *BDARO*, vol. I, pp. 309–313. OAMCE stands for l'Organisation Africaine et Malgache de Coopération Economique.

144 Charter of the African and Malagasy Union, Tananarive, September 8, 1961. *BDARO*, vol. I, p. 352. UAM stands for l'Union Africaine et Malgache.

145 Article 3, *Ibid.*, p. 310.

146 Article 4, *Ibid.*

147 Article 2, *Ibid.*, p. 352.

148 Borella, François. 'Le régionalisme africain en 1964.' *AFDI*, vol. X, 1964, p. 632. Wodie, Francis. *Les institutions internationales régionales en Afrique occidentale et centrale*, Paris, Librairie générale de droit et de jurisprudence, 1970, p. 49.

149 The *Union africaine et malgache des postes et télécommunications* (UAMPT), the *Union africaine et malgache de banques pour le développement*, the *Office africaine et malgache de la propriété industrielle* and *Air Afrique*.

150 Borella, François, *op. cit.*, p. 633. UAMCE stands for *l'Union Africaine et Malgache de Coopération Economique*.

151 *BDARO*, vol. I, p. 257.

152 Borella, François, *op. cit.*, pp. 633–634. Ranjeva, Raymond, *op. cit.*, pp. 109–110. For the text of the Charter of the UAMCE see Wodie, Francis, *op. cit.*, pp. 66–70.

153 Final Communiqué of the Nouakchott Conference, February 12,

1965, *Nations Nouvelles, Revue de l'UAMCE*, March 1965, p. 9. OCAM stands for *l'Organisation Commune Africaine et Malgache*.

154 Borella, François. 'Le régionalisme africain en crise.' *AFDI*, vol. XII, 1966, p. 777. *ILM*, 1967, pp. 53–56.

155 *BDARO*, vol. I, p. 257. Wodie, Francis, *op. cit.*, p. 55.

156 OCAM Res. No. 3/APJ/KINSHASA. Reproduced in Ranjeva, Raymond, *op. cit.*, p. 2A, note 41.

157 *Ibid.*, p. 348. Wodie, Francis, *op. cit.*, p. 64.

158 Ranjeva, Raymond, *op. cit.*, pp. 372 and 378. Wodie, Francis. *loc. cit.*

159 Article 387 of the Treaty of Versailles, *op. cit.*

160 Article 399, *Ibid.*

161 Articles 393, 405, 412 and 415, *Ibid.*

162 Tortora, Manuela. *L'OIT, Institution spécialisée et le système de l'organisation internationale*, Bruxelles, Bruylant, 1980, p. 106–110.

163 Ghebali, Victor-Yves. *Organisation internationale et Guerre Mondiale. Le cas de la Société des Nations et de l'Organisation internationale du Travail pendant la Seconde Guerre Mondiale*, Thèse, Université de Grenoble, 1975, pp. 33–36.

164 *Ibid*, p. 36.

165 *Ibid*. p. 39. Tortora, Manuela, *op. cit.*, p. 50.

166 Resolution Concerning the Constitution and Constitutional Practice of the International Labour Organisation and its Relationship with Other International Bodies. International Labour Conference, 26th Session, Philadelphia, 1944. Record of Proceedings, Appendix XI, III, para. 4, p. 527.

167 Instrument of Amendment and Recommendation adopted by the Conference, November 7, 1945, *UNTS*, vol. 2, pp. 17–25.

168 International Labour Organisation Instrument for the Amendment of the Constitution, Montreal, October 9, 1946, *UNTS*, vol. 15, pp. 32–122.

169 Convention for the Partial Revision of Convention . . . , Montreal, October 9, 1946, *UNTS*, vol. 38, pp. 3–15.

170 LN Doc. No. A/33, April 18, 1946, Resolution for the Dissolution of the League of Nations.

171 Agreement between the League of Nations and the International Labour Organisation Concerning the Transfer of Certain Properties, Geneva and Montreal, May 17, 1946, *UNTS*, vol. 19, p. 189.

172 LN Doc. No. C.5.M.5., July 31, 1947, Final Report of the Board of . Liquidation, pp. 22–23.

173 *UNTS*, vol. 15, p. 36, note 1.

174 Article 2, Pact of the League of Arab States, Cairo, March 22, 1945, *UNTS*, vol. 70, pp. 249–263.

175 Boutros-Ghali, Boutros. 'The Arab League (1945–1970).' *Revue égyptienne de droit international*, vol. 25, 1969, p. 681.

176 McDonald, Robert W. *The League of Arab States, A Study in the Dynamic of Regional Organization*, Princeton, New Jersey, Princeton University Press, 1965, p. 173.

177 Charter of Arab Cultural Unity, Baghdad, February 29, 1964. *IGO*,

Part III–IV, pp. 34–35. Constitution of the Arab League Educational, Cultural and Scientific Organization, Baghdad, February 29, 1964. *Ibid.*, pp. 30–38. Article 3 of the Charter provides that the 'Member States agree to develop the cultural organs of the League of Arab States (the Cultural Department, the Institute of Arabic Manuscripts and the Institute of Higher Arabic Studies) into one comprehensive organization within the framework of the League of Arab States to be called "The Arab League Educational, Cultural and Scientific Organization".' *Ibid.*, p. 25. Article 10 of the Constitution provides that 'The Arab League Educational, Cultural and Scientific Organization is a specialized agency, within the context of the League of Arab States.' *Ibid.*, p. 36.

178 *Ibid.*, p. 21.
179 UNGA Res. No. 2152(XXI). Resolution on Establishment of the United Nations Industrial Development Organization, 17 November 1966.
180 Article 1, *Ibid.*
181 UNGA Res. No. 3201 (S-VI). Declaration on the Establishment of a New International Economic Order, 1 May 1974. UNGA Res. No. 3281(XXIX). Charter of Economic Rights and Duties of States, 12 December 1974.
182 Bretton, Philippe. 'La transformation de l'ONUDI en institution spécialisée.' *AFDI*, vol. XXV, 1979, p. 568.
183 *Ibid.*
184 *YBUN*, Vol. 33, 1979, p. 618.
185 *Ibid.* UN Doc. A/CONF. 90/19, April 8, 1979. The rules of the Conference provided for adoption of the constitution by a two thirds majority of those present and voting. Bretton, Philippe. *op. cit.*, p. 569.
186 UN Doc. A/CONF. 90/19.
187 UNGA Res. No. 34/96, 13 December 1979.
188 *Ibid. YBUN*, Vol. 39, 1985, p. 591.
189 WEU Doc. No. 130, 'Rationalization of European Institutions other than those of the Six.' Assembly of the Western European Union, Proceedings, Fifth Ordinary Session, 1st Part, vol. I, June 1959, p. 140.
190 *Ibid.*
191 Wigny Plan, *Ibid.*, Appendix I, pp. 140–145.
192 WEU Doc. No. 149, Transfer of Cultural and Social Activities of the Western European Union to the Council of Europe. Report submitted on behalf of the General Affairs Committee by Mr. Kopf, Rapporteur, *Ibid.*, 2nd Part, vol. I, December 1959, p. 97.
193 *Ibid.*, p. 99.
194 WEU Doc. No. 130, *op. cit.*, p. 147. The President of the WEU Assembly addressed a letter to the Chairman of the WEU Council on May 25, 1959 which declared that this decision represented 'a very serious infringement of the rights of the Assembly of Western European Union to be consulted before any decision, even of principle, is reached concerning a modification or the application

of the Treaty of Brussels, to ensure the observance of which the Assembly was set up.' *Ibid.*

195 *EY*, 1960, vol. VIII, 1961, p. 199.

196 Wiebringhaus, Hans. 'A propos du transfert de compétences entre organisations internationales. Le cas du transfert de certaines activités de l'UEO au Conseil de l'Europe.' *AFDI*, vol. VII, 1961, p. 549.

197 Articles 2 (1) and (2), Convention Establishing an International Relief Union, Geneva, July 12, 1927. *LNTS*, vol. 135, 1932, pp. 249–265.

198 UN Doc. No. E/4227, Transfer to the United Nations of the Responsibilities and Assets of the International Relief Union, p. 2.

199 *Ibid.*

200 *Ibid.*

201 UN Doc. No. E/4402, Transfer to the United Nations of the Responsibilities and Assets of the International Relief Union, Report by the Secretary-General, p. 3.

202 ECOSOC Res. No. 1268 (XLIII), August 4, 1967, Transfer to the United Nations of the Responsibilities and Assets of the International Relief Union.

203 Article I, Agreement between UNESCO and the International Relief Union, UNESCO Doc. No. 15 C/ 85, Annex II, p. 3.

204 Article III, *Ibid.*, p. 4.

205 *Yearbook of International Organizations*, 1984/85, Union of International Associations, vol. I, entry C2411.

206 UNRRA Res. No. 94, Relating to the Health Activities of the Administration. Woodbridge, George. UNRRA, *The History of the United Nations Relief and Rehabilitation Administration*, vol. III, pp. 157–158. Agreement between the Interim Commission of the World Health Organization and UNRRA, December 9, 1946. *Ibid.*, pp. 352–354.

207 UNRRA Res. No. 102, Relating to Agricultural Production. *Ibid.*, p. 167. Agreement between the FAO and UNRRA, February 19, 1947, *Ibid.*, p. 354.

208 UNRRA Res. No. 95, Relating to the Social Welfare Activities of the Administration, *Ibid.*, p. 159. UNGA Res. No. 58(I), Transfer to the United Nations of the Advisory Social Welfare Functions of UNRRA, December 14, 1946. UNRRA Res. No. 103, Relating to the Rehabilitation of the Children and Adolescents of Countries which were Victims of Aggression, *Ibid.*, p. 167. Transfer to the United Nations of the Residual Assets and Activities of UNRRA, September 27, 1948, *UNTS*, vol. 27, pp. 350–397.

209 UNRRA Res. No. 99, Relating to Displaced Persons Operations, Woodbridge, George, *op. cit.*, p. 162. Agreement between the PCIRO and UNRRA, June 29, 1947, *Ibid.*, p. 357. The IRO was also intended to be a temporary organization and the same situation arose as in the case of the UNRRA when its functions were in turn split between the Intergovernmental Committee for European Migration and the United Nations High Commissioner for Refugees and several local governments. See IRO Doc. No. GC/SR/30,

Termination of the IRO Programmes, Second Session of the General Council. *Summary Record of the Thirtieth Meeting*, April 6, 1949, Annex, p. 5. IRO Res. Doc. No. 39, Completion of the Programme of the Organization, Holborn, Louise W. *The International Refugee Organization. A Specialized Agency of the United Nations*, London, New York, Toronto, Oxford University Press, 1956, pp. 725–726. IRO GC Res. No. 40, Future International Action Concerning Refugees, *Ibid.*, pp. 727–728. IRO GC Res. No. 106, Disposal of Assets, *Ibid.*, p. 748. IRO GC Res. No. 108, Establishing a Board of Liquidation. *Ibid.*, pp. 748–749. *International Refugee Organization in Liquidation, Report of the Liquidation*, July 31, 1953. Agreement between the French Government and the IRO Regarding the Transfer to the French Government of the Care and Maintenance Responsibilities of the IRO, February 28, 1950, Holborn, Louise. *loc. cit.*, pp. 629–630, and the Supplementary Agreement between the Italian Government and the IRO Relating to IRO Operations in Italy During the Supplementary Period 1950–51, November 14, 1950, *Ibid.*, pp. 634–635.

210 For a history of the evolution of the Pan American Union see Pan American Union v. American Security and Trust Company, *ILR*, 1951, pp. 441–443. The court concluded in this case that: 'The Charter of the organization of American States made no change in the name of the Pan American Union. There is nothing in the Charter to indicate any alteration of the identity of the Pan American Union.' See p. 443.

211 Hahn, Hugo J. *op. cit.*, p. 220.

212 Article 15, Convention on the Organization for Economic Cooperation and Development. *IGO*, Part I, vol. II, p. 1157: 'When this Convention comes into force the reconstitution of the Organization for European Economic Cooperation shall take effect, and its aims, organs, powers and name shall thereupon be as provided herein. The legal personality possessed by the Organization for European Economic Cooperation shall continue in the Organization but decisions, recommendations and resolutions of the Organization for European Economic Cooperation shall require approval of the Council to be effective after the coming into force of this Convention.'

213 Convention Relating to Certain Institutions Common to the European Communities, Rome, March 25, 1957, *UNTS*, vol. 298, pp. 267–274.

214 Treaty Establishing a Single Council and a Single Commission of the European Communities, Brussels, April 8, 1965, *ILM*, vol. 4, 1965, pp. 776–791.

215 Noël-Emile. 'Les institutions de la Communauté européenne.' *Documentation européenne*, 1988, p. 5. Reuter, Paul. *Organisations européennes*. 2e édition, Paris, Presses universitaires de France, 1970, pp. 190–191. Although the Single European Act, signed February 17, 1986, introduced certain modifications in the com-

petences of the three communities, it did not affect their structures. See *Bulletin of the European Communities*, Supplement 2/86.
216 Rideau, Joël. 'Les institutions internationales de la protection de la propriété intellectuelle.' *RGDIP*, 1968, vol. 72, pp. 733–734.
217 Voyame, Josephs. 'Organisation Mondiale de la Propriété Intellectuelle,' *AFDI*, 1967, vol. XXIV, p. 28.
218 *Ibid*. See also Article 3, Convention Establishing the World Intellectual Property Organization, July 14, 1967, in *IGO*, Part III - IV, p. 474.
219 Articles 9 and 21, *loc. cit.*, pp. 480 and 487–488.

CHAPTER III THE LEGAL BASIS OF SUCCESSION BETWEEN INTERNATIONAL ORGANIZATIONS

1 *Supra.*, p. 4.
2 Article IV, Agreement for the Establishment of the Caribbean Organization, Washington, June 21, 1960, *UNTS*, vol. 418, p. 112.
3 Article III, *Ibid*.
4 Article 97, paragraph 1, Treaty for East-African Co-operation, Kampala, June 6, 1967, *IGO*, Part I, p. 423.
5 Article 43, paragraph 2(a), *BDARO*, vol. III, pp. 1171 and 1243–1244.
6 Annex XV, *Ibid.*, p. 1268.
7 Article XXI, paragraph 2, Convention for the Establishment of a European Space Agency, Paris, May 30, 1975, *IGO*, part III–IV, p. 178.
8 Article XIX. *Ibid.*, p. 177.
9 For OIRSA see *20 Anios de OIRSA*, 1953–1973, OIRSA, p. 27. For OAMCE see Ranjeva, Raymond, *op. cit.*, p. 348 and Wodie, Francis, *op. cit.*, p. 64.
10 The Electricity Company of Sofia and Bulgaria (Preliminary Objections), *PCIJ*, 1939, Series A/B, No. 77, p. 92.
11 UN Doc. No. A/Conf. 39/27.
12 Waldock, Sir Humphrey. 'Third Report on the Law of Treaties,' *YILC*, 1964 II, p. 35. This rule was codified in Article 30, paragraph 4 of the 1969 Vienna Convention on the Law of Treaties, *loc. cit.*
13 Article XVI, Section 2 and Schedule E of the Articles of Agreement of the International Monetary Fund, *IGO*, Part I, pp. 1036, 1059–1061.
14 *IL*, vol. VIII, p. 214.
15 Article 13, Agreement Concerning the Establishment of an International Patents Bureau, *UNTS*, vol. 46, p. 261.
16 Article XIX, Convention for the Establishment of a European Space Research Organization, Paris, May 30, 1975, *IGO*, Part III–IV, p. 178. Other examples are Article XIV, Convention for the Establishment of a European Organization for Nuclear Research, July 1, 1953, *IGO*, Part III–IV, p. 87. Article XXV, Convention for the Establishment of a European Space Agency, May 30, 1975, *Ibid.* p. 179. Article XXXVIII, Convention Establishing the International

Organization of Legal Metrology, October 2, 1955, *Ibid.*, p. 333. Article XXII, paragraph 1, Agreement creating the International Migratory Locust Control Organization for Central and Southern Africa, September 16, 1970, *Ibid.*, p. 301.

17 Article VIII, Agreement for the Establishment of the International Office of Public Health, Rome, December 9, 1907, *AJIL* Supplement, vol. 3, 1909, p. 154.

18 Article 18, Convention Establishing the World Intellectual Property Organization, July 14, 1967, *IGO*, Part III–IV, p. 474.

19 Article 5, Constitution of the International Labour Organisation, *IGO*, Part III–IV, p.485.

20 See for example Article XXXII, Charter of the Organization of African Unity, *IGO*, Part I, p. 1170. Article 95, Convention on International Civil Aviation, *IGO*, Part IV, p. 421. Article 30, Convention of the World Meteorological Organization, *IGO*, Part IV, p. 485. Article XXI, Agreement for the Establishment of the Caribbean Commission, *UNTS*, vol. 27, p. 92. Article 33, Agreement Establishing the Caribbean Free Trade Association, *IGO*, Part I, p. 1434. A slight variation on this procedure appears in the UNESCO constitution which provides that withdrawal will take effect on December 31st of the year following that during which the notice was given. See Article II.b., Constitution of the United Nations Educational Scientific and Cultural Organization, *IGO*, Part III, p. 441.

21 *LNTS*, vol. 11, p. 198.

22 ICAN Res. No. 1167, *Official Bulletin of the ICAN*, No. 28, 1945, p. 22. This action was presaged in Article 80 of the Convention on International Civil Aviation which provided that 'Each contracting state undertakes, immediately upon the coming into force of this Convention, to give notice of denunciation of the Convention relating to the Regulation of Aerial Navigation signed at Paris on October 13, 1919.' For a summary of the evolution of this article see *Proceedings of the International Civil Aviation Conference*, United States Government Printing Office, 1948, vol. II, p. 1393.

23 In the case of the International Commission for Air Navigation, Bulgaria, Estonia, Japan, Lettonia and Uruguay had not given notice of denunciation at the time the Liquidation Committee completed its work on December 31, 1948. See ICAN Doc. No. 4813 C/603, Report of the Secretary General on the Liquidation of the International Commission for Air Navigation, Annex I and ICAO Doc. No. C-WP/233, Final Report of the Secretary General on the Liquidation of ICAN, Appendix A.

24 Protocol for the Dissolution of the International Institute of Agriculture and the Transfer of its Functions and Assets to the Food and Agriculture Organization of the United Nations, Rome, 30th March 1946, *GBTS*, No. 29, Cmd 7413. *Ibid.*, p. 3: 'When the duties assigned to it by Article II of this Protocol have been completed, the Permanent Committee of the Institute shall forthwith, by circular letter, notify the Members of the Institute of the dissolution of

the Institute . . . and of the transfer of the functions and assets thereof to the Organization. The date of such notification shall be deemed to be the date of termination of the Convention of 7th June 1905, and also the date of the dissolution of the Institute . . .'.

25 *Ibid.*, p. 4, note 3.
26 *Ibid.*, p. 3, note 3.
27 *Actes de la Seizième Assemblée générale*, 8 et 9 juillet 1946, p. 51.
28 FAO Doc. No. 1249, Report of the Activities of the FAO European Regional Office 1948/1949, Fifth Session, p. 33.
29 Article 3, Protocol Concerning the *Office international d'hygiène publique*, New York, July 22, 1946, *UNTS*, vol. 9, p. 66.
30 EB2 Res. No. 50, Denunciation of Rome Agreement and Transfer of OIHP Assets to WHO, *Handbook of Resolutions and Decisions of the World Health Assembly and Executive Board*, vol. I, 1948–1972, WHO, Geneva, 1973, p. 361.
31 EB3 Res. No. 47, *Ibid.*
32 WHA.2. Res. No. 83, *Ibid.*
33 These were Germany, Japan, Spain, Rumania, Poland, Uruguay and Sudan. Cf. Compte rendu de la réunion de la Commission des finances et du transfert de l'Office international d'hygiène publique, 4 mai 1950, *Procès-verbaux des Séances du Comité permanent*, Session de Mai 1950, p. 4.
34 WHO Doc. No A3/46. Add.1, Rev. 1, 18th May 1950, The Position as Regards the Office international d'hygiène publique, p. 1.
35 Procès-verbaux des séances du Comité permanent, *loc. cit.*: 'La Commission étant d'accord sur la possibilité d'une terminaison de facto, la discussion s'ouvre sur la destination des avoirs de l'Office au cas où cette dissolution se réaliserait.'
36 WHO Doc. No. A3/46. Add. l, Rev. 1, *loc. cit.*, p. 3.
37 WHA Res. No. 58, *op. cit.*, p. 362 and EB8 Res. No. R. 5, *Ibid.*
38 WHO Res. Nos. EB9, R. 6 and WHA. 5.40, *Ibid.*
39 *LN Official Journal*, Special Supplement No. 194, p. 84.
40 *Ibid.*, p. 79. The vote was taken by roll-call. The states present were Afghanistan, the Union of South Africa, Argentina, Australia, Belgium, Bolivia, United Kingdom, Canada, China, Cuba, Denmark, Dominican Republic, Egypt, Ecuador, Finland, France, Greece, India, Iran, Luxembourg, Mexico, Norway, New Zealand, Panama, the Netherlands, Poland, Portugal, Sweden, Switzerland, Czechoslovakia, Turkey, Uruguay and Yugoslavia.
41 See Kiss, Alexandre-Charles. 'Quelques aspects de la substitution d'une organisation une autre.' *AFDI*, vol. VII, 1961, p. 469: 'L'argument avancé par le texte de cette même Résolution, selon lequel l'Assemblée était investie par l'article 3 al. 3 du Pacte de compétences si larges qu'elles comprenaient même la dissolution de toute l'organisation, ne paraît pas suffisant pour justifier cette procédure.' Schwarzenberger, Georg. *International Law as Applied by International Courts and Tribunals*, vol. III, London, Stevens and Sons Ltd., 1976, p. 97.
42 *Loc. cit.*

43 Article 54, Vienna Convention on the Law of Treaties, *op. cit.* See also Judge Read, Separate Opinion on the International Status of South-West Africa, *op. cit.*, p. 167: 'Any legal position, or system of legal relationships, can be brought to an end by the consent of all persons having legal rights and interests which might be affected by their termination.'

44 'Draft Articles on the Law of Treaties with Commentaries.' *YILC*, 1966 II, p. 249: 'The states concerned are always free to choose the form in which they arrive at their agreement to terminate the treaty. In doing so, they will doubtless take into account their own constitutional requirements, but international law requires no more than they should consent to the treaty's termination.' Fitzmaurice, Sir Gerald. 'Second Report on the Law of Treaties.' *YILC*, 1957 II, p. 46: 'The correct view is that, since the agreement of all the parties is required, they can, adopt . . . such form as may be appropriate for constitutional or other reasons. In law, however, all that is required is agreement, and the form in which it is embodied is immaterial, provided it is adequate to make clear the character and intention of the transaction.' Kiss, Alexandre-Charles, *op. cit.*, p. 464: 'C'est un des principes incontestés du droit international public qu'un traité international ne saurait être abrogé ou modifié que par le consentement des Etats entre lesquels il est intervenu. Un autre principe, celui de l'autonomie de la volonté des Etats contractants, apporte une atténuation à la rigueur de cette règle: les Etats contractants sont libres d'adopter, par accord mutuel, des procédures spéciales permettant de modifier, voire d'abroger un traité sans qu'un acte formel de consentement soit nécessaire de la part de chacun d'eux.' Leca, Jean. *Les techniques de révision des conventions internationales*, Paris, Librairie générale de droit et de jurisprudence, 1961, p. 152: 'Le droit international ne soumet la conclusion, l'abrogation ou la révision du traité aucune condition de forme particulière.'

45 Protocol of Signature of the Statute of the Permanent Court of International Justice, 16th December 1920.

46 UN Doc. No. PC/20, Report of the Preparatory Commission of the United Nations, 23rd December 1945, p. 57. See also the recommendation of the Executive Committee of the Preparatory Commission in UN Doc. No. PC/EX/Rev. 1, 12th November 1945, Report of the Executive Committee to the Preparatory Commission of the United Nations, p. 8.

47 *LN Official Journal*, Special Supplement No. 194, p. 277–278. For the legislative history of this resolution see *loc. cit.*, pp. 73–74.

48 Cf. Article 39, Treaty of Peace with Italy, Paris, February 1947, *European Peace Treaties After World War II*, edited by Amelia C. Leiss, Worcester, Massachusetts, World Peace Foundation, 1954, p. 179: 'Italy undertakes to accept any arrangements which have been or may be agreed for the liquidation of the League of Nations, the Permanent Court of International Justice and also the International Financial Commission in Greece.' Article 7, Treaty of

129

Peace with Bulgaria. *Ibid.*, p. 253: 'Bulgaria undertakes to accept any arrangements which have been or may be agreed for the liquidation of the League of Nations and the Permanent Court of International Justice.' Identical language was also used in Article 9 of both the Treaty of Peace with Hungary and the Treaty of Peace with Rumania. *Ibid.*, pp. 277 and 307 respectively.

49 Charter of the United Nations, *IGO*, Part I, p. 1318.

50 An international organization may be dissolved even though several member states object to its termination. In the case of the International Danube Commission, Italy, Belgium, France, the United Kingdom, Austria and Germany objected to abrogation of the 1921 Convention Instituting the Definitive Statute of the Danube. Nevertheless, the seven riparian states, the USSR, the Ukranian SSR, Bulgaria, Rumania, Yugoslavia, Czechoslovakia and Hungary signed an agreement that declared the 1921 Convention to be 'no longer in force'. The western states attempted to maintain the International Danube Commission in existence, at least long enough to allow its liquidation, but they were unable to prevent its ultimate demise.

51 Agreement Concerning the Execution of the Transfer to the United Nations of Certain Assets of the League of Nations, Geneva, July 19, 1946, *UNTS*, vol. 1, pp. 110–117. Arrangement to Give Practical Effect to Certain Provisions of the Agreement of July 19, 1946, Dealing with the Execution of the Transfer of League Assets to the United Nations, Geneva, July 31, 1946, *Ibid.*, pp. 120–129. Protocol (No. I) Concerning the Execution of Various Operations in the Transfer to the United Nations of Certain Assets of the League of Nations, Geneva, August 1, 1946, *Ibid.*, pp. 132–133. Protocol (No. II) on the Transfer of Certain Services from the League of Nations to the United Nations, Geneva, August 1, 1946, *Ibid.*, pp. 136–137. Protocol Concerning the Transfer of the International Press House Fund from the League of Nations to the United Nations, Geneva, April 11, 1947, *UNTS*, vol. 4, pp. 444–447. Protocol Concerning the Transfer of the Library Endowment Fund from the League of Nations to the United Nations, Geneva, April 14, 1947, *Ibid.*, pp. 450–457. Protocol Concerning the Transfer of the Administration of the Léon Bernard Fund from the League of Nations to the United Nations, Geneva, June 27, 1947, *UNTS*, vol. 5, p. 390–393. Protocol Concerning the Transfer of the Administration of the Darling Foundation from the League of Nations to the United Nations, Geneva, June 27, 1947, *Ibid.*, pp. 396–399.

52 Agreement between the Interim Commission of the World Health Organization and UNRRA, December 9, 1946, in Woodbridge, George, *op. cit.*, vol. III, pp. 552–554.

53 Arrangement between the Food and Agriculture Organization (FAO) of the United Nations and UNRRA, February 19, 1947, *Ibid.*, pp. 354–356.

54 Agreement between the Preparation Commission for the Inter-

national Refugee Organization (PCIRO) and UNRRA, June 29, 1947, *Ibid.*, pp. 356–358.

55 Agreement between UNRRA (United Nations Relief and Rehabilitation Administration) and the United Nations Concerning the Transfer to the United Nations of the Residual Assets and Activities of the United Nations Relief and Rehabilitation Administration, September 27, 1948, *UNTS*, vol. 27, pp. 250–297.

56 Agreement between the League of Nations and the International Labour Organisation Concerning the Transfer of Certain Properties, Geneva, May 4, 1946 and May 17, 1946, *UNTS*, vol. 19, pp. 189–191.

57 Agreement between the United Nations Educational, Scientific and Cultural Organization and the International Institute for Intellectual Cooperation, December 1946, UNESCO Doc. No. IC/30, General Conference, First Session, November 20 December 10, 1946, pp. 241–242.

58 Agreement for the Transfer to the Interim Commission of the World Health Organization of the Duties and Functions of the *Office international d'hygiène publique*, Geneva, January 27, 1948, *Official Records of the WHO*, No. 7, Annex, pp. 203–204.

59 Draft Agreement between UNESCO and the International Bureau of Education, November 16, 1968, UNESCO Doc. No. 15C/83, Annex II.

60 Draft Agreement between UNESCO and the International Relief Union, December 16, 1968, UNESCO Doc. No. 15C/85, Annex II, p. 3.

61 Draft Agreement on the Integration of the International Patent Institute into the European Patent Office, September 29, 1977, Interim Committee for the European Patent Organization, Doc. No. CI/Final 23/77.

62 Paragraph 2, *LN Official Journal*, Special Supplement, No. 194, p. 281.

63 Paragraph 13, *Ibid.* '(1) The Board (of liquidation) shall in due course transfer to the International Labour Organisation its appropriate share in the Renovation Fund and any other fund in which it may have an interest. (2) The balances of the International Labour Organisation for the financial years 1941, 1943, 1944 shall be transferred from the suspense account in which they are at present placed to a special reserve fund for the International Labour Organisation.'

64 Paragraph 14, *Ibid.* 'An agreement to cause the full ownership of the land and buildings at present occupied by the International Labour Organisation to vest in that Organisation shall be concluded between the Secretary-General of the League and the Acting Director of the International Labour Office and all the steps which, under the law of the Republic and Canton of Geneva or of the Swiss Confederation, are necessary to give effect to the agreement shall be taken as soon as possible.'

65 UNRRA Res. No. 94, Relating to the Health Activities of the Administration. *UNRRA Resolutions on Policy*, 1946, p. 1.

66 UNRRA Res. No. 95, Relating to the Social Welfare Activities of the Administration, *Ibid.*,pp. 2–3.

67 UNRRA Res. No. 102, Relating to Agricultural Production, *Ibid.*, p. 14.

68 UNRRA Res. No. 99, Relating to Displaced Persons Operations, *Ibid.*, pp. 6–7.

69 UNRRA Res. No. 103, Relating to the Rehabilitation of the Children and Adolescents of Countries which were Victims of Aggression. *Ibid.*, pp. 15–16.

70 Section I, 1(a). Protocol on the Centralization of the European Patent System and on Its Introduction, *op. cit.*, p. 151.

71 Final Instruments of the Conference, *Report of the International Health Conference*, Annex 2, p. 61.

72 FAO Constitution, *IGO*, Part II, p. 101: 'The Conference may approve arrangements placing other international organizations dealing with questions relating to food and agriculture under the general authority of the Organization on such terms as may be agreed with the competent authorities of the organization concerned.'

73 UNESCO Constitution, *IGO*, Part III–IV, p. 447: 'Whenever the General Conference of this Organization and the competent authorities of any other specialized intergovernmental organizations or agencies whose purposes and functions lie within the competence of this Organization, deem it desirable to effect a transfer of their resources and activities to this Organization, the Director General, subject to the approval of the Conference, may enter into mutually acceptable arrangements for this purpose.'

74 Agreement for UNRRA, in Woodbridge, George, *op. cit.*, vol. III, p. 26.

75 IRO Constitution, in Holborn, Louise W. *op. cit.*, p. 582: 'The Organization may assume all or part of the functions, and acquire all or part of the resources, assets and liabilities of any intergovernmental organization or agency the purposes and functions of which lie within the scope of the Organization.'

76 Article 6, Vienna Convention on the Law of Treaties Between States and International Organizations or Between International Organizations. UN Doc. A/CONF. 129/15: 'The capacity of an international organization to conclude Treaties is governed by the relevant rules of that organization.'

77 UNGA Res. No. 24 (I), 12th February 1946, Transfer of Certain Functions, Activities and Assets of the League of Nations, Section II, UN Doc. No. A/64, Resolutions Adopted by the General Assembly During the First Part of its First Session, 10th January to 14th February 1946, p. 35.

78 LN Res. 3, The Assumption by the United Nations of Activities Hitherto Performed by the League, *LN Official Journal*, Special Supplement No. 194, p. 278.

79 UNGA Res. No. 51(I), UN Doc. No. A/66/Add. 1 p. 78. See also ECOSOC Res. No. 23(III), 2nd October 1946, UN Doc. No. E/245/ Rev. 1, pp. 50–69.
80 LN Doc. No. C.5.M.5., July 31, 1947, Final Report of the Board of Liquidation, p. 16.
81 *Ibid.*
82 *LN Official Journal*, Special Supplement No. 194, pp. 271–272.
83 ILO Res. No. 6; 9th October 1946, Résolution concernant l'adoption du Règlement révisé de la Caisse des pensions du personnel presentée par la Commission des finances des représentants gouvernementaux. Compte Rendu des Travaux de la vingt-neuvième session de la Conférence internationale du Travail, Montréal, 1946, pp. 531–532. Also see LN Doc. No. C.3.M.3., 1st March 1947, Third Interim Report of the Board of Liquidation, p.16.
84 With respect to the Judges' Pensions Fund, see paragraph 18 of the dissolution resolution, *op. cit.*, p. 272; LN Doc. No. C.4.M.4., 1st May 1947, Fourth Interim Report of the Board of Liquidation, pp. 4–5; and LN Doc. No. C.5.M.5., 31st July 1947, Final Report of the Board of Liquidation, pp. 14–15. Regarding the Working Capital Fund see paragraph 20 of the dissolution resolution, *loc. cit.*; LN Doc. No. C.4.M.4., *op. cit.*, pp. 3 and 8; and LN Doc. No. C.5.M.5., *op. cit.*, p. 14. For the Renovation Fund see paragraph 13(1) of the dissolution resolution, *op. cit.*, p. 270; LN Doc. No. C.4.M.4., *op. cit.*, p. 3; and LN Doc. No. C.5.M.5., *op. cit.*, p. 12.
85 OIHP Permanent Committee, Resolution of October 31, 1946, *Procès-verbaux des Séances du Comité permanent*, Session Ordinaire Octobre 1946, p. 140.
86 *Official Records of the World Health Organization*, No. 5, pp. 110–111. Rapport du Président de la Commission des finances et du transfert sur le fonctionnement de *l'Office international d'hygiène publique*, novembre 1946–avril 1950.
87 *OIHP Procès-verbaux des Séances du Comité permanent*, session mai 1950, p. 26.
88 Arrangement of July 22, 1946, *Official Records of the World Health Organization*, No. 7, Annex 28, pp. 203–204.
89 Paragraph 2, OIHP Permanent Committee Res. of May 6, 1950, WHO Doc. No. A3/46, Add.1, Rev.1, p.3. WHO Doc. No. A4/27, Transfer of the Assets of the *Office international d'hygiène publique* April 30, 1951, pp. 1–2.
90 Other examples of this procedure are the transfer of the ownership of certain assets of the IIIC from the United Nations to UNESCO, UN Res. No. A/ 591 (VI), Questions Concerning the Liquidation of the International Institute of Intellectual Cooperation, the transfer of certain funds from the League of Nations to the ILO, LN Doc. No. A/32, (1946) X, Resolution for the Dissolution of the League of Nations, p. 14, the transfer of the functions of the League of Nations Health Organization from the United Nations to the World Health Organization. ECOSOC Res. No. 20 (III),

World Health Organization, UN DOC. No. E/245/ Rev.1., the transfer of ICAN's library, documentation and office furnishings to ICAO, ICAO Doc. No. 4813, C/603, October 26, 1948, Liquidation Plan of the International Commission for Air Navigation. *ICAN Official Bulletin*, No. 29, pp. 11–12 and the transfer of the social and cultural activities of the Western European Union to the Council of Europe. *Supra.*, p. 17.

91 Hudson, Manley O. 'The Succession of the International Court of Justice to the Permanent Court of International Justice.' *AJIL*, vol. 51, 1957, p. 571.

92 Article 92, Charter of the United Nations: 'The International Court of Justice shall be the principal judicial organ of the United Nations. It shall function in accordance with the annexed Statute, which is based upon the Statute of the Permanent Court of International Justice and forms an integral part of the present Charter.'

93 *Case concerning the Aerial Incident of July 27, 1955 (Israel v. Bulgaria)*, Preliminary Objections. *ICJ Reports 1959*, p. 139. *Case concerning the Barcelona Traction, Light and Power Company, Limited (Belgium v. Spain)*, Preliminary Objections. *ICJ Reports 1964*, p. 31.

94 *ICJ Reports 1959*, p. 139: ' . . . to restrict the application of Article 36, paragraph 5, to the states signatories of the statute is to take into account the purpose for which this provision was adopted;' and p. 141, ' . . . Article 36, paragraph 5, was designed to govern the transfer dealt with in that provision only as between the signatories of the statute . . . '. See also the *Case concerning the Temple of Preah Vihear (Cambodia v. Thailand)*, Preliminary Objections. *ICJ Reports 1961*, p. 25: ' . . . the Court, interpreting paragraph 5 of Article 36, came to the conclusion that it did not apply indiscriminately to all states which, having accepted the compulsory jurisdiction of the former Permanent Court, might at any subsequent date become parties to the statute of the Court, but only to such states as were original parties.'

95 *ICJ Reports 1959*, p. 137. *ICJ Reports 1961*, p. 25.

96 *Loc. cit.*, pp. 35–36.

97 The Court also said that the possibly 'far-reaching effects' of its decision should not 'be allowed to influence the legal character of that decision: but it does constitute a reason why the decision should not be regarded as already predetermined by that which was given in different circumstances in the Israel v. Bulgaria Case.' *Ibid.*, pp. 29–30. For a critique of this decision see Schwarzenberger, Georg. *International Law as Applied by International Courts and Tribunals*. vol. III, London, Stevens & Sons Ltd., 1976, pp. 109–112.

98 International Opium Convention, January 23, 1912, *NTS*, vol. 8, pp. 189–239. Agreement concerning the Suppression of the Manufacture of Internal Trade in and Use of, Prepared Opium, February 11, 1925, *LNTS*, vol. 51, pp. 338–347. International Opium Convention, February 19, 1925, *LNTS*, vol. 81, pp. 319–358. Convention for Limiting the Manufacture and Regulating the Distribution of Narcotic Drugs, July 13, 1931, *LNTS*, vol. 139, pp. 302–349. Agree-

ment Concerning the Suppression of Opium Smoking, November 27, 1931, *LNTS*, vol. 177, pp. 375–380. Convention for the Suppression of the Illicit Traffic of Dangerous Drugs, June 26, 1936, *LNTS*, vol. 198, pp. 301–323. For a complete inventory of the functions entrusted to the League under these conventions see UN Doc. No. 1116, pp. 23–31.

99 Draft Protocol Amending the Conventions on Narcotic Drugs Concluded at The Hague on January 23, 1912 and Geneva on February 19, 1925, July 13, 1931 and June 26, 1936, UN Doc. No. E/116. Draft Protocol Amending the Agreements, Conventions and Protocols on Narcotic Drugs Concluded at The Hague on January 23, 1912, at Geneva on February 11, 1925 and February 19, 1925, and July 13, 1931, at Bangkok on November 27, 1931, and at Geneva on June 26, 1936, UN Doc. No. E/168/Rev. 2, October 9, 1946, Report and Resolutions of the Economic and Social Council to the General Assembly on the Transfer to the United Nations of the Powers Exercised by the League of Nations under the International Agreements, Conventions and Protocols on Narcotic Drugs.

100 UNGA Res. No. 54(1), November 19, 1946, Transfer to the United Nations of the Powers Exercised by the League of Nations Under the International Agreements, Conventions and Protocols on Narcotic Drugs, UN Doc. No. A/64/ Add. 1, January 31, 1947, Resolutions Adopted by the General Assembly during the Second Part of the First Session, pp. 8–89.

101 Protocol signed at Lake Success, New York on December 11, 1946, Amending the Agreements, Conventions and Protocols on Narcotic Drugs Concluded at The Hague on January 23, 1912, at Geneva on February 11, 1925 and February 19, 1925, and July 13 1931, at Bangkok on November 27, 1931 and at Geneva on June 26, 1936, *UNTS*, vol. 12, pp. 180–187 and Annex to the Protocol, *Ibid.*, pp. 198–210.

102 Convention on the Suppression of Traffic in Women and Children, September 30, 1921, *IL*, vol. I, pp. 726–733. Convention on the Suppression of the Circulation of and Traffic in Obscene Publications, September 12, 1923, *IL*, vol. VI, pp. 469–476. Convention for the Suppression of the Traffic in Women of Full Age, October 11, 1933, *IL*, vol. II, pp. 1051–1062.

103 ECOSOC Res. No. 43 (IV), March 29, 1947, Suppression of Traffic in Women and Children, UN Doc. No. E/437, Resolutions Adopted by the Economic & Social Council During its Fourth Session, p. 24.

104 UNGA Res. No. 126 (II), October 20, 1947, Draft Protocol to Amend the Convention for the Suppression of the Traffic in Women and Children, Concluded at Geneva on September 30, 1921, and the Convention for the Suppression of Traffic in Women of Full Age, Concluded at Geneva on October 11, 1933, UN Doc. No. A/519, *Official Records of the Second Session of the General Assembly, Resolutions*, pp. 32–36; and Draft Protocol to Amend the International Convention for the Suppression of the Circulation

and Traffic in Obscene Publications, Opened for signature at Geneva on September 12, 1923, *Ibid.*, pp. 36–38.

105 *UNTS*, vol. 53, pp. 14–19.

106 *UNTS*, vol. 30, pp. 4–9.

107 UN Doc. No. E/264, February 18, 1947, Report of the Statistical Commission of the Economic and Social Council, paragraph 18, p. 8.

108 Articles 8, 11, 12, 13 and 16, *LNTS*, vol. 110, pp. 171–283.

109 ECOSOC Res. No. 114 (VL), March 2, 1948, Report of the Second Session of the Statistical Commission, UN Doc. No. E/777, *Resolutions Adopted by the Economic and Social Council During its Sixth Session*, pp. 11–16.

110 UNGA Res. No. 255 (III), November 18, 1948, Transfer to the United Nations of Functions and Powers Previously Exercised by the League of Nations under International Conventions Relating to Economic Statistics, signed at Geneva on December 14, 1928, UN Doc. No. A/810, *Official Records of the Third Session of the General Assembly*, Part I, Resolutions, pp. 160–164.

111 Protocol Amending the International Convention Relating to Economic Statistics, December 14, 1948, *UNTS*, vol. 20, p. 230.

112 *IL*, vol. III, pp. 1902–1974.

113 *IL*, vol. VI, pp. 292–321.

114 UNRRA Council Res. No. 52: Modification of the International Sanitary Convention, 1926, and the International Sanitary Convention for Aerial Navigation, 1937, Woodbridge, George, *op. cit.*, pp. 93–94.

115 Article 26, International Sanitary Convention, Washington, December 15, 1944, *IL*, vol. IX, p. 249. Article 23, International Sanitary Convention for Aerial Navigation, Washington, December 15, 1944, *IL*, vol. IX, p. 271. The incapacity of the OIHP was regarded as only temporary. See UNRRA Council Res. No. 52, paragraph 6, *op. cit.*, p. 94. ' . . . the Council authorizes the Director General, at the time when the emergency Conventions come into force, to undertake the functions set out therein for the period for which the emergency amendments are to remain in force, at the end of which time it is hoped the International Office of Public Health will be able to exercise its full functions,' and paragraph 2 of the preamble of the two 1944 Conventions, *op. cit.*, pp. 237–238 and 255–256: 'Having entrusted the task of solving this temporary problem by the preparation of emergency agreements and arrangements for the notification of epidemic diseases and for uniformity in quarantine regulations to the United Nations Relief and Rehabilitation Administration . . . in accordance with Resolution No. 8 (2) adopted by the Council of UNRRA at its First Session, without prejudice however to the States of the International Office of Public Health which it is hoped will be able at the expiry of the present Convention to assume the above-mentioned duties and functions . . . '.

116 Protocol to Prolong the Duration of the International Sanitary

Convention, 1944, Washington, April 23, 1946, *IL*, vol. IX, pp. 251–254 and Protocol to Prolong the Duration of the International Sanitary Convention for Aerial Navigation of 1944, Washington, April 23, 1946, *IL*, vol. IX, pp. 272–275.

117 Letter from Fiorello H. Laguardia to Brock Chisholm, Executive Secretary, Interim Commission of the World Health Organization, October 22, 1946, Woodbridge, George, *op. cit.*, vol. III, p. 352: ' . . . the Interim Commission will undertake to carry out as of November 1, 1946, the duties and functions which have been performed by the United Nations Relief and Rehabilitation Administration under these International Sanitary Conventions . . . I shall be glad, with your permission to arrange with Dr. W. A. Sawyer, Director of Health, UNRRA, the practical arrangements for the transfer of these functions, together with the relevant materials, records and equipment . . . '. See also Article 2, Protocol Concerning the Office International d'hygiène public, *UNTS*, vol. 9, p. 66: 'The parties to this Protocol further agree that, as between themselves, from the date when this Protocol comes into force, the duties and functions conferred upon the Office by the agreements listed in Annex 1 shall be performed by the Organization or its Interim Commission.'

118 International Convention for Locust Control, Rome October 31, 1920. International Convention for Plant Protection, Rome, April 16, 1929. International Convention Concerning the Marketing of Eggs in International Trade, Brussels, December 11, 1931. International Convention for the Standardisation of the Methods of Cheese Analysis, Rome, April 26, 1934, International Convention for the Standardisation of Methods of Analysing Wines, Rome, June 5, 1935. International Convention for the Standardisation of the Methods of Keeping and Utilising Herdbooks, Rome, October 14, 1936. See Protocol for the Dissolution of the International Institute of Agriculture, Annex, *op. cit.*, p. 8.

119 Article IV, *Ibid.*, p. 3.

120 Convention for the Partial Revision of the Convention Adopted by the General Conference of the International Labour Organisation at its First Twenty-eight Sessions for the Purpose of Making Provisions for the Future Discharge of Certain Chancery Functions Entrusted by the said Conventions to the Secretary-General of the League of Nations and Introducing Therein Certain Further Amendments Consequential Upon the Dissolution of the League of Nations and the Amendment of the Constitution of the International Labour Organisation, Montreal, October 9, 1946, *UNTS*, vol. 38, pp. 3–15.

121 See Article 40, paragraph 4 of the Vienna Convention on the Law of Treaties which provides that 'The amending agreement does not bind any State already a party to the treaty which does not become a party to the amending agreement,' and Article 30, paragraph 4(b) which provides that 'When the parties to the later treaty do not include all the parties to the earlier one: . . . as between a

State party to both treaties and a State party to only one of the treaties, the treaty to which both States are parties govern their mutual rights and obligations.' U.N. Doc. A/CONF. 39/27.

122 Article 44, The Vienna Convention on the Law of Treaties, *op. cit.*

123 The problems that can arise when the members of the two organizations are substantially different was illustrated by the replacement of the International Danube Commission by the Danube Commission. The Convention Regarding the Régime of Navigation on the Danube and its Supplementary Protocol, signed by seven riparian states and the Soviet Union in Belgrade on August 18, 1948, provided for the abrogation of the régime established by the Definitive Statute of the Danube of July 23, 1921 and the replacement of the International Danube Commission by a new body called the Danube Commission. The western European states that had signed the 1921 Statute were either not invited to sign or refused to sign the new convention and claimed that the old treaty still remained in effect. As a result, a curious situation arose when the new Danube Commission came into being on May 11, 1949. The western powers transferred the old Commission to Rome where it could exercise its authority over the western occupied zone, while the new Commission established its authority in the Soviet occupied zone. The assets of the International Danube Commission in the eastern zone were taken over by the Danube Commission, while those that had been moved to Rome were liquidated by the European and International Danube Commissions and used to settle pension claims. See Kunz, Joseph L. 'The Danube Régime and the Belgrade Conference.' *AJIL*, vol. 43, 1949, pp. 110–111. Articles 21 and 22, Convention Regarding the Régime of Navigation on the Danube, August 18, 1948, *UNTS*, vol. 23, pp. 207–221. Article 1, Supplementary Protocol to the Convention Regarding the Régime of Navigation on the Danube, August 18, 1948, *Ibid.*, p. 223. Sinclair, I. M. 'Danube Conference of 1948,' *BYBIL*, vol. XXV, 1948; pp. 403–404. CD. Doc. No. SES 2/19, Procès-Verbaux de la Commission du Danube, Tome 1, 1951, p. 190. Gorove, Stefan. *Law and Politics of the Danube*, The Hague, Martinus Nijhoff, 1964; p. 148.

124 *Supra.*, p. 4.

125 Some of these customary rules have been codified in the 1978 Vienna Convention on Succession of States in Respect of Treaties and the 1983 Vienna Convention on Succession of States in Respect of State Property, Archives and Debts. Supra., p. 6.

126 LN Doc. No. 21/31/14D. Mandate for German South West Africa, Art. 1: 'The territory over which a Mandate is conferred upon His Britannic Majesty for and on behalf of the Government of the Union of South Africa (hereinafter called the Mandatory) comprises the territory which formerly constituted the German Protectorate of South West Africa.'

127 UN Doc. No. A/334, 1st August 1947, Communication from the

Union of South Africa on the Future Status of South West Africa of 23rd July 1947, p. 2.

128 International Status of South-West Africa, Advisory Opinion, *ICJ Reports 1950*, p. 129.

129 *Ibid.*, p. 131.

130 *Ibid.*, p. 132.

131 *Ibid.*, p. 133.

132 *Ibid.*

133 *Ibid.*, Article 80, paragraph 1 of the Charter reads as follows: 'Except as may be agreed upon in individual trusteeship agreements under Articles 77, 79 and 81, placing each territory under the trusteeship system, and until such agreements have been concluded, nothing in this chapter shall be construed in or of itself to alter in any manner the rights whatsoever of any states or any peoples or the terms of existing international instruments to which Members of the United Nations may respectively be parties.'

134 *Loc. cit.*, p. 134.

135 *Ibid.*, p. 135.

136 *Ibid.*, p. 136.

137 *Ibid.*

138 *Ibid.*

139 *Ibid.*, p. 137.

140 *Ibid.*

141 In particular the Court mentioned the following resolutions: UNGA Resolution 141 (11) of November 1, 1947, which urged 'the Government of the Union of South Africa to propose for the consideration of the General Assembly a trusteeship agreement for the territory of South West Africa'and authorized the Trusteeship Council 'in the meantime to examine the report on South West Africa recently submitted by the Government of the Union of South Africa and to submit its observations thereon to the General Assembly.' UNGA Resolution of November 26, 1948, which reiterated the General Assembly's previous recommendations 'that South West Africa be placed under the Trusteeship System'and requested that the Union of South Africa 'continue to supply annually information on its administration of the Territory'of South West Africa and that the Trusteeship Council 'continue to examine such information and to submit its observations thereon to the General Assembly.' UNGA Resolution 337(IV) of December 6, 1949, which expressed regret that the Union of South Africa had announced it would no longer submit reports on its administration of the Territory of South West Africa and invited the Union of South West Africa to resume submitting reports and to act in accordance with the decisions of the General Assembly expressed in its earlier resolutions relating to South West Africa.

142 *Ibid.*

143 Separate Opinion by Judge Read. *ICJ Reports* 1950, pp. 164, 166, 168, 169.

144 *Ibid.*, pp. 164, 169.

145 *Ibid.*, p. 165.
146 *Ibid.* It could also be said that the mandatories were all totally preoccupied with the war and could not give much attention to the mandated territories. It was only after the war that the powers could turn their attention to the future of the territories.
147 *Ibid.*, p. 169.
148 *Ibid.*, p. 171.
149 *Ibid.*
150 *Ibid.*, p. 172.
151 *Ibid.* Resolution XVI(I), February 12, 1946, clause 3C.
152 *Ibid.*, p. 173.
153 Separate Opinion by Sir Arnold McNair. *ICJ Reports 1950*, p. 154.
154 *Ibid.*, p. 157.
155 *Ibid.*, p. 159.
156 *Ibid.* Article 37 of the Statute of the International Court of Justice provides that 'whenever a treaty or convention in force provides for reference of a matter to a tribunal to have been instituted by the League of Nations, or to the Permanent Court of International Justice, the matter shall, as between the parties to the present Statute, be referred to the International Court of Justice.'
157 *Ibid.*, p. 160.
158 *Ibid.*, p. 161.
159 *Ibid.*
160 *Ibid.*
161 *Ibid.*
162 *Ibid.*, p. 158.
163 Hudson, Manley O. 'The Twenty-Nineth Year of the World Court,' *AJIL*, vol. 45, 1951; p. 13.
164 *Ibid.*
165 *Ibid.*
166 *Ibid.*. p. 14.
167 *Ibid.*
168 *ICJ Reports 1956*, p. 65.
169 *Ibid.*, p. 66.
170 *ICJ Reports 1962*, p. 539.
171 *Ibid.*
172 *Ibid.*, p. 540.
173 Dissenting Opinion of Judge Van Wyk, South West Africa Cases, *ICJ Reports 1962*, p. 639.
174 *Ibid.*
175 *Official Records of the Second Session of the General Assembly*, Supplement No. 11, UN Doc. No. A/364, p. 43.
176 *Loc. cit.*, p. 639.
177 Separate Opinion of Judge Van Wyk, South West Africa. Second Phase, *ICJ Reports 1966*, p.108.
178 *Ibid.*, p. 109.
179 Dissenting Opinion of Judge Alvarez, *ICJ Reports 1950*, p. 181.
180 *Ibid.*, p. 182.
181 *Ibid.*, p. 181.

182 Separate Opinion of Sir Hersch Lauterpacht, *ICJ Reports 1956*, p. 46.
183 *Ibid.*, p. 48.
184 *Ibid.* 'The essence of such instruments is that their validity continues notwithstanding changes in attitudes, or the status, or the very survival of individual parties or persons affected. Their continuing validity implies their continued operation and the resulting legitimacy of the means devised for that purpose by way of judicial interpretation and application of the original instrument.'
185 *Ibid.* The word 'succession' in this context is used in the sense of 'automatic succession'.
186 Fitzmaurice, Sir Gerald. 'The Law and Procedure of the International Court of Justice: International Organizations and Tribunals,' *BYBIL*, vol. 29, 1952, p. 8.
187 *Ibid.*, pp. 8–9.
188 *Ibid.*, p. 9.
189 *Ibid.*
190 UNGA Res. No. 2145(XXI), paragraphs 3 and 4.
191 UNSC Res. No. 276(1970).
192 *Legal Consequences for States of the Continued Presence of South Africa in Namibia (South West Africa) notwithstanding Security Council Resolution 276(1970), ICJ Reports 1971*, p. 17.
193 *Ibid.*, p. 29.
194 *Ibid.*
195 *Ibid.*, p. 32. The Court said: 'To the question whether the continuance of a mandate was inseparably linked with the existence of the League, the answer must be that an institution established for the fulfilment of a sacred trust cannot be presumed to lapse before the achievement of its purpose. The responsibilities of both mandatory and supervisor resulting from the mandates institution were complementary, and the disappearance of one or the other could not affect the survival of the institution.'
196 *Ibid.*, p. 33.
197 *Ibid.*
198 For the text of this provision see *Supra.*, p. 139, note 133.
199 *Loc. cit.*, p. 34.
200 Article 80, paragraph 2 reads as follows: 'Paragraph 1 of this Article shall not be interpreted as giving grounds for a postponement of the negotiation and conclusion of agreements for placing mandated and other territories under the trusteeship system as provided in Article 77.'
201 *Loc. cit.*, p. 35. The Court cited Article 76(d) of the charter as another example of a clause that be deprived of any practical effect if the negative interpretation of Article 80, paragraph 1 were accepted.
202 *Ibid.*, p. 37.
203 *Ibid.*
204 Dissenting Opinion of Judge Sir Gerald Fitzmaurice, *ICJ Reports 1971*, p. 227.

205 *Ibid.*, p. 236.

206 *Ibid.*

207 *Ibid.*, p. 237.

208 *Ibid.*, pp. 237–238.

209 *Ibid.*, p. 238.

210 *Ibid.*, p. 240.

211 *Ibid.*

212 *Ibid.*, p. 242.

213 *Ibid.*, p. 248.

214 *Ibid.*, p. 250. The Court had addressed this issue in its opinion and rejected the argument on the grounds that:

The fact that a particular proposal is not adopted by an international organ does not necessarily carry with it the inference that a collective pronouncement is made in a sense opposite to that proposed. There can be many reasons determining rejection or non-approval. For instance, the Chinese proposal, which was never considered but was ruled out of order, would have subjected mandated territories to a form of supervision which went beyond the scope of the existing supervisory authority in respect of mandates, and could have raised difficulties with respect to Article 82 of the Charter, Cf. *ICJ Reports 1971*, p. 36.

215 *Loc. cit.*, p. 252.

216 *Ibid.*, p. 254. In Fitzmaurice's opinion, South Africa had never demonstrated a 'positive expression of recognition or acceptance,' but in fact had repeatedly denied any accountability to the United Nations. *Ibid.*, p. 262.

217 *Ibid.*, p. 263.

218 *ICJ Reports 1971*, p. 37, paragraph 72: 'Since a provision of the Charter – Article 80, paragraph 1–had maintained the obligations of the Mandatory, the United Nations had become the appropriate forum for supervising the fulfilment of those obligations. Thus, by virtue of Article 10 of the Charter, *South Africa agreed* (emphasis added) to submit its administration of South West Africa to the scrutiny of the General Assembly, on the basis of the information furnished by the Mandatory or obtained from other sources.'

219 *Ibid.*, p. 40, paragraph 76 and *ICJ Reports 1950*, p. 142.

220 *Loc. cit.*, p. 132.

221 *ICJ Reports 1962*, p. 330.

222 *Ibid.*, p. 331.

223 'Report of the International Law Commission to the General Assembly.' *YILC*, 1974, Vol. II, Part one, pp. 196–197.

224 *Ibid.*, p. 204.

225 *Ibid.*, pp. 197, 205. The Commission also cited the cases of the separation Belgium from Holland, the neutralization of Chablais and Faucigny and the régimes of free navigation on the Congo and Niger rivers. *Loc. cit.*

226 *Ibid.*, p. 206. The Commission went on to say that 'this course was also strongly indicated by the decisions of the Commission and of

the United Nations Conference on the Law of Treaties with regard to treaties providing for such régimes in codifying the general law of treaties.'

227 *Ibid.*

228 *Ibid.*, p. 196: 'Article 12. Other territorial régimes, 1. A succession of states does not as such affect: (a) obligations relating to the use of any territory, or to restrictions upon its use, established by a treaty for the benefit of any territory of a foreign state and considered as attaching to the territories in question; (b) rights established by a treaty for the benefit of any territory and relating to the use, or to restrictions upon the use, of any territory of a foreign state and considered as attaching to the territories in question. 2. A succession of states does not as such affect: (a) obligations relating to the use of any territory, or to restrictions upon its use, established by a treaty for the benefit of a group of states or of all states and considered as attaching to that territory; (b) rights established by a treaty for the benefit of a group of states or of all states and relating to the use of any territory, or to restrictions upon its use, and considered as attaching to that territory.'

229 Article 12, Vienna Convention on Succession of States in Respect of Treaties, UN. Doc. A/CONF.80/31, August 22, 1978.

230 Article 12, paragraph 3, *Ibid.* 'The provisions of the present article do not apply to treaty obligations of the predecessor state providing for the establishment of foreign military bases on the territory to which the succession of states relates.' The discussions that led up to the insertion of this paragraph are related by Zidane Meriboute in *La succession d'Etats en matière de traités la lumière des travaux de la Commission du droit international et de la conférence de Vienna de 1978*, Thèse IUHEI No. 363, Genève, 1983, pp. 202–204.

231 *ICJ Reports 1950*, p. 156.

232 *Ibid.*

233 *Ibid.*, p. 159.

234 *ICJ Reports 1962*, p. 333.

235 *ICJ Reports 1950*, p. 136.

236 *ICJ Reports 1962*, p. 334.

237 *ICJ Reports 1971*, p. 42.

238 *Ibid.*

239 *ICJ Reports 1950*, p. 136.

240 *Ibid.*, p. 137.

241 *Ibid.*

242 *Ibid.*

243 *ICJ Reports 1956*, p. 28.

244 *ICJ Reports 1950*, p. 136.

CHAPTER IV THE EFFECTS OF SUCCESSION BETWEEN INTERNATIONAL ORGANIZATIONS

1 Supervision of the mandate over South West Africa was, of course, a political function. The General Assembly of the United Nations

in its Resolution of February 12, 1946 distinguished between 'functions and powers of a technical and non-political character' which would be examined by the Economic and Social Council and 'functions and powers under treaties, international conventions, agreements and other instruments having a political character' which the General Assembly would examine or submit to the appropriate organ on the condition that a specific request was made to the United Nations from the parties concerned. See UNGA Res. No. 24 (I), February 12, 1946, Transfer of Certain Functions, Activities and Assets of the League of Nations, Sections B and C.

2 See for example the debates in the United Nations General Assembly over the transfer of the IRO's functions relating to the legal protection of refugees in *Official Records of the General Assembly*, Fifth Session, Summary Records of the Third Committee, Meetings, September 20 to December 11, 1950, p. 332, paragraph 58 and p. 337, paragraph 22 and 325th Plenary Meeting, *Official Records of the United Nations General Assembly*, p. 671, paragraphs 87 and 88 and p. 673, paragraph 114.

3 Article III, Protocol for the Dissolution of the International Institute of Agriculture and the Transfer of its Functions and Assets to the Food and Agriculture Organization of the United Nations, *GBTS*, No. 29, Cmd 7413, 1948.

4 Article 1, Protocol Concerning the *Office international d'hygiène publique*, *UNTS*, vol. 9, p. 66.

5 Article 2, Agreement between the United Nations Educational, Scientific and Cultural Organization and the International Bureau of Education, in UNESCO No. 15C/83, Annex II, p. 2: 'The IBE transfers to UNESCO the functions which have been conferred upon it under its statutes.'

6 Article 43, paragraph 2(a) Treaty of East African Co-operation, *IGO*, Part I, vol. I, p. 403.

7 Article XIX, Convention for the Establishment of a European Space Agency, *IGO*, Parts III–IV, p. 177.

8 LN Doc. No. C.5.M.5., Final Report of the Board of Liquidation, 31 July 1947, p.6. The functions assumed by the League under six treaties on narcotic drugs signed between 1912 and 1942 included communicating the texts of regulations and statistical information regarding trade in drugs, determining whether the provisions of the convention apply to certain preparations containing narcotic substances and appointing the members and staff of two technical bodies, the Permanent Central Opium Board and the Supervisory Body. See Art. 21, International Opium Convention of January 23, 1912; Art. 30, International Opium Convention of February 19, 1925; Art. 16, Convention for the Suppression of the Illicit Traffic in Dangerous Drugs of June 26, 1936; *Ibid*. Articles 8 and 10, International Opium Convention of February 19, 1925; Art. 11, Convention for Limiting the Manufacture and Regulating the Distribution of Narcotics Drugs of July 13, 1931; *Loc. cit*. Articles 19 and 20, International Opium Convention of February 19, 1925;

Loc. cit. Art. 5, Convention for the Manufacture and Regulating the Distribution of Narcotic Drugs of July 13, 1931; *Loc. cit.* For a complete inventory of the functions entrusted to the League under the narcotic conventions see UN Doc. No. E/116, 10 September 1946, Transfer to the United Nations of Powers Exercised by the League of Nations Under the Conventions on Narcotic Drugs, Annex III, pp. 23–31.

9 *Supra.*, pp. 52–53.
10 *ICJ Reports 1950*, p. 137.
11 *Ibid.*, p. 138.
12 *South-West Africa Voting Procedure*, Advisory Opinion of June 7, 1955, *ICJ Reports 1955*, p. 70. The rule that was adopted by the General Assembly on October 11, 1954 reads as follows: 'Decisions of the General Assembly on questions relating to reports and petitions concerning the Territory of South-West Africa shall be regarded as important questions within the meaning of Article 18, paragraph 2 of the Charter of the United Nations.' See UNGA Res. 844 (IX), October 11, 1954, Procedure for the Examination of Reports and Petitions Relating to the Treaty of South-West Africa.
13 *ICJ Reports 1955*, p. 74.
14 *Ibid.*, p. 75.
15 *ICJ Reports 1950*, p. 137.
16 *ICJ Reports 1955*, p. 76. Judge Lauterpacht, in his separate opinion, agreed that the competence of the United Nations to exercise supervisory functions derived from its constituent instrument but thought that it was possible to approximate the procedure of the Council. See Separate Opinion of Judge Lauterpacht, *Ibid.*, p. 112.
17 *Admissibility of Hearings of Petitioners by the Committee on South-West Africa*, Advisory Opinion of June 1, 1956, *ICJ Reports 1956*, p. 24.
18 *Ibid.*, p. 28.
19 *Ibid.*, p. 29.
20 *Ibid.*
21 *Ibid.*, p. 30.
22 *Ibid.*
23 *Ibid.*
24 Separate Opinion of Sir Hersch Lauterpacht, *ICJ Reports 1956*, p. 41. This view is repeated by Judge Fitzmaurice in his 1971 Dissenting Opinion where he affirmed that changing the supervisory organ changes also the nature of the obligation itself. See *ICJ Reports 1971*, p. 233.
25 *EY 1961*, vol. VIII, p. 197.
26 *Ibid.*
27 *Ibid.*
28 *Manual of the Council of Europe, Structure, Functions and Achievements*, Steven & Sons, Ltd., London/Fred. B. Rothman and Co., South Hachensack, NJ, 1970, p. 184.
29 *EY 1961*, vol. VIII, p. 197.
30 On the question of impossibility of performance see *Supra.*, pp. 48–49.

31 *Supra.*, pp. 56–58.
32 See Articles 36, paragraph 5 and 37 of the Statute of the International Court of Justice.
33 Article 74, paragraph 2. Vienna Convention on the Law of Treaties between States and International Organizations or between International Organizations, March 21, 1986. UN Doc. No. A/CONF. 129/ 15.
34 Article 73, Vienna Convention on the Law of Treaties, UN Doc. No. A/CONF. 39/27, p. 298.
35 Article 70, paragraph 2, Vienna Convention on the Law of Treaties, *Loc. cit.* Art. 70, paragraph 2, Draft Articles on the Law of Treaties Between States and International Organizations, *Loc. cit.*
36 Article 17, Vienna Convention on the Succession of States in Respect of Treaties, UN Doc. A/CONF. 80, 31, 22 August 1978.
37 *Supra.*, pp. 74–75.
38 South West Africa Cases, *ICJ Reports 1962*; p. 331.
39 *Supra.*, p. 77.
40 Articles 8 and 9, Vienna Convention on Succession of States in Respect of Treaties, *Loc. cit.*
41 Article 2, paragraph 1, Agreement Concerning the Execution of the Transfer to the United Nations of Certain Assets of the League of Nations, Geneva, July 19, 1946, *UNTS*, vol. 1, p. 110 and Art. 2(a), Agreement Between the United Nations and the Swiss Confederation on the Ariana Site, Berne, June 11, 1946 and New York, July 1, 1946, *UNTS*, vol. I, p. 155.
42 Article 2, Agreement Between the League of Nations and the International Labour Organisation for the Transfer of Certain Properties, Montreal, May 17, 1946, LN Doc. No. C.83.M.83. September 1, 1946, First Interim Report of the Board of Liquidation, Annex 3, p. 16.
43 Article 1, paragraph 3, Agreement Concerning the Execution of the Transfer to the United Nations of Certain Assets of the League of Nations, *Loc. cit.*
44 Article 1, paragraph 2, *Ibid.*
45 Article 1, paragraph 4, *Ibid.*
46 *Ibid.*
47 LN Doc. No. C.83.M.83, September 1, 1946, *Loc. cit.*
48 Ranjeva, Raymond, *op. cit.*, p. 345.
49 *Ibid.*, p. 348, Wodie, Francis, *op. cit.*, p. 64.
50 Ranjeva, Raymond, *Loc. cit.*
51 Article 2, Agreement on the Integration of the International Patent Institute into the European Patent Office, Munich, October 19, 1977, EPO Doc. No. CI Final, 23/27, p. 4.
52 Letter dated April 30, 1947 from M. Segnier, Chairman of the Liquidation Committee to Mr. Bedin, Regional Representative for PICAO, in Liquidation Plan of the International Commission for Air Navigation Adopted by the Liquidation Committee During its Meetings of January 7 and 8, 1947, ICAO Doc. No. 4813, C/603,

October 26, 1947, pp. 15–17. ICAO Doc. No. 6280, C/717, Minutes of the Eighteenth Meeting, p. 9. ICAO Doc. No. 6437, A4–P/8, Reports on Suspension of Financial Regulations, p. 1.

53 Rapport du Président de la Commission des finances et du transfert sur le fonctionnnement de l'Office international d'hygiène publique, novembre 1946–avril 1950, *Procès-verbaux des Séances du Comité permanent*, Session de Mai 1950, p. 26. Official Records of the World Health Organization, No. 5, p. 110. WHO Res. No. EB 2.R50, *Handbook of Resolutions and Decisions of the World Health Assembly and the Executive Board*, vol. 1, 1948–1972, p. 361.

54 Article 2, Agreement Concerning the Execution of the Transfer to the United Nations of Certain Assets of the League of Nations, Geneva, July 19, 1946, *UNTS*, vol. 1, p. 112. Schedule attached to the Common Plan for the transfer of the League of Nations Assets, *LN Official Journal*, Special Supplement No. 194, p. 274. Art 1, Agreement between the League of Nations and the International Labour Organisation Concerning the Transfer of Certain Properties, Geneva and Montreal, May 17, 1946, *UNTS*, vol. 19, p. 189.

55 Paragraphs 5 and 6, Liquidation Plan of the International Commission for Air Navigation Adopted by the Liquidation Committee During its Meetings of January 7 and 8, 1947, in ICAO Doc. No. 4813, C/603, October 26, 1947, p. 11.

56 Paragraph 7, *Ibid.*

57 Article II (a), Protocol for the Dissolution of the International Institute of Agriculture and the Transfer of its Functions and Assets to the Food and Agriculture Organization of the United Nations, Rome, March 30, 1946, *GBTS*, No. 29 (1948), Cmd. 7413, p. 3.

58 Exchange of letters between the Director General of the FAO and the President of the Permanent Committee of the IIA, *Actes de la Seizième Assemblée générale*, 8 & 9 juillet 1946, pp. 371–373.

59 Article 2, Agreement on the Integration of the International Patent Institute into the European Patent Office, EPO Doc. No. CI/Final 23/77, p. 4.

60 Article 29, *Ibid.*, p. 27.

61 WHO Res. No. EB 2, R50. *Handbook of Resolutions and Decisions of the World Health Assembly and the Executive Board*, vol. I, 1948–1972, p. 361.

62 Rapport du Président de la Commission des finances et du transfert sur le fonctionnement de l'Office international d'hygiène publique, novembre 1946–avril 1950, *OIHP Procès-verbaux des Séances du Comité permanent*, Session mai 1950, p. 26. Rapport de la Commission des Avoirs, soumis la Commission des Transferts, *Ibid.*, p. 5.

63 *Loc. cit.*, *Official Records of the World Health Organization*, No. 5, p. 112.

64 Paragraph 3, OIHP Permanent Committee Res. of May 6, 1950, in WHO Doc. No. A3/46, Add. 1, Rev. 1, p. 3. WHO Doc. No. A4/27. Transfer of the Assets of the *Office international d'hygiène publique*, p. 2.

65 LN Doc. No. C.5.M.5, July 31, 1947, Final Report of the Board of Liquidation, p. 28. The only members of the League that did not settle their debts were Albania, Bulgaria, Ethiopia, Liberia, Paraguay and Spain. These debts only represented 0.82 percent of the outstanding debts. The other 6.16 percent had been cancelled because of war or other such calamities. *Ibid.*

66 Projet de lettre à adresser à Sir John Boyd Ore, Directeur général de la FAO, Washington, D.C., *Actes de la Seizième Assemblée générale*, pp. 373–374: 'il a des créances très considérables, principalement auprès des Etats-membres, qui doivent des arriérés de contributions pour un montant de 5,768,295 francs suisses (sans compter les contributions pour l'année en cours qui se chiffrent 1,634,760 francs suisses).'

67 *Ibid.*, p. 374.

68 FAO Doc. No. C49/25, Report on the Liquidation of the International Institute of Agriculture and the International Forestry Center, November 14, 1949, Appendix II, p. 9.

69 Czechoslovakia and Hungary claimed that they were prevented from fulfilling their obligations because of an absolute lack of foreign exchange. *Ibid.*, p. 10.

70 *Ibid.*, Appendix I, p. 61. The Director General of the FAO accepted the offer of the IIA's Liquidation Commission on the following terms: 'It is with pleasure that I confirm that the FAO is prepared to assume responsibility for those matters that will remain to be dealt with after the formal liquidation, namely: (1) To collect arrears of contributions still outstanding; (2) As and when necessary funds become available, to make further payments to the staff in accordance with the statute of final liquidation granted to the personnel by the General Assembly of July 1946 . . .'.

71 *Handbook of Resolutions and Decisions of the World Health Assembly and Executive Board*, p. 363; see also the reports cited therein.

72 *Supra.*, p. 87.

73 Negotiations with the *Office international d'hygiène publique*, Official Records of the World Health Organization, No. 5, pp. 110–111.

74 Rapport du Président de la Commission des finances et du transfert sur le fonctionnement de l'Office international d'hygiène publique (novembre 1946–avril 1950). *OIHP Procès-verbaux des Séances du Comité permanent*, Session Mai 1950, p. 27.

75 *Ibid.*, p. 12.

76 LN Doc. No. C.5.M.5, *op. cit.*, p. 13. The Darling Foundation and the Léon Bernard Fund amounted to 12,926.76 and 16,165.55 Swiss francs respectively.

77 *Ibid.* The sum transferred was 92,030.60 Swiss francs.

78 LN Doc. No. A.19. 1946, Report of the Supervisory Commission on the Work of its One-hundredth Session, p. 6.

79 LN Doc. No. C.5.M.5, *op. cit.*, p. 19.

80 *Ibid.*, p. 14.

81 *Ibid.* Paragraph 20. Resolution for the Dissolution of the League of Nations, *op. cit.,* p. 284.

82 Paragraph 18, Resolution for the Dissolution of the League of Nations, *Loc. cit.*

83 *Ibid.*

84 *Loc. cit.,* pp. 19 and 22. The balance of these three funds were as follows: the Reserve Fund, 174,000 Swiss francs, the Exchange Fund, 285,000 Swiss francs and the Staff Provident Fund, 48,000 Swiss francs.

85 *Ibid.,* p. 23.

86 Paragraph 16, *Ibid.* The amount transferred was 2,400,064.50 Swiss Francs. See LN Doc. No. C.5.M.5. *op. cit.,* p. 15.

87 *OIHP Procès-verbaux des Séances du Comité permanent,* Session 1950, p. 26. Official Records of the World Health Organization, No. 5, pp. 111 and 112.

88 WHO Res. No. EB 23. R24, in *Handbook of Resolutions and Decisions of the World Health Assembly and the Executive Board,* p. 363.

89 Woodbridge, George, vol. III, *op. cit.,* p. 353.

90 *Ibid.,* pp. 354 and 510.

91 *Ibid.,* p. 509.

92 *Official Records of the World Health Organization,* No. 7, Annex 28, pp. 203–204 and No. 10, p. 81. See also WHA Res. No. 3.53 and EB Res. Nos. 3.R13 and 5.R56 in *Handbook of Resolutions and Decisions of the World Health Assembly and the Executive Board,* vol. I, 1948–1972.

93 Paragraph 7, The Common Plan, *op. cit.,* p. 273.

94 LN Doc. No. A.32 (I), 1946, Report of the Finance Committee, April 18, 1946.

95 LN Doc. No. C.5.M.5, *op. cit.,* p. 8.

96 *Ibid.,* p. 9.

97 Paragraphs 9 and 10. Liquidation Plan of the International Commission for Air Navigation Adopted by the Liquidation Committee During its Meetings of January 7 and 8, 1947, ICAO Doc. No. 4813, C/ 603, October 26, 1947, p. 12.

98 Paragraph 11, *Ibid.*

99 These included Bulgaria, Estonia, Finland, Japan, Latvia, Rumania, Hungary and Czechoslovakia, *Ibid.,* p. 39.

100 ICAO Doc. No. 6280, C/717, Fifth Session of the ICAO Council, November 16, 1948, pp. 2 and 9.

101 FAO Doc. No. C49/25, Report on the Liquidation of the International Institute of Agriculture and the International Forestry Center, November 14, 1949, p. 3.

102 The United Kingdom expressed this view before the sixteenth General Assembly in July 1946 and again at the time it paid its arrears. Australia offered to discharge its obligations 'provided that an arrangement could be made for the transfer to an account with the United Nations Organization for Food and Agriculture of any residual amount that may stand to our credit when the Institute is wound up'. Burma specified that 'any residual amount that may stand to its credit at the conclusion of the operations for

liquidation of the Institute, shall be paid over to the Government direct and to the United Nations Organization for Food and Agriculture', *Ibid.*, pp. 8 and 9. *Actes de la seizième Assemblée générale, op. cit.*, pp. 41–42.

103 Article 1, paragraph 1, *op. cit.*, p. 2.
104 Article XIX, *op. cit.*, p. 177.
105 *Supra.*, pp. 41–42.
106 Common Plan, *op. cit.*, p. 219.
107 Paragraph 6, Agreement between UNRRA and the United Nations Concerning the Transfer to the United Nations of the Residual Assets and Activities of UNRRA, *UNTS*, vol. 27, p. 352.
108 Paragraph 9, *Ibid.*, p. 354.
109 *Supra*, pp. 22, 25.
110 Wencak v. United Nations, United States, Supreme Court of New York, January 18, 1956, *ILR*, 1956, pp. 509–510.
111 LN Doc. No. C.5.M.5, *op. cit.*, pp. 16–17. LN Doc. No. C.89.M.89, December 1, 1946, Second Interim Report of the Board of Liquidation, p. 3. LN Doc. C. 83.M.83. *op. cit.*, p. 6.
112 ICAN Doc. No. 4813, C/603, p. 3.
113 IIA. Res. No. 4, Additional Resolution Relative to the Dissolution of the International Forestry Center (C.I.S.), *Actes de la Seizième Assemblée générale*, pp. 67–69. FAO Doc. C.49/25, *op. cit.*, p. 14.
114 *LN Official Journal*, Special Supplement No. 19, Annex 24, pp. 252, 254 and 279.
115 *Supra.*, pp. 31–33.
116 Ranjeva, Raymond. *op. cit.*, p. 279.
117 Article 71, paragraph 2. Treaty for East-African Co-operation, *IGO*, Part I, vol. I, p. 415. Ranjeva, Raymond, *op. cit.*, p. 282.
118 LN Doc. No. C.5.M.5, *op. cit.*, p. 21.
119 ICAN Res. No. 1,167. Review of the Twenty-eighth Session of the International Commission for Air Navigation, London, August 21–25, 1945, *Official Bulletin of CINA*, No. 28, 1945, p. 22; See also Report by the General Secretary on the Work Executed Since the End of the Twenty-eighth Session and the Internal Situation at the Opening of the Twenty-Ninth Session, October 28, 1946. *Official Bulletin of the CINA*, No. 29, 1946, p. 29.
120 Rapport du Président de la Commission des finances et du transfert sur le fonctionnement de l'Office international d'hygiène publique, novembre 1946–avril 1950, *OIHP Procès-verbaux des Séances du Comité permanent*, Session de Mai 1950, p. 26. By April 1950, the OIHP had only three employees left.
121 Rapports présentés à la XVIe Assemblée générale, supplément No. 11 au Rapport financier, p. 353: 'Le 1er août, la FAO prendra sa charge tout l'Institut. Elle offrira un contrat provisoire au personnel, avec le traitement actuel, jusqu' à la notificaton aux Etats, qui étaient membres de l'Institut, dès la dissolution définitive de celui-ci.'
122 Article 4, Protocol on the Centralization of the European Patent System and on Its Introduction, *op. cit.*, p. 153.

123 Article 7, Agreement between UNESCO and the International Bureau of Education, UNESCO Doc. No. 15C/83, Annex II, p. 3.

BIBLIOGRAPHY

I. SUCCESSION IN MUNICIPAL LAW

A. Sources

Bonjean, L.B. *Institutes de l'Empereur Justinien. traduites en franais avec texte en regard*, Paris, Videcoq, 1838, 464 p.

Bürgerliches Gesetzbuch. München, C.H. Bech'sche Verlags-buchhandlung, 1977, v – 1128 p.

Code Civil. 77e édition, Paris, Dalloz, 1977–1978, vi – 1309 p.

Code civil néerlandais. traduit en français et mis en concordance avec le Code civil belge par P.H. Haanebrink, Bruxelles, Etablissement Emile Bruylant/ Paris, Librairie générale de droit et de jurisprudence, 1921, v–423 p.

Codice civile con la constituzione e le principali leggi speciali. Milano, Dott. A. Guiffrè, 1975.

Les codes et les lois spéciales les plus usuelles en vigueur en Belgique. 30e édition, Tome I, Bruxelles, Etablissement Emile Bruylant, 1961, 718 p.

Codigo civil. Madrid, Boletin oficial del Estado, 1972, 784 p.

Corpus Iuris Civilis. edited by Paul Krueger and Theodor Mommsen, Berlin, Weidmannsche Verlagsbuchhandlung, 1954, 3 vols.

Recueil systématique du droit fédéral. vol. 2/1, Berne, Chancellerie fédérale suisse, 1978.

Tissot, P.A. *Les douze livres du Code de l'Empereur Justinien.* 2e édition, Tome 3, Metz, Behemer, 1807, 484 p.

Zulueta, Francis de. *The Institutes of Gaius.* Parts I and II, Oxford, The Clarendon Press.

B. Works

Austin, John. *Lectures on Jurisprudence.* 5th edition, revised and edited by Robert Campbell, vol. I, London, John Murray, 1929, 2 vols.

Ballantine, Henry W. *On Corporations.* revised edition, Chicago, Callaghan and Co., 1946, xx – 992 p.

Buckland, W.W. and McNair, Arnold D. *Roman Law and Common Law*

152

BIBLIOGRAPHY

– *A Comparison in Outline*. 2nd edition, revised by F. H. Lawson, Cambridge, University Press, 1965, ix 439 p.

Capitaine, Georges. *La liquidation officielle d'une succession en droit suisse*. Genève, Imprimerie Atar, 1935, 201 p.

Capitant, Henri. *Introduction l'étude du droit civil*. 5e édition, Paris, A. Pédone, 1929, 483 p.

Carbonnier, Jean. *Droit civil*. 9e édition, Tome 1er, Paris, Presses Universitaires de France, 1971, 316 p.

Carbonnier, Jean. *Théorie des obligations*. Paris, Presses Universitaires de France, 1963, 572 p.

Coissoro, Narana. The Customary Laws of Succession in Central Africa. Lisbon, Centro de Estudos Politicos e Socialis, 1966, vii – 412 p.

Colin, Ambroise and Capitant, Henri. *Traité de droit civil*. refondu par Léon Julliot de la Morandière, Tome II, Paris, Librairie Dalloz, 1959, v – 1006 p.

Coq, Edouard. *Manuel des institutions juridiques des romains*. 2e édition, Paris, Librairie Plon/Librairie générale de droit et de jurisprudence, 1928, i – 956 p.

David, René. *Les contrats en droit anglais*. Paris, Librairie générale de droit et de jurisprudence, 1973, 482 p.

Eliachevitch, Basil. *La personnalité juridique en droit privé romain*. Paris, Librairie du Recueil Sirey, 1942, xiii – 400 p.

Engel, Pierre. *Traité des obligations en droit suisse*. Neuchâtel, Ides et Challandes, 1973, 668 p.

Family Law in Asia and Africa. edited by J.N.D. Anderson, London, George Allen and Unwin Ltd., 1968, 301 p.

Frank, W. F. *The General Principles of English Law*. 5th edition, London, Toronto, Wellington, Sydney, George G. Harrap and Co. Ltd., 1971, 219 p.

Gaudement, Jean. *Le droit privé romain*. Paris, Armand Colin, 1974, 416 p.

Girard, Paul Frédéric. *Manuel élementaire de droit romain*. 7e édition, Paris, Librairie Arthur Rousseau et Cie, 1924, vi – 1158 p.

Gutteridge, H. C. *Comparative Law. An Introduction to the Comparative Method of Legal Study and Research*. Cambridge, University Press, 1946, ix – 208 p.

Hazard,John N. and Shapiro, Issac. *The Soviet Legal System*. New York, Oceana Publications Inc., 1962, xv – 186 p.

Hémard, Jean, Terre, François et Mabilat, Pierre. *Sociétés commerciales*. 3e édition entièrement nouvelle de G. Hureau, Paris, Dunod, 1969, 3 vols.

Henn, Harry G. *Handbook of the Law of Corporation and Other Business Enterprises*. 2nd edition, St.Paul, Minn. West Publishing Co., 1970, xxxi – 956 p.

Holmes, Oliver Wendell, Jr. *The Common Law*. Boston, Little, Brown and Company, 1881, 422 p.

Huvelin, Paul. *Cours élémentaire de droit romain*. Tome 1er, Paris, Recueil Sirey, 1927, 761 p.

153

Ickowicz, Marc. *De l'exhérédation en droit suisse*. Genève, Georg et Co., 1930, 116 p.

James, Phillip S. *Introduction to English Law*. 9th edition, London, Butterworth and Co., 1976, xxxvii – 498 p.

Jenks, Edward. *The Book of English Law*. 6th edition, revised by Paul B. Fairest, London, John Murray, 1967, xvi – 376 p.

Jhering, Rudolph von. *L'évolution du droit (Zweck im Recht)*. traduit sur la 3e édition allemande par O. de Neulenaere, Paris, Librairie A. Maresca, 1901, iii – 400 p.

Jolowicz, H.F. *Historical Introduction to the Study of Roman Law*. 2nd edition, Cambridge, University Press, 1952, xv – 596 p.

Jolowicz, H.F. *Roman Foundations of Modern Law*. Oxford, The Clarendon Press, 1957, v – 217 p.

Josserand, Louis. *Cours de droit civil positif français*. Tome III, Paris, Librairie du Recueil Sirey, 1940, vii – 1172 p.

Kaser, Max. *Römisches Privatrecht*. 9. Auflage, München, C.H. Beckschen Verlagsbuchhandlung, 1976, vi – 371 p.

Kirkpatrick, Robert E. *Initiation du droit anglais*. Bruxelles, Maison Ferd. Larcier, S.A., 1964, 302 p.

Lattin, Norman. *The Law of Corporations*. 2nd Edition, New York, The Foundation Press, 1971, xxiii – 690 p.

The Law of Inheritance in Eastern Europe and in the People's Republic of China. Edited by Z. Szirmai, Leyden, A.W. Sijthoff, 1961, 373 p.

Lee, Robert W. *Elements of Roman Law*. Cambridge, Mass., Harvard University Press, 1950, v – 499 p.

Lee, Robert W. *The Elements of Roman Law with a Translation of the Institutes of Justinian*. 4th Edition, London, Sweet and Maxwell Ltd., 1956, v – 499 p.

Maine, Sir Henry Sumner. *Ancient Law. Its Connection with the Early History of Society and its Relation to Modern Ideas*, London, John Murray, 1916, v – 426 p.

Martin, Alfred. *Le Code des Obligations. Théorie des obligations*. Genève, Société anonyme des éditions Sonor, 1919, 280 p.

Mazeaud, Henri, Léon et Jean. *Leons de droit civil*. Tome IV, vol. II, 2e édition, Paris, Editions Montchrestien, 1971, 994 p.

Mellows, Anthony R. *The Law of Succession*. 3rd Edition, London, Butterworths, 1977, v – 843 p.

Michoud, Léon. *La théorie de la personnalité morale et son application au droit français*. 3e édition par Louis Trotabas, 2e partie, Paris, Librairie générale de droit et de jurisprudence, 1932, 540 p.

Monier, Raymond. *Manuel élémentaire de droit romain*. Tome I, réimpression de la 6e édition, Paris 1947, Aalen Sciencia Verlag 1970, vii – 551 p.

Parry, Sir David Hughes. *The Law of Succession. Testate and Intestate*. 6th Edition, London, Sweet and Maxwell Ltd., 1972, v – 376 p.

Paton, George Whitecross. *A Textbook of Jurisprudence*. Oxford, Clarendon Press, 1946, v – 528 p.

Piotet, Paul. *Précis de droit successoral*. Berne, Editions Staemspfli, 1976, 210 p.

Planiol, Marcel et Ripert, Georges. *Traité pratique de droit civil français*. Tome 1er, 2e édition par René Savatier, Paris, Librairie générale de droit et de jurisprudence, 1952, v – 974 p.

Redmond, P.W.D. *General Principles of English Law*. 2nd Edition, London, Sweet and Maxwell, Ltd., 1972, vii – 331 p.

Ripert, Georges et Boulanger, Jean. *Traité élmentaire de droit civil*. 3e édition, Tome III, Paris, Librairie générale de droit et de jurisprudence, 1948, vii – 1308 p.

Ripert, Georges et Boulanger, Jean. *Traité général de droit civil d'après le Traité de Planiol*. Tome IV, Paris, Librairie générale de droit et de jurisprudence, 1959, ix – 1320 p.

Roguin, Ernest. *Trait de droit civil comparé. Les succession*. Tome I, Paris, Librairie générale de droit et de jurisprudence/Lausanne, Librairie F. Rouge et Cie, 1989, v – 503 p.

Saleilles, Raymond. *De la personnalité juridique*. Paris, Librairie nouvelle de droit et de jurisprudence Arthur Rousseau, 1910, v – 673 p.

Savigny, Frédéric Charles de. *Traité de droit romain*. traduit de l'allemand par Charles Guenoux, 2e édition, tome 3, Paris, Librairie de Firmin Didot Frères, 1851.

Smith, Kenneth and Keenan, Denis J. *Company Law*. 3rd Edition, London, Pitman Publishing, Ltd., 1977, x – 510 p.

Stevens, Robert S. *Handbook on the Law of Private Corporations*. 2nd Edition, St. Paul Minn., West Publishing Co., 1949.

Stone, Julius. *Social Dimensions of Law and Justice*. London, Stevens and Sons, Ltd., 1966, vii – 933 p.

Thomas, J.A.C. *Textbook of Roman Law*. Amsterdam, New York, Oxford, North-Holland Publishing Company, 1976, v – 562 p.

Toumbouros, George. *Parallel Legislations*. vol. I, *The Laws of Ancient Greece*. Munich, Süddeutscher Verlag Press, 1959, v – 388 p.

Treitel, G.H. *The Law of Contracts*. 4th Edition, London, Stevens and Sons, Ltd., 1965, xlix – 721 p.

Vecchio, Giorgio del. *Humanité et unité de droit*. Paris, Librairie générale de droit et de jurisprudence, 1963, 310 p.

Watson, Alan. *The Law of Succession in the Later Roman Republic*. Oxford, Clarendon Press, 1971, xi – 209 p.

Watson, Alan. *Legal Transplants: An Approach to Comparative Law*. Edinburgh, Scottish Academic Press, 1974, ix – 106 p.

Weill, Alex. *Droit civil. Les Biens*. Paris, Dalloz, 1970, 612 p.

Weill, Alex. *Droit civil. Les Obligations*. Paris, Dalloz, 1971, 1058 p.

Williston, Samuel. *Treatise on the Law of Contracts*. 3rd Edition, by Walter H.E. Jaeger, vol. 1, New York, Baker, Voohis and Co., Inc., 1957, vii – 221 p.

II. SUCCESSION IN INTERNATIONAL LAW

A. Sources

Bedjaoui, Mohamed. 'First, Second, Third, Fourth, Fifth, Sixth and Seventh Reports on Succession of States in Respect of Matters other than Treaties.' *YILC*, 1968, vol. II (pp. 94–117), 1969, vol. II (pp. 69–100), 1970, vol. II (pp. 131–169), 1971, vol. II (pp. 157–192), 1972, vol. II (pp. 61–70), 1973, vol. II (pp. 3–74), 1974, vol. II (pp. 91–116).

The Effects of Independence on Treaties. A handbook published under the auspices of the International Law Association, prepared by the Committee on State Succession to Treaties and Other Governmental Obligations, London, Stevens & Sons, 1965, xvi – 391 p.

Castrén, Eric. 'The Succession of States and Governments: The Limits and Methods of Research.' *YILC*, vol. II, 1963; pp. 290–293.

Lachs, Manfred. 'Working Paper.' *YILC*, 1963, vol. II, pp. 297–300.

Report by Mr. Manfred Lachs, Chairman of the Sub-Committee on Succession of States and Governments, 7 June 1963, *YILC*, vol. II, 1963: pp. 260–262.

Vallat, Sir Francis. 'First Report on Succession of States in Respect of Treaties.' *YILC*, 1974, vol. II, pp. 1–88.

Vienna Convention on Succession of States in Respect of Treaties, 22 August 1978, UN Doc. A/CONF. 80/31.

Vienna Convention on Succession of State Property, Archives and Debts. 1983, UN Doc. A/CONF. 117/14.

Waldock, Sir Humprhey. 'First, Second, Third, Fourth and Fifth Reports on Succession in Respect of Treaties.' *YILC*, 1968, vol. II (pp. 87–93), 1969, vol. II (pp. 45–69), 1970, vol. II (pp. 25–60), 1971, vol. II (pp. 143–156), 1972, vol. II (pp. 1–60).

B. Works

1. Books

Guggenheim, Paul. *Beitrége zur völkerrechtlichen Lehre vom Staatenwechsel.* Berlin, F. Vahlen, 1925, 200 p.

Huber, Max. *Die Staatensuccession.* Leipzig, Verlag von Dunker & Humblot, 1898; xxii – 319 p.

Marcoff, Marco-G. *Accession à l'indépendance et succession d'Etat aux traités internationaux.* Fribourg, Editions universitaires, 1969, 388 p.

Marek, Krystyne. *Identity and Continuity of States in Public International Law.* 2e édition, Genève, Librairie Droz, 1968; 619 p.

Mériboute, Zidane. *La codification de la succession aux traités. Décolonisation, sécession, unification.* Paris, Presses universitaires de France, 1984. 270 p.

Mochi-Onory, Andrea Giuseppe. *La succession d'Etat aux traités.* Milano, Dott. A. Guiffrè editore, 1968; 168 p.

Muralt, R.W.G. *The Problem of State Succession with Regard to Treaties.* The Hague, W.P. van Stokman & Sons, 1954, 165 p.

Nguyen, Huu-Tru. *Quelques problèmes de succession d'Etat concernant le Viet-Nam.* Bruxelles, Bruylant, 1970; 323 p.

O'Connell, D.C. *State Succession in Municipal Law and International Law.* Cambridge, University Press, 1967, 2 vols.

Pereira, André G. *La succession d'Etat en matière de traité.* Paris, A. Pédone, 1969; 232 p.

Pufendorf, Samuel. *De jure naturae et gentium.* Washington, D.C., Carnegie Institute of Washington/Oxford, the Clarendon Press, 1934, 2 vols.

Udokang, Okon. *Succession of New States to International Treaties.* Dobbs Ferry, NY, Oceana Publications, Inc., 1972, 525 p.

Vattel, Emer de. *Le droit des gens, ou Principes de la loi naturelle, appliqués à la conduite et aux affaires des nations et les souverains.* Washington, The Carnegie Institution of Washington, 1916, 3 vols.

2. *Articles*

Bartos, M. 'Les Nouveaux Etats et les traités internationaux.' *Jugoslavensk revija za medjunarodno Prava*, No. 2, 1962, pp. 185–197.

Bedjaoui, Mohammed. 'Problèmes récents de succession d'Etat dans les Etats nouveaux.' *RCADI*, vol. 130, 1970 II, pp. 455–586.

Caflisch, Lucius. 'The Law of State Succession: Theoretical Observations.' *Netherlands International Law Review*, 1963, pp. 337–366.

Castrén, E. 'Aspects récents de la succession d'Etats.' *RCADI*, vol. 78, 1951 I, pp. 279–506.

Castrén, E. 'On State Succession in Practice and Theory.' *Acta Scandinavica iuris gentium*, vol. 24, 1954, Nos. 3–4, pp. 55–75.

Cavaglieri, Arrigo. 'Note in materia successione di stato a stato.' *Rivista di Diritta Internazionale*, vol. 16, 1924, pp. 26–46.

Jenks, C. Wilfred. 'State Succession in Respect of Law-making Treaties.' *BYBIL*, 1952, pp. 105–144.

Keith, K.J. 'Succession to Bilateral Treaties by Succeeding States.' *AJIL*, vol. 61, 1967.

Kelsen, Hans. 'Théorie générale du droit international public. Problèmes choisis.' *RCADI*, vol. 42, 1934, pp. 121–351.

O'Connell, D.P. 'Independence and Succession to Treaties.' *BYBIL*, vol. 38, 1962, pp. 84–180.

Rousseau, Charles. 'La pratique récente en matière de succession d'Etats.' *Annales de droit et des sciences politiques*, tome 12, 1962, pp. 3–17.

Schermers, Henry G. 'Succession of States and International Organizations.' *NYIL*, vol. 6, 1975, pp. 103–119.

Vallat, Francis. 'Some Aspects of the Law of State Succession.' *Transactions of the Grotius Society*, vol. 41, 1955, pp. 123–135.

Udina, Manlio. 'La succession des Etats quant aux obligations internationales autres que les dettes publiques.' *RCADI*, 1933 II, pp. 669–773, 684–689.

Zemanek, K. 'State succession after decolonization.' *RCADI*, vol. 116, 1965 III, pp. 187–298.

III.THE LAW OF INTERNATIONAL ORGANIZATIONS

A. Sources

1. Documents

Annuaire des Organisations Internationales. Bruxelles, Union des Associations Internationales 1980.

El-Erian, Abdullah. 'First and Second Reports on Relations Between States and International Organizations.' *YILC*, 1963, vol. III, pp. 159–186 and 1967 vol. II, pp. 133–153.

European Peace Treaties after World War II, edited by Amelia C. Leiss, Worchester, Mass., World Peace Foundation, 1954, v – 341 p.

Hall, H. Duncan. *Mandates, Dependencies and Trusteeships*. Washington, Carnegie Endowment for International Peace / London, Stevens & Sons, Ltd., 1948, vii – 429 p.

Reuter, Paul. 'First, Second, Third and Fourth Reports on the Question of Treaties Concluded Between States and International Organizations or Between Two or More International Organizations.' *YILC*, 1972, vol. II (pp. 171–198), 1973, vol. II (pp. 75–94), 1974, vol. II (pp. 135–150), 1975, vol. II (pp. 25–44).

United Nations Yearbook. 1947–1948, Department of Public Information, United Nations, Lake Success, New York, 1949, v. 1126 p.

Vienna Convention on the Law of Treaties. UN Doc. No. A/ CONF. 39/27, 23 May 1969.

Vienna Convention on the Law of Treaties between States and International Organizations or between International Organizations. UN Doc. A/CONF. 129/15, 20 March 1986.

Waldock, Sir Humphrey. 'First, Second and Third Reports on the Law of Treaties.' *YILC*, 1962, vol. II (pp. 27–83), 1963, vol. II (pp. 36–94), 1974, vol. II (pp. 5–65).

2. Cases

Reparation for Injuries Suffered in the Service of the United Nations. ICJ Reports 1949, p. 180.

B. Works

1. Books

Amaducci, Sandro. *La nature juridique des traités constitutifs des organisations internationales*, Bruxelles, 1971, 156 p.

Bastid, Suzanne. *Droit international; le droit des organisations internationales*. Paris, Cours de droit, 1968, 333 p.

Bowett, D.W. *The Law of International Institutions*. 3rd edition, London, Stevens & Sons, 1975, v – 382 p.

Cahier, Philippe. *Etude des accords de siège entre les organisations internationales et les Etats ou elles résident. Milano, Dott.A. Guiffr', 1959, viii – 451 p.

Cheng, Bin. *General Principles of Law as Applied by International Courts and Tribunals*. London, Stevens & Sons Ltd., 1953–vii – 490 p.

Claude, Inis L. Jr. *Swords to Plowshares. The Problems and Progress of International Organizations*. 2nd edition, New York, Random House, 1962, xiv – 537 p.

Colliard, Claude-Albert. *Institutions des relations internationales*. 7e édition, Paris Dalloz, 1978, xx – 964 p.

Detter, Ingrid. *Law-Making by International Organizations*. Stockholm, P.A. Norstedt & Šners Forlag, 1965, 353 p.

Elias, T.O. *The Modern Law of Treaties*. Dobbs Ferry, N.Y., Oceana Publications Inc. / Leiden, A. W. Sijthoff, 1974, 272 p.

Geiser, Hans Jürg. *Les effets des accords conclus par les organisations internationales*. Bern, Herbert Lang, 1977, xii – 260 p.

Grotius, Hugo. *De Jure belli ac pacis libri tres*. Washington D.C., Carnegie Institution of Washington / Oxford, the Clarendon Press, 1916–1925, 2 vols.

Hoyt, Edwin C. *The Unanimity Rule in the Revision of Treaties. A Reexamination*. The Hague, Martinus Nijhoff, 1959, v – 263 p.

Jenks, C. Wilfred. *The Proper Law of International Organisations*. London, Stevens & Sons, 1962, vii – 282 p.

Kelsens, Hans. *Principles of International Law*. 2nd edition, New York, Holt, Reinhart & Winston, Inc., 1966, 602 p.

Lauterpacht, Sir Hersch. *The Development of International Law by the International Court*. London, Stevens & Sons, Ltd., 1958, xx – 408 p.

Lecca, Jean. *Les techniques de révision des conventions internationales*. Paris, Librairie générale de droit et de jurisprudence, 1961, iv – 330 p.

O'Connell, Daniel P. *International Law*. London, Stevens & Sons, 2nd edition, 1970, 2 vols.

Oppenheim, L. *International Law. A Treatise*. 8th edition, edited by Hersch Lauterpacht, London, Longmans, Green & Co., Ltd., 1963, vol. I, vii – 1072.

Reuter, Paul. *Institutions Internationales*. Paris, Presses Universitaires de France, 7e édition, 1972, 348 p.

Rouyer-Hammeray, Bernard. *Les compétences implicites des organisations internationales*. Paris, Librairie générale de droit et de jurisprudence, 1962, 111 p.

Schwarzenberger, Georg. *International Law as Applied by International Courts and Tribunals. International Constitutional Law*. London, Stevens & Sons Ltd., 1976, vol. III, ix – 680 p.

Virally, Michel. *L'organisation mondiale*. Paris, Librairie Armand Colin, 1972, 589 p.

2. Articles

Abi-Saab, Georges. 'The Concept of International Organization: A Synthesis.' *The Concept of International Organization*, Paris, UNESCO, 1981, pp. 9–24.

Bastid, Suzanne. 'Place de la notion d'institution dans une théorie générale des organisations internationales.' *L'Evolution du droit public. Etudes en l'honneur d'Achille Mestre*, Paris, Sirey, 1956, pp. 43–51.

Chaumont, Charles M. 'La signification du principe de spécialité des organisations internationales.' *Mélanges offerts H. Rolin*, Paris, 1964, pp. 55–66.

Engel, Salo. ' "Living" International Constitutions and the World Court (The Subsequent Practice of International Organs under their Constituent Instruments).' *ICLQ*, 1967, vol. 16, pp. 865–910.

Friedman, Wolfgang. 'The Use of General Principles in the Development of International Law.' *AJIL,*. 1963, pp. 279–299.

Hardy, Michael. 'The United Nations and General Multilateral Treaties Concluded under the Auspices of the League of Nations.' *BYBIL*, vol. 29, 1963, pp. 425– 440.

Jenks, C. Wilfred. 'Coordination: the New Problem of International Organisation.' *RCADI*, vol.77, 1950 II, pp.

Jennings, Robert V. 'General Course on Principles of International Law.' *RCADI*, vol. 121, 1967 II, pp. 327–605.

Kaufmann, Wilhelm. 'Les Unions internationales de nature économiques.' *RCADI*, vol.3, 1924 II, pp.181–289.

Kraus, Herbert. 'Système et fonction des traités internationaux.' *RCADI*, vol. 50, 1934 IV, pp. 317–399.

Lauterpacht, E. 'The Legal Effects of Illegal Acts of International Organisations.' *Cambridge Essays in International Law*. London, Stevens & Sons / New York, Dobbs Ferry, 1965, pp. 88–121.

Mann, F.A. 'The Proper Law of Contracts Concluded by International Persons.' *BYBIL*, vol. 35, 1960, pp.34–57.

Monaco, Riccardo. 'Le caractère constitutionnel des actes institutifs d'organisations internationales.' *Mélanges offerts Charles Rousseau*, Paris, A. Pédone, 1974, pp. 277–300.

Parry, Clive. 'Constitutions of International Organizations.' *BYBIL*, vol. XXIII, 1946, pp. 394–396.

Reuter, Paul. 'Le droit des traités et les accords internationaux conclus par les organisations internationales.' *Miscellanea W.J. Ganshof van der Meersch. Studia ab discipulis amicusque in honorem agregi professoris edita*, Bruxelles, Bruylaut, 1972, pp. 195–215.

Sorensen, Max. 'Principes de droit international public.' *RCADI*, vol. 101, 1960 III, pp. 1–251.

Virally, Michel. 'La notion de fonction dans la théorie de l'organisation international.' *Mélanges offerts Charles Rousseau*, Paris, A.Pédone, 1974, pp. 277–300.

Wolff, Karl. 'Les principes généraux du droit applicables dans les rapports internationaux.' *RCADI*, vol.36, 1931 II, pp. 483–553.

IV. SUCCESSION BETWEEN INTERNATIONAL ORGANIZATIONS

A. General

Chiu, Hungdah. 'Succession in International Organizations.' *ICLQ*, vol. 14, 1965, pp. 83–120.

Fitzmaurice, Sir Gerald. 'The Law and Procedure of the International Court of Justice: International Organizations and Tribunals.' *BYBIL*, vol. 29, 1952, pp. 1–62.

Hahn, Hugo J. 'Continuity in the Law of International Organization.' *OZFOR*, Band XII, 1964; pp. 167–239.

Hudson, Manley O. 'The Succession of the International Court of Justice to the Permanent Court of International Justice.' *AJIL*, vol. 51, 1957, pp. 569–573.

Hurst Cecil. 'State Succession in Matters of Tort.' *BYBIL*, vol. 5, 1924, pp. 163–178.

Jenks, C. Wilfred. 'Some Constitutional Problems of International Organizations.' *BYBIL*, vol. 12, 1945, pp. 11–72.

Kiss, Alexandre-Charles. 'Quelques aspects de la substitution d'une organisation à une autre.' *AFDI*, vol. VII, 1961; pp. 463–491.

Mochi-Onory, Andrea Giuseppe. 'The Nature of Succession Between International Organizations: Functions and Treaties.' *RHDI*, vol. 21, 1968, pp. 33–48.

Ranjeva, Raymond. *La succession d'organisations en Afrique.* Paris, A. Pédone, 1978, xiii – 418 p.

B. Examples

1. The Bureau International Pour la Protection de la Propriété Intellectuelle / The World Intellectual Property Organization

Sources

Bern Convention for the Protection of Literary and Artistic Works. 14 July 1967, Stockholm, *IGO*, Part III–IV, pp. 513–540.

Convention Establishing the World Intellectual Property Organization. 14 July 1967, Stockholm, *IGO*, Part III–IV, pp. 474–487.

Paris Convention for the Protection of Industrial Property. 14 July 1967, Stockholm, *IGO*, Part III–IV, pp. 488–512.

Works

Calvocoressi, Peter. *Survey of International Affairs 1947–1948.* London, New York, Toronto, Oxford University Press, 1952, v – 581 p.

Desbois, Henri. 'La Conférence de Stockholm relative aux droits intellectuels.' *AFDI*, vol. XIII, 1967, pp. 7–46.

Voyaume, Joseph. 'Organisation Mondial de la Propriété Intellectuelle.' *ASDI*, vol. XXIV, 1967, pp. 25–42.

2. The Caribbean Commission / The Caribbean Organization

Sources

Agreement for the Establishment of the Caribbean Commission. Washington, 30 October 1946, *UNTS*, vol. 27, pp. 77–93.
Declaration of Barbados, 16 December 1956, *AFDI*, vol. VI, 1960, p. 698.
Statute of the Caribbean Organization, Washington, 2 June 1960, *UNTS*, vol. 418, pp. 124–139.

Works

Crassweller, Robert D. *The Caribbean Community. Changing Societies and US Policy.* New York, Washington, London, Praeger Publishers, 1972, v – 470 p.
Leprette, Jacques. 'De la Commission des Caraïbes à l'Organisation des Caraïbes.' *AFDI*, vol. VI, 1960, pp. 685–706.

3. The Caribbean Free Trade Association / The Caribbean Community

Sources

Agreement Establishing the Caribbean Free Trade Association. March 1968, *IGO*, Part I, vol. II, pp. 1417–1432.
Treaty Establishing the Caribbean Community, Port of Spain, 4 July 1973, *ILM*, vol. XII, No. 5, 1973, pp. 1033–1074.

Works

Geiser, Hans J., Alleyne, Pamela and Gajraj, Caroll. *Legal Problems of Caribbean Integration. A Study on the Legal Aspects of CARICOM.* Leyden, Sijthoff, 1976, v – 275 p.

4. The Commonwealth Telecommunications Board/The Commonwealth Telecommunications Organization

Sources

Agreement Terminating the Commonwealth Telegraphs Agreement signed at London on 11 May 1948 and 25 July 1963. *GBTS*, No. 53 (1969) Cmd. 3988.
Commonwealth Telegraphs Agreement (with Schedules and Protocol). London, 11 May 1948, *UNTS*, vol. 500, pp. 268–294.
Commonwealth Telegraphs Agreement. London, 25 July 1963, *UNTS*, vol. 500, pp. 294–314.
Constitution of the Commonwealth Telecommunications Organization. London, 1966, *IGO*, Part V, pp. 286–293.

BIBLIOGRAPHY

5. *European Communities*

Sources

Convention Relating to Certain Institutions Common to the European
Communities. Rome, 25 March 1967, *UNTS*, vol. 298, pp. 267–274.
Treaty Establishing a Single Council and a Single Commission of the
European Communities, Brussels, 8 April 1965, *ILM*, vol. 4, 1965,
pp. 776–791.

Works

Gaudet, Michael and Amphoux, Jean. 'La fusion des institutions des
Communautés européennes.' *EY*, vol. XVI, 1968, pp. 17–58.
Palmer, Michael and Lambert John. European Unity. *A Survey of Euro-
pean Organizations*. London, George Allen & Unwin Ltd., 1968, 519 p.
Robertson, A.H. *European Institutions: Co-operation, Integration, Unifi-
cation*. 3rd edition, London, Stevens & Sons, Ltd./New York, Mathew
Bender, 1973, vii – 478.
Weil, Gordon L. 'The Merger of the Institutions of the European Com-
munities.' *AJIL*, vol. 61, 1967, pp. 57–65.

6. *The East African Common Services Organization / The East African Community*

Sources

The Annual Register. World Events in 1976, edited by H.V. Hodson,
London, Longman, 1977, p. 353.
The Annual Register. World Events in 1977, edited by H.V. Hodson,
London, Longman, 1978, p. 353.
Agreement for the Establishment of the East African Common Services
Organization. Dar-Es-Salam, 9 December 1961, *UNTS*, vol. 437,
pp. 48–54.
The Constitution of the East African Common Services Organization.
Dar-Es-Salam, 9 December 1961, *UNTS*, vol. 437, pp. 54–109.
Treaty of East African Co-operation. Kampala, Uganda, 6 June 1967,
BDARO, vol. III, pp. 1145–1269.

7. *The European Space Research Organization / The European Organization
for the Construction and Development of Space Vehicle Launchers / The European Space Agency*

Sources

Annual Report of the European Space Vehicle Launcher Development
Organization. *EY*, 1973, pp. 833–869.
European Space Agency. *EY*, 1975, pp. 821–824.

163

European Space Vehicle Launcher Development Organization. *EY*, 1966, pp. 736–789.

Agreement Setting up a Preparatory Commission to Study the Possibilities of European Collaboration in the Field of Space Research. 1 December 1960, *EY*, 1962, vol. II, pp. 1110–1115.

Convention for the Establishment of a European Space Agency. Paris, 30 May 1975, *IGO*, Part III–IV, pp. 166–180.

Convention for the Establishment of a European Space Research Organization. Paris, 14 June 1962, *EY*, 1962, vol. II, pp. 1115–1141.

Protocol Establishing a Preparatory Group with a View to the Creation of a European Organization for the Development and Construction of Space Vehicle Launchers. *EY*, 1962, vol. II, pp. 1203–1206.

Res. No. 1 of the Final Text of the Conference of Plenipotentiaries for the Establishment of a European Space Agency. *ILM*, vol. XIV, No. 4, 1975, pp. 857–858.

Assumption of the Rights and Obligations of ELDO, Final Act of the European Space Conference. Paris, 30 May 1975, *ILM*, vol. XIV, No. 4, 1975, p. 858.

Works

Chappez, Jean. 'La Création de l'Agence spatiale européenne.' *AFDI*, vol. XXI, 1975, pp. 801–813.

Chappez, Jean. 'La cessation des activités de l'ELDO et la relance de l'Europe spatiale.' *AFDI*, vol. XIX, 1973, pp. 941–956.

Dreyfus, Bernard. 'L'Organisation européenne de recherche spatiales.' *EY*, 1962, vol. I, The Hague, Martinus Nijhoff, 1963, pp. 151–175.

8. The International Bureau of Education / UNESCO

Sources

Agreement between the United Nations Educational, Scientific and Cultural Organization and the International Bureau of Education, 14 November 1968, UNESCO Doc. No. 15C/83.

Bulletin of the International Bureau of Education. No. 13, September 1929, pp. 3–5.

Le Bureau international d'éducation au service du mouvement éducatif. Paris, UNESCO, 1979, 153 p.

Provisional Agreement between the United Nations Educational, Scientific and Cultural Organization and the International Bureau of Education. UNESCO Doc. No. 1c/7, Chapter IV, Annex 3.

Statutes of the International Bureau of Education, Geneva, 25 July 1929, *UST*, vol. 14, 1963, pp. 315–318.

Statutes of the International Bureau of Education. UNESCO Records of the General Conference, Fifteenth Session, 1968, Resolutions, pp. 109–110.

Summary Records of the Legal and External Relations Sub-Commission, Fourth Meeting, 2 December 1946. UNESCO Doc. 1C/30.

BIBLIOGRAPHY

Report of the Director General on the Activities of the Organization in 1947. UNESCO Doc. No. 2 C/4.

Agreements now in Force with Certain Inter-Governmental Organizations. UNESCO Doc. No. 7C/ADM/25.

Transfer to UNESCO of the Resources and Responsibilities of other International Organizations, International Bureau of Education. UNESCO Doc. No. 15C/Resolutions.

9. The International Commission for Air Navigation / The International Civil Aviation Organization

Sources

Convention Relating to the Regulation of Aerial Navigation. Paris, 13 October 1919, *LNTS*, vol. 11, pp. 190–198.

History of the PICAO. *PICAO Journal*, vol. I. No. 1.

The Ibero-American Convention for Air Navigation. Madrid, November 1926, *IL*, vol. III, pp. 2027–2029.

ICAN Resolutions Nos. 1167, 1218, 1219, 1220, 1221, 1222 in *Official Bulletin of the ICAN*, No. 28, 1945, p. 22 and No. 29, 1946, pp. 43–45.

ICAO Doc. Nos. C-WP/33, 4007 (A1–LE/1), 4023 (A1–P/3), 4029 (A1–CP/2), 4031 (A1–CP/4), 4553, 4813 (C/603), 6280 (C/717), 6437 (A3–P/8), 6772.

The Pan American Convention on Commercial Aviation, Havana, 1928, *IL*, vol. IV, pp. 1336–2369.

Proceedings of the International Civil Aviation Conference, Chicago, November 1–December 7, 1944, Washington, United States Government Printing Office, 1948, 2 vols.

Works

Jennings, Robert Y. 'International Civil Aviation and the Law.' *BYBIL*, vol. 22, 1945, pp. 181–209.

Jennings, Robert Y. 'Some Aspects of the International Law of the Air.' *RCADI*, vol. 75, 1949 II, pp. 513–588.

Schenkmann, Jacob. *International Civil Aviation Organization*. Geneva, Librairie Droz, 1955, viii – 414 p.

Tombs, Laurence. C. *International Organization in European Air Transport*. New York, Columbia University Press, 1936, xx – 219 p.

10. The International Danube Commission / The Danube Commission

Sources

Docments

CD Doc. No. SES 2/19. Procès-Verbaux de la Commission du Danube, Tome I, 1951, p. 190.

Convention Instituting the Definitive Statute of the Danube. Paris, 23 July 1921, *IL*, vol. I, pp 681–699.

Convention Regarding the Régime of Navigation on the Danube. Belgrade, 18 August 1948, *UNTS*, vol. 33, pp. 297–321.

Treaty of Berlin. 13 July 1878, *NRG*, Series II, vol. II, pp. 463–464.

Treaty of London. 13 March 1871, *NRG*, Series I, vol. XVIII, pp. 305–306.

Treaty of London. 10 March 1883, *NRG*, Series II, vol. IX, pp, 393–394.

Treaty of Paris. 30 March 1856, *NRG*, Series I, vol. XV, pp. 770.

Supplementary Protocol to the Convention Regarding the Régime of Navigation on the Danube. Belgrade, 18 August 1948, *UNTS*, vol. 33, p. 223.

Cases

Jurisdiction of the European Commission of the Danube Between Galatz and Braila. PCIJ Reports, Series B No. 14, 1927, pp. 6–14.

Works

Gorove, Stephan. *Law and Politics of the Danube*. The Hague, Martinus Nijhoff, 1964, xiv – 171 p.

Kunz, Joseph L. 'The Danube Régime and the Belgrade Conference.' *AJIL*, vol. 43, 1949, pp. 104–113.

Sinclair, I.M. 'Danube Conference of 1948.' *BYBIL*, vol. XXV, 1948, pp. 398–404.

11. The International Institute of Agriculture / The Food and Agriculture Organization of the United Nations

Sources

Convention for the Establishment of an International Institute of Agrculture. Rome, 7 June 1905, *NRG*, 3rd series, vol. 2, pp. 238–243.

Additional Resolution Relative to the Dissolution of the International Forestry Center (CIS).

IIA Resolution No. 4. *Actes de la Seizième Assemblée générale*, pp. 65–67.

Anglo-French Resolution Regarding International Institute of Agriculture, FAO Doc. No. 41.

Extinction of the International Convention of 1905 and the Dissolution of the International Institute of Agriculture. I.I.A. Resolution No. 3, *Actes de la Seizième Assemblée générale*, 8 et 9 juillet 1946, pp. 63–65.

First Report to the Governments of the United Nations by Interim Commission on Food and Agriculture. Washington, 1944, 55 p.

Protocol for the Dissolution of the International Institute of Agriculture and the Transfer of its Functions and Assets to the Food and Agriculture Organization of the United Nations. *GBTS*, No. 29, Cmd 7413, 1948, p. 55.

Rapport sur le projet de résolution présenté au nom du Comité perma-

nent pour l'extinction de la Convention internationale de 1905. *Actes de la Seizième Assemblée générale*, 8 et 9 juillet 1946, pp. 40–60.
Report of Commission B to the Conference. FAO doc. No. 206.
Report of Committee I of Commission B, Second Session. FAO Doc. No. 61.
Report of the Activities of the FAO European Regional Office, Fifth Session. FAO Doc. No. 1249.
Report on Liquidation of the International Institute of Agriculture and the International Forestry Center. FAO Doc. No. C49/25.
Report to Committee B on Work of Committe IV. FAO Doc. No. 171.
Seat of the European Center of the FAO. IIA Res. No. 5, *Actes de la Seizième Assemblée générale*, 8 et 9 juillet 1946, pp. 67–69.
Second Report to the Governments of the United Nations by the Interim Commission on Food and Agriculture, Washington, July 1945.
Tasks in Connection with the Liquidation of the IIA, *Actes de la Seizième Assemblée générale*, 8 et 9 juillet 1946, pp. 71–73.
United Nations Conference on Food and Agriculture. Text of the Final Act. *AJIL Supplement*, Official Documents, vol. 37, 1943, pp. 159–192.

Works

Villa, Cino. 'La coopération internationale en matière d'agriculture.' *RCADI*, vol. 56, 1936 II, pp. 305–415.

12. The International Institute of Intellectual Co-operation / UNESCO

Sources

Agreement between UNESCO and the IIIC. 9 December 1946, UNESCO Doc. No. IC/30.
International Act Converning Intellectual Co-operation. Paris, 3 December 1938, *IL*, vol. VIII, pp.209–215.
Institut international de coopération intellectuelle 1925–1946. Paris, 1956, 599 p.
Liquidation of the International Institute of Intellectual Co-operation. UNESCO Doc. 29 EX/38, 5 p.
Liquidation of the International Institute of Intellectual Co-operation. UNESCO Doc. No. 29 EX/38 Add., 1 p.
Liquidation of the Institute. UNESCO Doc. No. 29 EX/ Decisions, p. 17.
Liquidation of the International Institute of Intellectual Co-operation, Final Report. UNESCO Doc. No. 42 EX/41, 1 p.
Mandate of the Liquidator of the International Institute of Intellectual Co-operation. UNESCO Doc. No. 30 EX/ Decisions, p. 16.
Questions Concerning the Liquidation of the International Institute of Intellectual Co-operation. UN Doc. No. A/ 2119, pp. 80–81.
Report of the Preparatory Commission on General Arrangements, Legal Questions, and External Relations. UNESCO Doc. No. IC/7, Chapter IV, Annex 3, 8 p.

Statut organique de l'Institut international de coopération intellectuelle. Paris, 8 décembre 1924. *LN Official Journal*, No. 2, 1924, pp. 285–289.

Transfer to UNESCO of the Functions and Activities and Utilization by UNESCO of the Assets of the Institute Transferred to the United Nations by the League of Nations. UN Doc. No. A/136, 6 p.

Utilization of the property rights of the League of Nations in the International Institute of Intellectual Cooperation. ECOSOC Res. No. 24 (II), UN Doc. E/245/ Rev. 1.

Utilization by UNESCO of the Property Rights of the League of Nations in the International Institute of Intellectual Co-operation. UN Res. No. A/71 (I), UN Doc. No. 4/64/Add. 1, p. 133.

13. *International Labour Organisation / League of Nations*

Sources

Agreement between the League of Nations and International Labour Organisation concerning the Transfer of Certain Properties, Geneva and Montreal, 17 May 1946, *UNTS*, vol. 19, pp. 188–191.

Convention for the Partial Revision of the Conventions Adopted by the General Conference of the International Labour Organisation at its First/Twenty-eighth Sessions, Montreal, 9 October 1946, *UNTS*, vol. 38, pp. 3–15.

Instrument of Amendment and Recommendation Adopted by the Conference. Paris, 7 November 1945, *UNTS*, vol. 2, pp. 17–25.

International Labour Organisation, Articles 387–427 of the Treaty of Versailles, in Strupp, Karl. *Documents pour servir l'histoire du droit des gens*, Tome IV, 1923, pp. 537–565.

International Labour Conference. Twenty-sixth Session, Philadelphia, 1944, Record of Proceedings, p. VII.

International Labour Organisation. Instrument for the Amendment of the Constitution, Montreal, 9 October 1946, *UNTS*, vol. 15, pp. 32–122.

Reports of the Conference Delegation on Constitutional Questions. Part I, International Labour Conference, 29th Session, Montreal, 1946, 197 p.

Resolution Concerning the Constitution and Constitutional Practice of the International Labour Organisation and its Relationship with Other International Bodies. International Labour Conference, 26th Session, Philadelphia, 1944, Record of Proceedings, pp. 526–627.

Résolution concernant l'adoption du Règlement révisé de la Caisse des pensions du personnel. Conférence internationale du Travail, 29e session, Montréal, 1946, pp. 531–532.

Works

Ghebali, Victor-Yves. Organisation internationale et Guerre mondiale. Le cas de la Société des Nations et de l'Organisation internationale du travail pendant la Seconde Guerre Mondiale. Thèse, Université de Grenoble, 1975, 1051 p.

Ghebali, Victor-Yves. 'La transition de la Société des Nations l'organisation des Nations Unies.' *La Société des Nations: rétrospective, Actes du Colloque Walter de Gruyter*, Berlin/New York, 1983, pp. 73–92.

Jenks, C. Wilfred. 'The Revision of the Constitution of the International Labour Organisation.' *BYBIL*, vol. 23, 1946, pp. 303–317.

14. The International Patent Institute / The European Patent Organization

Sources

Agreement Concerning the Establishment of an International Patents Bureau, The Hague, 6 June 1947, *UNTS*, vol. 46, pp. 258–261.

Convention on the Grant of European Patents (European Patent Convention), Munich, 5 October 1973, *IGO*, Part III–IV, pp. 93–151.

Draft Agreement on the Integration of the International Patent Institute into the European Patent Office. 29 September 1977, Interim Committee for the European Patent Organization Doc. No. CI/Final 23/77.

Protocol on the Centralization of the European Patent System and its Introduction (Protocol on Centralization). *IGO*, Part III–IV, pp. 151–155.

Official Journal of the European Patent Office, Year 2/ November 5, 1978.

Works

Benthem, J.B. van. 'The State of the European Patent System.' *Revue et Bulletin de la Fédération internationale des Conseils en propriété industrielle*, No. 31, mars 1979, pp. 69–91.

Merle, Daniel. *L'Institut international des Brevets: Règle, Organisation, Fonctionnement*, La Haye, 1962.

15. The International Relief Union / UNESCO

Sources

Convention Establishing an International Relief Union. Geneva, 12 July 1927, *UNTS*, vol. 135, pp. 249–265.

Draft Agreement between UNESCO and the International Relief Union. UNESCO Doc. No. 15C/85, Annex II, pp. 3–4.

International Relief Union. UNESCO Doc. No. 15C/ Resolutions, pp. 110–111.

Transfer of UNESCO of Certain Responsibilities and Assets of the International Relief Union. UNESCO Doc. No. 78 EX/19, p. 4. UNESCO Doc. No. 78/EX/19 Add., 6p. UNESCO Doc. No. 15C/19, 6 p. UNESCO Doc No. 15C/85, 4 p.

Transfer to the United Nations of the Responsibilities and Assets of the International Relief Union. ECOSOC Res. No.1153 (XII), UN Doc. E/4264, Resolutions, p.38.

16. The International Refugee Organization / The Intergovernmental Committee for European Migration / The United Nations High Commissioner for Refugees

Sources

Preliminary Recommendations of the Director-General with View to Termination of the IRO Programmes. IRO Doc. No. GC/W/3.

Acceptance of Transfer to IRO of Property, Assets and Records of the Preparatory Commission and Ratification of Acts. IRO Doc. No. GC/19.

Completion of the Programmes of the Organization. IRO GC Res. Nos. 39, 54, 76.

Constitution of the International Refugee Organization. 15 December 1946, *UNTS*, vol. 18, pp. 3–24.

Continuation of the Organization's Operations. IRO GC Res. No. 78.

Defining the Powers of the Liquidator. IRO GC Res. No. 110.

Disposal of Assets. IRO GC Res. No. 106. Establishing a Board of Liquidation. IRO GC Res. No. 108.

Future International Action Concerning Refugees. IRO GC Res. No. 40.

International Refugee Organization in Liquidation. Report of the Liquidator, 31 July 1953.

Resolution to Establish a Provisional Intergovernmental Committee for the Movement of Migrants from Europe. December 1951, *IGO*, vol. I, pp. 875–877.

Refugees and Stateless Persons. UNGA Res. No. 319 (IV), UN Doc. No. A/1251.

Statute of the Office of United Nations High Commissioner for Refugees. UNGA Res.No 428 (V), UN Doc.No.A/1775.

Termination of the IRO Programmes. IRO Doc. No. GC/SR/30, Annex.

Works

Holborn, Louise W. *The International Refugee Organization. A Specialized Agency of the United Nations*. London/New York/Toronto, Oxford University Press. 1956,v – 805 p.

17. The League of Nations / The United Nations

Sources

Documents

Agreement Concerning the Execution of the Transfer to the United Nations of Certain Assets of the League of Nations. Geneva, 19 July 1946, *UNTS*, vol. 1, pp. 111–117.

Annotated Provisional Agenda of the Assembly. LN Doc. A.2. 1946, 2 p.

Approval of Trusteeship Agreements. UNGA Res. No. 63 (I), UN Doc. No. A/64/Add. 1, p. 122.

Arrangement to Give Practical Effect to Certain Provisions of the Agreement of July 19th 1946, Dealing with the Execution of the Transfer of League Assets to the United Nations. Geneva, 31 July 19046, *UNTS*, vol. 1, pp. 120–129.

Assumption by the United Nations of Activities Hitherto Performed by the League. *LN Official Journal*, Special Supplement No. 194, LN Res. NO. 3, 18 April 1946.

Attribution to the Assembly of the Responsibilities of the Council. LN Doc. No. A.26. 1946.

Charter of the United Nations. *IGO*, Part I, vol. 2, pp. 1301–1332.

Common Plan for the Transfer of League of Nations Assets. LN Doc. No. A. 8. 1946, UN Doc. No. A/18/Add. 2, 28 January 1946.

Communication from the Union of South Africa on the Future Status of South West Africa of 23 July 1947. UN Doc. No. A/334.

Consideration of Proposed New Trusteeship Agreements, if any: Question of South West Africa. UNGA Res. No. 141 (II), UN Doc. No. A/519.

Covenant of the League of Nations. *IL*, vol. I, 1931, pp. 2–17.

Draft General Report of the Social Commission. UN Doc. No. E/260, 11 February 1947, 30 p.

Draft Protocol Amending the Agreement, Convention and Protocols on Narcotic Drugs. UN Doc. No. E/168/ Rev.2.

Future Status of South West Africa. UNGA Res. No. 65 (I), UN Doc. No. A/64/ Add. 1.

International Convention Relating to Economic Statistics. Geneva, 14 December 1928, *LNTS*, vol. 110, pp. 172–283.

Non-Political Functions and Activities of the League Other than those belonging to the League under International Agreements. ECOSOC Res. No. 23 (III), UN Doc. E/245/Rev. 1.

Non-Political Functions and Activities of the League of Nations. Resolutions Adopted by the Economic and Social Council During its First Session, 23 January to 18 February 1946, ECOSOC Res. No. 1/12.

Non-Self-Governing Peoples. UNGA Res No.9 /I), UN Doc. A/64.

Powers Exercised by the League of Nations Under the International Agreements, Conventions and Protocols on Narcotic Drugs. ECOSOC Res. No. 12 (III), UN Doc. No. E/125/ Rev. 1.

Protocol Amending the Agreement for the Suppression of the Circulation of Obscene Publications. Lake Success, New York, 4 May 1949, *UNTS*, vol. 30, pp. 4–9.

Protocol Amending the Convention for the Suppression of the Traffic in Women and Children and the Convention for the Suppression of the Traffic of Women of Full Age. Lake Success, New York, 20 November 1947, *UNTS*, vol. 53, pp. 14–19.

Protocol Amending the International Convention Relating to Economic Statistics. Paris, 9 December 1948, *UNTS*, vol. 20, pp. 230–234.

Protocol (No. I) Concerning the Execution of Various Operations in the Transfer to the United Nations of Certain Assets of the League of Nations, Geneva, 1 August 1946, *UNTS*, vol. 1, pp. 131–133.

Protocol Concerning the Transfer of the Administration of the Darling Foundation from the League of Nations to the United Nations. Geneva, 27 June 1947, *UNTS*, vol. 5, pp. 396–399.

Protocol Concerning the Transfer of the Administration of the Léon Bernard Fund from the League of Nations to the United Nations. Geneva, 27 June 1947, *UNTS*, vol. 5, pp. 390–393.

Protocol (No. II) on the Transfer of Certain Services from the League of Nations to the United Nations. Geneva, 1 August 1946, *UNTS*, vol. 1, pp. 135–137.

Recommendation of the Subcommittee on Trusteeship, Draft Resolution for the General Assembly. 20 December 1945. UN Doc. No. PC/TC/41.

Report and Resolution of the First Committee on the Dissolution of the Permanent Court of International Justice. 17 April 1946, LN Doc. No. A.35. 1946.

Reports of the League of Nations Board of Liquidation: First Interim Report. LN Doc. No. C.83.M.83. Second Interim Report. LN Doc. No. C.89.M.89. Third Interim Report. LN Doc. No. C. 3.M. 3 Fourth Interim Report. LN Doc. No. C. 4.M. 4. Final Report. LN Doc. No. C. 5.M. 5.

Report of the Committee Set up by the Preparatory Committee to Discuss and Establish a Common Plan for the Transfer of the Assets of the League of Nations. UN Doc. No. A/18, 28 January 1946.

Report of the Executive Committee to the Preparatory Commission of the United Nations. UN Doc. No. PC/EX/113/Rev. 1, 12 November 1945.

Report of the Finance Committee to the Assembly. LN Doc. No. A.32. 1946.

Report of the Preparatory Commission to the United Nations. LN Doc. NO. PC/20, 23 December 1945.

Report of the Second Session of the Statistical Commission. ECOSOC Res. No. 114 (VI), UN Doc. No. E/777.

Report of the Sixth Committee to the Third Committee with Respect to the Conventions on Narcotic Drugs. UN Doc. No. A/C.6/65.

Report of the Supervisory Commission on the Work of its 100th Session. LN Doc. No. A.19. 1946.

Report of the Temporary Social Commission. UN Doc. No.E/41.

Report of the Temporary Transport and Communications Commission to the Economic and Social Council. UN Doc. E/42.

Report on the Work of the League During the War Submitted to the Assembly by the Acting Secretary-General, LN Doc. No. A.6. 1946.

Request for an Advisory Opinion of the International Court of Justice: Question of South West Africa. UNGA Res. No. 338 (IV), UN Doc. No. A/1215, 28 December 1949.

Resolution on Custody of the Original Texts of International Agreements. 18 April 1946, LN Official Journal, Special Supplement No. 194, p. 278.

Resolution on Functions and Powers Arising Out of International Agreements of a Technical and Non-Political Character. 18 April 1946, LN Official Journal, Special Supplement No. 194, p. 278.

Resolution on Mandates. 18 April 1946, LN Official Journal, Special Supplement No. 194, pp. 278–279.

Resolution on the Assumption by the United Nations of Activities Hitherto Performed by the League. 18 April 1946, LN Official Journal, Special Supplement No. 194, p. 278.

Resolution for the Dissolution of the League of Nations. 18 April 1946. LN Official Journal, Special Supplement No. 194, pp. 281–284.

Responsibilities of the League Arising Out of Articles 22 (Mandates). Report by the Council of the Assembly. LN Doc. No. 20/48/61.

Supervisory Commission, General Summarized Report on its Work During the Period of Emergency 1940–1946. LN Doc. No. A.5. 1946.

Supervisory Commission, Report on Discussions with the Representatives of the United Nations on Questions of the Transfer of League of Nations Assets. LN Doc. No. A.8. 1946.

Transfer of Certain Functions, Activities and Assets of the League of Nations. UNGA Res. No. A/24 (I), UN Doc. No. A/64.

Transfer to the United Nations of Certain Non-Political Functions and Activities of the League of Nations, Other than those Pursuant to International Agreements. UNGA Res. No. 51 (I), UN Doc. No. A/66/Add. 1, UN Doc. No. E/177.

(a) Cases

International Status of South West Africa, Advisory Opinion. ICJ Reports 1950, pp. 128–219.

Voting Procedure on Questions Relating to Reports and Petitions Concerning the Territory of South West Africa, Advisory Opinion. ICJ Reports 1955, pp. 67–123.

Admissibility of Hearings of Petitioners by the Committee on South West Africa, Advisory Opinion. ICJ Reports 1956, pp. 23–71.

South West Africa Case (Ethiopia v. Union of South Africa). ICJ Reports 1961, pp. 3–15.

South West Africa Cases (Ethiopia v. South Africa; Liberia v. South Africa), Preliminary Objections. ICJ Reports 1962, pp. 319–662.

South West Africa, Second Phase, Judgment. ICJ Reports 1966, pp. 6–505.

Legal Consequences for States of the Continued Presence of South Africa in

Namibia (South West Africa) notwithstanding Security Council Resolution 276 (1970), Advisory Opinion. *ICJ Reports 1971*, pp. 16–345.

18. The League of Arab States / The Arab League Educational Scientific and Cultural Organization

Sources

Charter of Arab Cultural Unity. Baghdad, 29 February 1964, *IGO*, Part III – IV, pp. 24–29.

Constitution of the Arab League Educational, Cultural and Scientific Organization. Baghdad, 29 February 1964, *IGO*, Part III – IV, pp. 30–38.

Pact of the League of Arab States. Cairo, 22 March 1945, *UNTS*, vol. 70, pp. 249–263.

Works / Articles

Boutros-Ghali, Boutros. 'The Arab League (1945–1970).' *Revue égyptienne de droit international*, vol. 25, 1969, pp. 67–118.

MacDonald, Robert W. *The League of Arab States. A Study in the Dynamics of Regional Organizations.* Princeton, New Jersey, Princeton University Press, 1965, v – 407 p.

19. The African and Malagasy Organization for Economic Cooperation / The Union of African and Malagasy States / The Common African, Malagasy and Mauritanian Organization

Sources

Charter of the African and Malagasy Union. Tananarive, 8 September 1961, *BDARO*, vol. I, p. 357.

Charter of the African and Malagasy Common Organization. 27 June 1966, *ILM*, vol. VI, No. 1, 1967, pp. 53–56.

Final Communiqué of the Nouakchott Conference. 12 February 1965, Nations Nouvelles, *Revue de l'OCAM*, mars 1965, p. 9.

Treaty Establishing the African and Malagasy Organization for Economic Cooperation. Tananarive, 12 September 1961, *BDARO*, vol. I, pp. 309–313.

Articles

Feurer, Guy. 'Les conférences africaines et l'organisation de la communauté africano-malgache d'expression française.' *AFDI*, vol. VII, 1961, pp. 762–786.

20. *OECE / OCDE*

Sources

Convention on the Organization for Economic Co-operation and Development. Paris, 14 December 1960, *IGO*, Part I, vol. II, pp. 1154–1160.

Works / Articles

Hahn, Hugo J. 'Reconstruction de l'OECE et continuation de l'OCDE.' *AFDI*, vol. VIII, 1962, pp. 751–762.

21. *The Office International d'Hygiène Publique / UNRRA / WHO*

Sources

Adjustment of Pensions for Retired OIHP Staff Members. WHO Res. No. EB 23.R.24.

Agreement for the Establishment of the International Office of Public Health. Rome, 9 December 1907, *AJIL*, Supplement, vol. 3, 1909, pp. 152–158.

Agreement for the Transfer to the Interim Commission of the World Health Organization of the Duties and Functions of the OIHP. Geneva, 27 January 1948, *Official Records of the WHO*, No. 7, Annex, pp. 203–204.

Denunciation of the Rome Agreement and Transfer of OIHP Assets to WHO. WHAI Res. Nos. 1/84, 3/98, 4/58, 5/40 and E.B. Res. Nos. 2/R50, 2/83, 3/R47, 9/R6.

Establishment of the World Health Organization. UNGA Res. No. 61 (1), UN Doc. No. A/64/Add. 1.

Extension of the International Sanitary Convention, 1944, and the International Sanitary Convention for Aerial Navigation, 1944. UNRRA Council Res. No. 85.

Final Act of the International Health Conference. New York, 22 July 1946, *UNTS*, vol. 9, pp. 4–7.

International Health Conference. ECOSOC Res. No. 2/1.

International Sanitary Convention. 21 June 1926, *IL*, vol. III, pp. 1902–1980.

International Sanitary Convention for Aerial Navigation. 12 April 1933, *IL*, vol. VI, pp. 292–320.

International Sanitary Convention 1944. Washington, 15 December 1944, *UNTS*, vol. 17, pp. 306–355.

International Sanitary Convention for Aerial Navigation, 1944. Washington, 15 December 1944, *UNTS*, vol. 16, pp. 248–309.

Negotiations with the OIHP. *Official Records of the WHO*, No. 5, Annex 14.

The Position as Regards the OIHP. WHO Doc. No. A/3/46, Add. I, Rev. 1.

Protocol Concerning the OIHP. New York, 22 July 1946, *UNTS*, vol. 9, pp. 66–68.

Protocol to Prolong the Duration of the International Sanitary Convention, 1944. Washington, 23 April 1944, *IL*, vol. IX, pp. 251–254.

Protocol to Prolong the Duration of the International Sanitary Convention for Aerial Navigation, 1944. Washington, 23 April 1946, *IL*, vol. IX, pp. 272–275.

Rapport de la Commission des Avoirs, soumis la Commission des Transferts. *OIHP Procès-Verbaux des séances du Comité permanent*, session mai 1950, p. 5.

Rapport du Président de la Commission des finances et du transfert. *OIHP Procès-verbaux des séances du Comité permanent*, session mai 1950, p. 26.

Report of the International Health Conference. UN Doc. No. E/772.

Office international d'hygiène publique. Official Records of the World Health Organization, No. 10.

Report of the Committee on Relations on the Agreement with the OIHP, *Official Records of the World Health Organization*, No. 7.

Resolution Calling for an International Health Conference. ECOSOC Res. No. 1/1.

Transfer of the Assets of the OIHP. WHO Doc. No. A/4/27.

World Health Organization. ECOSOC Res. No. 20 (III), UN Doc. E/245/Rev. 1.

22. Permanent Court of International Justice/International Court of Justice

Sources

(a) Documents

Protocol of Signature of the Permanent Court of International Justice. Geneva, 16 December 1920, *IL*, pp. 529 et seq.

Resolution on the Dissolution of the Permanent Court of International Justice. 18 April 1946, LN Official Journal, Special Supplement No. 194, pp. 277–278.

(b) Cases

Case Concerning the Aerial Incident of July 27th, 1955 (Israel v. Bulgaria), Preliminary Objections. *ICJ Reports 1955*, pp. 127–146.

Case Concerning the Barcelona Traction, Light and Power Company, Limited. (New Application: 1962) (Belgium v. Spain), Preliminary Objections. *ICJ Reports 1964*, pp. 6–47.

23. *The Equatorial Customs Union / The Economic Customs Union of Central Africa*

Sources

Convention relative l'Union douanière equatoriale, Brazzaville, Congo, 23 June 1959, *BDARO*, vol. II, 1977, pp. 676–685.
Convention and Statute of the Conference of Heads of State of Equatorial Africa. Brazzaville,Congo, 23 June 1959, *BDARO*, vol. II, pp. 642–650.
Treaty Instituting a Customs and Economic Union of Central Africa. Brazzaville, Congo, 8 December 1964, *BDARO*, vol. II, pp. 734–750.

24. *UNRRA / WHO / FAO / IRO / UN*

Sources

Agreement for the United Nations Relief and Rehabilitation Administration. Washington, 9 November 1943, *IL*, vol. IX, pp. 84–90.
Assumption by the United Nations of Certain Advisory Social Welfare Functions of UNRRA, Report and Recommendations of the Secretary-General. UN Doc. No. A/32.
Establishment of an International Children's Emergency Fund. UNGA Res. No. A/57 (I). 11 December 1946, UN Doc. No. A/64/Add. 1.
Transfer to the United Nations of the Advisory Social Welfare Functions of UNRRA. UNGA Res. No. A/58, 14 December 1946, UN Doc. No. A/64/Add. 1.
Transfer to the United Nations of the Residual Assets and Activities of UNRRA. UNGA Res. No. A/241 (III), UN Doc. A/810.
Transfer to the United Nations of the Residual Assets and Activities of UNRRA, 27 September 1948, *UNTS*, vol. 27, pp. 350–397.
UNRRA Res. No. 1. November 1943, Relating to the Scope of the Activities of the Administration.
UNRRA Res. No. 80. August 1945, Relating to Further Contributions.
UNRRA Res. No. 92. May 1946, Relating to Displaced Persons Operations.
UNRRA Res. No. 94. August 1946, Relating to the Health Activities of the Administration.
UNRRA Res. No. 95. August 1946, Relating to the Social Welfare Activities of the Administration.
UNRRA Res. No. 99. Relating to Displaced Persons Operations.
UNRRA Res. No. 102. Relating to Agricultural Production.
UNRRA Res. No. 103. Relating to Rehabilitation of Children and Adolescents of Countries which were Victims of Agression.
Welfare Activities Performed by UNRRA. ECOSOC Res. No. 11 (III), UN Doc. No. E/245/Rev. 1.

Works

Woodbridge, George. UNRRA. *The History of the United Nations Relief and Rehabilitation Administration.* New York, Columbia University Press, 1950, 3 vols. All of the Agreements between UNRRA and the WHO, FAO, IRO and the UN as well as the resolutions abolishing the organs of UNRRA and appointing an administrator for liquidation are reproduced in volume 3.

25. The United Nations / The United Nations Industrial Development Organization

Sources

UNGA Res. 2152(XXI). 17 November 1966. On the United Nations Industrial Development Organization.

UN Doc. No. A/CONF.90/19. Constitution of the United Nations Industrial Development Organization, 8 April 1979.

UNGA Res. 34/96. 13 December 1979. Transitional Arrangements Relating to the Constitution of the United Nations Organization for Industrial Development as a Specialized Agency.

YBUN, 1966, pp. 297–306. *YBUN*, 1979, vol. 33, pp. 607–624 *YBUN*, 1982, vol. 36, pp. 760–761. *YBUN*, 1983, vol. 37, pp. 584–585. *YBUN*, 1985, vol. 39, pp. 591–597. *YBUN*, 1986, vol. 40, p. 1201.

Bretton, Philippe. 'La transformation de l'ONUDI en institution spécialisée'. *AFDI*, vol. XXV, 1979; pp. 567–578.

26. The West African Customs Union / The West African Economic Community

Sources

Customs Union Convention. Paris, 9 June 1959, *BDARO*, vol. II, pp. 926–927.

Convention Establishing the West African Customs Union. Abidjan, Ivory Coast, 3 June 1966, *BDARO*, vol. II, pp. 928–932.

Protocol of Agreement on Creation of a West African Economic Community. Bamako, 21 May 1970, *IGO*, Part I, vol. II, pp. 1365–1367.

Works

Borella, François. 'Le régionalisme africain en 1964.' *AFDI*, vol. X, 1964, pp. 621–637.

Elias, T.O. 'The Economic Community of West Africa.' *The Yearbook of World Affairs*, London, Stevens and Sons, 1978, pp. 93–116.

Gautron, Jean Claude. 'La Communauté de l'Afrique de l'Ouest: Antécédants et Perspectives.' *AFDI*, vol. XXI, 1975, pp. 197–215.

Wodie, Francis. *Les institutions internationales régionales en Afrique occid-*

entale et centrale. Paris, Librairie générale de droit et de jurisprudence, 1970, 274 p.

26. The Western European Union / The Council of Europe

Sources

Assembly of Western European Union Proceedings. Fifth Ordinary Session, 1959:
First Part, vol. I, pp. 130–147. First Part, vol. II, pp. 49, 128–162 Second Part, vol. III, pp. 96–104 Second Part, vol. IV, pp. 44, 194–201.
Protocol Motifying and Completing the Treaty for Collaboration in Economic, Social and Cultural Matters and for Collective Self-Defence, signed at Brussels on 17 March 1948, Paris, 23 October 1954, *UNTS*, vol. 211, pp. 342–349.
Statute of the Council of Europe. London, 5 May 1948, *UNTS*, vol. 87, pp. 104–129.
Treaty for Collaboration in Economic, Social and Cultural Matters and for Collective Self-Defence, Brussels, 17 March 1948, *UNTS*, vol. 19, pp. 51–63.

Works

Manual of the Council of Europe, Structure, Functions and Achievements. London, Stevens & Sons Ltd., South Hackensack, N.J., Fred B. Rothman and Co., 1970, pp. vii – 322 p.
Robertson, A.H. *The Council of Europe. Its Structure, Functions and Achievements.* London, Stevens, 1965, xv – 288 p.
'Western European Union. Chronology of Principal Events in 1960.' *EY*, 1960, pp. 190–201.
Wiebringhaus, Hans. 'A propos du transfert de compétences entre organisations internationales.' *AFDI*, vol. VII, 1961; pp. 537–550.

INDEX

INDEX OF CASES

For Product Safety Concerns and Information please contact our EU
representative GPSR@taylorandfrancis.com
Taylor & Francis Verlag GmbH, Kaufingerstraße 24, 80331 München, Germany